Sarah Elizabeth Titcomb

Early New England People

Some Account of the Ellis, Pemberton, Willard, Prescott, Titcomb, Sewall, and Longfellow, and Allied Families

Sarah Elizabeth Titcomb

Early New England People
Some Account of the Ellis, Pemberton, Willard, Prescott, Titcomb, Sewall, and Longfellow, and Allied Families

ISBN/EAN: 9783337013493

Printed in Europe, USA, Canada, Australia, Japan

Cover: Foto ©Suzi / pixelio.de

More available books at **www.hansebooks.com**

Early New England People.

SOME ACCOUNT OF THE

ELLIS, PEMBERTON, WILLARD, PRESCOTT, TITCOMB, SEWALL AND LONGFELLOW,

AND

ALLIED FAMILIES.

By SARAH ELIZABETH TITCOMB.

BOSTON:
W. B. CLARKE & CARRUTH, PUBLISHERS,
340 Washington Street.
1882.

PREFACE.

The author having collected during a number of years, for her personal gratification, many facts relating to some of the early settlers of New England, has, at the earnest entreaties of friends, prepared them for publication.

She would express her thanks to all who have in any way aided her, and acknowledges herself under special obligations to the following persons: Hervey D. Ellis; Samuel Adams Drake; Samuel Green, M.D.; Joseph Titcomb of Kennebunk, Me.; Judge Samuel Titcomb; John C. Sibley; Major Ben. Perley Poor; William H. Whitmore; William R. Dean; Sereno D. Nickerson, Recording Grand Secretary of the Grand (Masonic) Lodge in Massachusetts; Benjamin Chase; Giles M. Kelley; N. W. Marston; Peter Thacher, Esq.; G. B. Bartlett; A. G. Lord; John Poor Titcomb; W. H. Montague; J. J. Dow; C. C. Chase; Rev. James Uniacke; Gen. T. K. Smith; Henry Pemberton; W. S. Ellis; Judge C. A. Bradley; Judge John K. Bartlett; Miss Maria G. Bradley; Miss Caroline Whiting, (the genealogist of the Whitings;) James Whitehouse; Rev. Stephen Allen; and Joseph Titcomb of Newburyport.

ELLIS.

THE name of Ellis is met with in France as early as the middle of the ninth century, but in England not before the time of William the Conqueror, a Norman of that name[1] (though differently spelled)[2] being in his train. William Smith Ellis, Esq., a barrister of the Middle Temple, London, Eng., author of "A Plea for the Antiquity of Heraldry,"[3] appears to have very thoroughly investigated the early records of the Ellises of France, England, Scotland, Ireland and Wales, the results being given to the public in his book entitled, "Notices of the Ellises of England, Ireland and Scotland," and the four supplements that have since appeared. He presents much evidence in support of the belief, entertained in England, that the Ellis and synonymous families of France are descended from the early kings of that country,—an origin countenanced by the fleurs-de-lis to be found in the arms of those families, the name being originally Elias or Louis. Mr. Ellis says: "A bearing like the fleur-de-lis,[4] having little intrinsic importance or meaning, but

[1] The name occurs in *Doomsday Survey* as Alis and Helias.

[2] From authentic written evidence, we know that the name of Ellis, like most names, was spelled in various ways; as, Alis, Halis, Helias, Hellys, Holys, Hillis, Eales, Ellis, Elias, Elys, etc.

[3] "Notwithstanding Voltaire's caustic remark that 'Heraldic knowledge is the science of fools with long memories,' it can not be denied that genealogical memoranda are serviceable auxiliaries to History," and that the blazoning of Arms and the compilation of Pedigrees are useful to identify dates and to avoid confusion in Biography.—*Visitations of Wales*, Vol. I., p. ix. By Samuel Rush Meyrick, K.N.T., K.H., LL. D., F. A. S.

[4] "The origin of the device of the *fleur-de-lis* has given rise to considerable speculation; but the popular notion of its deriving its name

obtaining its celebrity from the eminence of its first bearer and his descendants, and therefore jealously guarded from usurpation, is not likely to have been adopted in any of its numerous forms and positions, by any but those who had a legitimate right to do so according to the laws of heraldry."

In Wales, the name is met with at an early date. A.D.815, "Griffi, son of Cyngen, son of Cadell, was slain through the treachery of his brother Elisse." Roderick (Theodoric) the Great, King of Wales 843–76, had a grandson named Elis "who," in the words of Mr. Ellis, "not improbably was the prototype of the numerous Louises and Ellises to be found in that country."[1] It is supposed that Roderick was descended from the early kings of France, and thus have originated the coats of arms with the device of fleurs-de-lis in Wales. A descendant of Roderick, Gwynnedd, King of North Wales in the twelfth century, is said to have been the progenitor[2] of the Ellises of Glasfryn, county Caernarvon.

---

from Louis, and being the exclusive ensign of French domination, is totally erroneous. Montfaucon has shown that it was not only assumed by the Frankish, but also by the Lombard and other Teutonic princes. In his great work, he gives engravings of statues of the Merovingian and Capetian race of kings, on whose sceptres and crowns the *fleur-de-lis* is distinctly represented. It is to be met with in remains from Babylon, and in sculptures from Nineveh. There is little doubt that the lotus is the flower intended by it; and that, we know, was regarded as of peculiar mystic import in Egypt and throughout the East. In course of time, it seems to have become the settled and peculiar *armorial bearings* of the kings of France, certainly long before the time of Charlemagne, as the descent of the families bearing it from his ancestors will demonstrate."—*William Smith Ellis.*

[1] In the tenth century, the Christian names of the fathers were adopted by the sons as surnames.

[2] "The Welshman's Pedigree was his title-deed by which he claimed his birthright in the country. Every one was obliged to show his descent through nine generations, in order to be acknowledged a free native, and by which right he claimed his portion of land in the community. He was affected with respect to legal process in his collateral affinities through nine degrees. A person passed the ninth descent formed a new *pen cenedyl*, or head of a family. Every family was

Dr. Edward Ellis came to New England, it is said, from Wales, prior to 1652. He was married in Boston, Aug. 6, 1652, to Sarah, daughter of Robert and Susan Blott.

Mr. Blott came to Charlestown in 1634, and he probably removed to Concord, Mass., as the following deed, taken from the first volume of the "Suffolk Deeds," would indicate:

"Robert Blott of Boston in the Massachusetts granted unto Samuel Stretton of Concord his house and land in Concord granted by the town to the same forty Acres more or less wth all the appertenances & priviledges thereunto belonging & this was by a deed of sale dat. 29 (5) 1648

"Robert Blott & a seal

"Sealed & dd in p'sence of

"Wm Aspinwall

"Nicholas Bushie

"Edward ffletcher

"Also it was adjoyneing to m[r] Edw: Buckley on the north & goodman Pearsley south."

Mr. Blott, at the time of his daughter's marriage, was a resident of Boston, Mass., his house being on the corner of Newbury (now Washington) Street and Blott's Lane. The latter was called Blott's Lane, for Mr. Blott, until 1708, when it was named Winter Street. This property was inherited by Dr. Ellis, and the corner of Newbury and Winter Streets was called Ellis's Corner until 1732. The following is a copy of a part of Mr. Blott's will:

"I Robert Blott being in perfect memorye Doe make this my last will and testament.

"I make Edward Ellis my sonne-in-law, Husband to Sarah, my Daughter, my Executor, and give unto him my house and the lot belonging thereunto, with all the appurtenances, also

---

represented by its elder, and these elders from every family were delegates to the national council."—*History and Antiquities of the County of Cardigan.*

my will is, that he pay my daughter's children whose name was Woodford, of Connecticutt £3. My will is that my Sonne Edward Ellis shall give to my daughter Tosier's children £7, and 3 bushels of wheat and 2 of Indyan Corn, besides to her eldest Sonne, John Green, cloth to make him a Coate.

"My will is that the said Edward shall give to my daughter Lovett's children of Braintree £7 & 3 bushels of wheat & 2 bushels of Indyan, also to my sonne-in-law Daniel Turin's children £8; that my daughter Tosier and my daughter Lovett shall have half the household stuff equally Divided between them, and the other half to my daughter Ellis, also three bushels of Mault to be divided between my three daughters, also to Daniel Lovett my sonne-in-law I give my Best Coate. in witness whereof I have set my hand the 27th of third month called May 1662."

"I Edward Ellis by God's help shall pay these legacies without fraud or guile before twelve months after ye death of my father-in-law," etc.

A codicil is added which makes some changes in the legacies, as Mr. Blott did not die at that time.

I am indebted to Hervey D. Ellis, Esq., of Boston, Mass., genealogist of the early families of Massachusetts by the names of Allis, Eeles, Ells, Ellis, etc., for the following items from old records; also, for much of the information I possess of the descendants of Dr. Edward Ellis:

"(75) Division No. 8 Capt. Jno Hull's [military] co. Edward Ellis 1681.

"(127) Edward Ellis (Heads) Wharfes &c. (Cowes). 2. H.

"(144) Edward Ellis 1

"(156) Countrie rate 1691 Edward Ellis

"(161) 1695 Edward Ellis

"(162) " Robert Ellis Jr."[1]

Property belonging to the estate of Anne Wampus of Boston, in 1676, was given to Joshua Hughs, and the following testimony was taken in regard to it, Sept. 28, 1676:

[1] Report of the Board of Commissioners of Boston, taken from tax list of 1681-8.

"Sarah Ellis aged about 45 years testifyeth to the truth of what is above written and doth further add that in the time of her sickness she gave her the keys of her house, to deliver unto Joshua Hughs which she did after she was dead.

"taken upon oath," etc.

In Suffolk Probate Register,[1] the name of Edward Ellis appears in the transfers of land, etc.; and also the name of his wife Sarah with his, in the record of lands sold by them in 1677.

June 17, 1698, Sarah, widow of Edward Ellis (chirurgeon), of Boston, Robert Ellis (chirurgeon), William Rusk (mariner), and Mary (Ellis) Rusk, wife of William, the said Robert and Mary being the only surviving children of said Edward, mortgage land on Blott's Lane.

"An accomp' of what is due Edward Ellis[2] for the cure of Robert Munson and Gerimiah Bumsted & the said Ellis being imploid therein by order of the Counsell; 13 November 1670

"I' for curing Robert Munson his arm being broke and his hand being wounded by shot in money 03. 00. 00

"I' for curing Gerimyah Bumsted his thigh being much broken by shell in money 06. 00. 00

The Sume 09. 00. 00"

"Samuel Brown aged 20 years or theirabouts testifieth that some time in august last past he heard Robert Munson say that Edward Ellis had thoroughly cured him of his wound hee had received of the indians in the Country' Service

[1675]. "Samuell Browne"

"1643-75 The Companye the trayne band of Brantry having made Choyse of leuftenant Rich[d] Brackett for there chaplin and Sergent Ellis for there leuftenant, and prevayled with them not to withstand that service, Doe intreate this honnored Court for there aprobation and confermation in these places and we shall pray for your pease and prosperitie.

"ffrancis Eliot

"in the name of ye Company"

"(Allowed)"

---

[1] Liber 3, fol. 495, liber 4, fol. 250, liber 6, fol. 6, and liber 10, fol. 73.

[2] Colonial Records, State House, Boston.

Dr. Edward Ellis and his wife Sarah had ten children: Sarah, born July 1, 1654; Edward, born Nov. 26, 1656, died April 9, 1658; Anna, born Feb. 5, 1658, died Dec. 4, 1678; Lydia, born Nov. 17, 1661; Edward, born Mar. 16, 1663; Mary, born 1st mo. 28, 1666; Mary, born Dec. 11, 1667, married William Rusk; Lydia, born Mar. 15, 1669; Robert, born Sept. 24, 1671; James, born Feb. 14, 1674. Their baptisms are given in the record of the First Church in Boston.

Dr. Edward Ellis died April 23, 1695,[1] aged 74 years. Mrs. Ellis died Dec. 18, 1711.

Nothing further has been learned of Mary Ellis, who married William Rusk.

Robert Ellis, surgeon, son of Dr. Edward, was appointed "chirurgeon" for the expedition to Port Royal,[2] Aug. 19, 1710, William Rand and Wheatley Gooch being appointed his assistants.

In Suffolk Register,[3] we read that, on account of Robert Ellis having purchased lands on Conduit Street, he is to have one-half share in the conduit, and "liberty of the drawbridge for use of vessels."

It appears that Dr. Ellis was a merchant, as well as a physician. His name appears as a creditor in the settlements of some thirty or more estates in Boston.

Dr. Robert Ellis married, June 4, 1698, Elizabeth, daughter of James and Sarah Pemberton, of Boston. Their children were: Edward, born Feb. 23, 1698-9; William, born Dec. 28, 1700, died Jan. 19, 1700-1;

---

[1] "Apr. 23, 1695. Neighbor Ellis died to-day."—*Judge Samuel Sewall's Diary.*

[2] "I shall now give you a short acct. of the state of our people, truly as delivered me by Doctor Ellis. There is a considerable number of them visited with violent fluxes and although we have things proper to give them, yet we dare not do it, others taken with mighty swellings in their throats, others filled with terror at the consideration of a fatal event of the expedition, concluding that in a short time there will not be well enough to carry off the sick."—*Extract from Wainwright's letter in respect to troops sent to reduce Port Royal.*

[3] Book 22, pp. 418–421.

William, born March 17, 1701-2, died Jan. 1, 1702-3; Mary, born July 4, 1703-4, died Nov. 2, 1719; Thomas, born Jan. 23, 1705-6; Sarah, born Sept. 15, 1707, married Thomas, son of John and Rebecca (Simpkins) Kilby (see account of the Kilby family); Robert, born June 13, 1709, died, 1723; William, born July 12, 1712, died Aug. 2, 1712; William, born Dec. 13, 1714, died July 24, 1716; Elizabeth, born Jan. 27, 1716; and Samuel, born June, 1718.[1]

Dr. Ellis died April 7, 1720. His will was made Feb. 23, 1719, and probated April 19, 1720, of which the following is a copy:

"In the name of God Amen. I Robert Ellis of Boston in the co. of Suffolk & Province of the Mass. Bay in New England Chirurgeon and Surgeon being sick and week of Body but thro mercy of sound & disposing mind and memory Do make and Ordain in my last Will and Testament in manner and form following, Hereby revoking and making null and void all former and Other Wills by me heretofore made. First and *Principally* I commit my precious and Immortal Soule into the Hands of my God my Creator, relying Solely on his mercy through the merit & Satisfaction of the Lord Jesus Christ for the pardon of my sins and gracious acceptance with Him.

"My body I Commit to the Earth to be decently Burried at the direction of my Executors hereinafter named. And for my Temporal Goods & Estate I Will that they be employed and bestowed in manner as is hereinafter Expressed. That is to say, Imprimis; I Will that all of my Just Debts and Funeral Expenses be well & truly paid & ordained to be paid by my Executors with all convenient Speed next after my Interment.

"Item I give to my well-beloved Wife Elizabeth my large Silver Tankard Porringer and largest spoon in the house, & it is my Will that the rest of my Plate be Divided to and among all my Children part and part alike. Item One Third part of the Remainder of my Estate both Real and Personal

---

[1] The baptisms may be found on the records of the Old South Church, Boston.

whatsoever and wheresoever the same is or may be found I Give Devise and Bequeath the same to my Well-beloved Wife Elizabeth for her comfort and Support during her natural life and at her Death to be disposed of in such way and manner as she shall see cause. Item The Other Two thirds part of the Remainder of my Estate both Real and Personal wheresoever the same is or may be found I give devise and bequeath to my Six children Namely Edward Thomas Robert Samuel Sarah and Elizabeth in six equal parts to be divided to and between them part and part alike and to be holden by them and their heirs and assigns forever. Item my mind and will is in case my Executors find it necessary for the Support of my Wife the maintenance and bringing up of my younger children, I do then hereby authorize and Impower them by good and Sufficient Deeds or Deed in the Law to sell and Dispose of all or any part of my Real Estate to be applied only to the use & uses aforesaid and that before any division be made providing also that the division of my estate as aforesaid among my children be no longer or farther delayed than such time as my youngest child shall arrive to the age of fifteen years. Item I do hereby make appoint and constitute my well-beloved Wife Elizabeth and my good friend and brother-in-law Mr. James Pemberton to be the executors of this my last Will & Testament in proof whereof I do hereby put my hand and Seal.....the 23 Feb. 1719..... Robert Ellis and a seal.

"John Ruggles
"Wm. Blair
"Jos. Marion"

From the inventory, we learn that a dwelling-house and land in Ann Street were valued at £450; two houses "at the south end of the town, fronting on Newbury and Winter Streets, with the land thereunto belonging," were £800; while the household goods, including 132 ounces of silver, amounted to £394. 7. 8.

Mrs. Ellis and her family continued the business of the store, but we learn from the "Suffolk Probate Register"[1] that she was obliged to dispose of land on

[1] Book 35, p. 28; book 36, p. 127; book 40, p. 323; book 42, p. 98.

Winter and Newbury Streets, for the maintenance of herself and several children under age.

Mrs. Ellis died Sept. 11, 1737. Her will was probated Sept. 20, 1737. It was made the previous August. She left her estate to her four children, Edward, Samuel, Sarah Kilby, and Elizabeth Ellis. She appointed her "good friend" John Welsh of Boston sole executor; but we see by the records that "Edward Ellis Chirurgeon (her son) was executor, Joseph St. Lawrence Genl^{n} and Daniel Oliver Perurke Maker" signing the bonds.

Dr. Edward was the only son of Dr. Robert Ellis who is known to have had descendants.

In the list of those who received "commissions from Gov. Shirley at Louisburg in the train of artillery sent from the Massachusetts Province" is the name of Edward Ellis, Esq., commissioned Surgeon-General of the Massachusetts troops, Feb. 19, 1744.[1]

In the list of those who received commissions in the Third Mass. Regiment "whereof Jere. Moulton, Esq., is Colonel," Edward Ellis, Esq., was commissioned Major and Captain of the 3d company, Feb. 25, 1744.[2]

"On the 12th Oct., 1743, Bro. Price—probably Henry Price, the first Provincial Grand Master—proposed Doctor Edward Ellis in the First Lodge in Boston. He was accepted Oct. 26th, and made a Mason Nov. 9th, 1743."[3]

In Suffolk Probate Records, from 1728 to 1756, the name of Edward Ellis appears frequently in the settlement of estates.

Richard Gredley, in attesting to his signature in the will of A. Reller of Boston, which was probated Dec. 20, 1745, says of Edward Ellis, whose name is also in the will as a witness, that "said Ellis is now at Louisburg."[4]

[1] N. E. Gen. and Ant. Register, Vol. XXIV., p. 371. [2] Ibid., p. 376.

[3] S. D. Nickerson, Recording Grand Secretary of the Grand Lodge of Massachusetts. [4] Suffolk Probate Records.

"Feb. 7, 1752. On the night of the seventh of February occurred a destructive fire, near Marlborough-street. It took in an out-house, burnt two stables, Mr. Sellon's blacksmith shop, and the dwellings of Dr. Cutler, and Dr. Edward Ellis. The night was rainy, but it raged with great vehemence for two or three hours. Several people were injured by the falling of a brick wall, and a horse was burned to death." [1]

"John had sm[l] pox and got well. Our servant woman Mary had y[e] sm[l] pox full. not Inoculated It came out on her, in y[e] [ ] of God's providence and she recover'd

"May 29, (1752) Georg came out pretty full sm[l] pox In y[e] way of God's Providence did well Edward Elis our doctor for all 3 of y[m] above." [2]

"Feb. 3 1747. Edward Ellis of Boston Physician, petitions the Gen. Court in regard to his account and says that on the 3d of Dec. last a grant was made him of £234. & £90 old tenor as appears by the printed reports but before an order or warrant on the Treasury was obtained, his acct. and order thereon was consumed when the Court House was burnt."

Endorsed on the above Petition:

"Bos. Feb. 18, 1747. An order is given for £234. old tenor in full for his service as Surgeon at the Castle in 1744 it being in proportion to the allowance made him in 1743. Also that the sum of £90. in like tenor be allowed him for his care of the sick & wounded French Prisoners brought into this Port by Messrs Tyng and Spry." [3]

Dr. Edward Ellis married Mary, daughter of Daniel and Mary (Mills) Willard, granddaughter of Major Simon and Mary (Dunster) Willard, of Boston, and widow of a West Indian planter named Cuyler.

They had three daughters: Maria, born in May, 1730; Sarah, born Aug. 22, 1733; and Elizabeth, born March 22, 1735.

Mrs. Ellis died at the age of fifty.

---

[1] Drake's History of Boston. [2] "Memoir of the Walker Family."
[3] Colonial Records, State House, Boston, Mass.

Dr. Ellis afterwards married Mrs. Haliburton, a widow. She died in Newport, Nova Scotia.

Dr. Ellis died in Amsterdam, Holland.

The graves of the first Dr. Edward; his daughter Anne; "Mrs. Elizabeth Ellis, wife of Mr. Robert Ellis, Surgeon, aged 52 years 2 months and 10 days;" Mary, daughter of Robert and Elizabeth; Robert, son of Robert and Elizabeth; and their four infant sons named William Ellis, are in the Old Granary Burying-ground, in the north-east corner, under the only weeping-willow in the ground.

Maria, the eldest daughter of Dr. Edward and Mary Ellis, married, June 30, 1748–9, Capt. Watmough of the British Army. (For their descendants, see account of the Watmoughs). Sarah married Isaac Deschamps, Esq., King's Attorney, and afterwards Chief Justice of Nova Scotia. Elizabeth married, Sept. 25, 1757, Capt. Peter Jacob Dordin. Their children were: Mary, died in infancy; Sarah, died in infancy; Peter, died in childhood; Elizabeth, married Silas, son of Edward and Mary Dean of Taunton, Mass. (see account of the Deans); Peter Jacob, drowned when about fifteen; Edward Ellis, died in infancy; a second Edward Ellis, died in infancy; a third Edward Ellis, died in infancy; and two infants who were not named. Capt. Dordin died Jan. 23, 1769.

Mrs. Dordin was married in Newport, R. I., by the Rev. W. Bissell of the Episcopal Church, Jan. 17, 1773, to Peter Francis Christian, son of Gideon and Madelon (Martine) de Les Dernier of Windsor, Nova Scotia. Their children were: Mary, born May 20, 1774, died in infancy; Harriet, born May 29, 1775, married William Pepperrell, son of Henry and Mary (Newmarch) Prescott (for their descendants, see account of the Prescotts); Sarah, born June 27, 1776, died in infancy; Anne Maria, born Nov. 27, 1777, married Lieut. Pearson, son of John and Elizabeth (Pearson) Titcomb (for their descendants, see account of the Titcombs). Mr. de Les Dernier was at one time a merchant on Long Wharf, Boston, Mass. He died in Philadelphia, Penn., with the yellow fever.

Mrs. de Les Dernier spent the last twenty years or more of her life with her youngest daughter, Mrs. Titcomb. She was blind several years before her death, which occurred in Salem, N. H., in 1817.

Mrs. Elizabeth Ellis Betton, a granddaughter of Mrs. de Les Dernier, has the Ellis coat of arms, exquisitely embroidered by her grandmother in her girlhood. It is sable between three fleurs-de-lis, argent; no crest. The same coat of arms has come down in the Watmough family, engraved on the stone of a seal ring.

Mr. Hervey D. Ellis, who has the records of all the early families by the name of Ellis in Massachusetts, tells me that he thinks, without doubt, the Mary Ellis mentioned in the following document was a sister of Dr. Edward Ellis (the first), his family being the only one by that name in Boston at that early date.

Major-Gen. Edward Gibbons was probably a half brother to Mary Ellis, and Dorothy Blythe may have been his sister-in-law.

"The 2d of the first m.·1645

This wrigeting is to testifye & to Confyrm Mary Ellis one house that was formerly Lef[t] Thos. Savidge & by him sold to maior Nehemya Bourne & by him to Edward Gibbons of Boston, the said Edward Doth giue to the aboue said Mary and her assignes the said Dwelling-house & with what ground is from goodman Smith's pale to two pales beyond the said Dwelling-house, and this of a lyne to the bottome of the pale that now Incloses the garden, to hould foreuer without molestation from him or any of his as his hand Doth witness

Edw Gibons

"This is to testifye Before home it maj Concern y[t] whereas wee John Richards, Tho[s.] Lake & Joshua Scottow, being authorrised to administer upon y[e] Estate of maior genrall Edw. Gibons of Boston late Deseased having this Deed presented unto us by Mrs Mary Skarlett, upon our former Experience of ye said maiors wrigetings and comparring it with other wrigting are firmely perswaded that it is [his] hand & Deed. in witness whereof wee haue hereunto signed

"Made at Boston this 16 December 1654.

"Josh. Scottow John Richards Thomas Lake

"Entred and Recorded this 8 June 1655 at Request of Mr^s Mary Scarlett Edw Rawson Recorder"

"This testimony was annexed upon the presented Deed

"Dorrathy Blythe Deposed sayeth that shee was in maior gibons her brothers howse and hard him Acknowledg that the howse & land menshoned in this Deed hee had giuen to my Cosyn Mary Ellis now Skarlet & to her heyres and assignes. I praying him to giue mee a little peece of the land hee said jts out of my power I haue made my sister Ruler ouer all.

"taken upon oath this 8^h June 1655 before mee

"Anthony Stoddard Commissioner"

"Enterd & Recorde ye same day

"Edw. Rawson Recorder"[1]

Major-Gen. Edward Gibbons was in America prior to 1628, as it is stated that he was here when Gov. Endicott arrived, and "rendered much service in organizing his government, at Salem."

Joshua Scottow, in his "Narrative of the Planting of the Massachusetts Colony in 1628,"[2] has given the following account of the change which took place in Mr. Gibbons's views after associating with the people at Salem:

"These prudent Undertakers sent forth their *Forlorn Hope* in two ships Laden with Passengers and Servants: two years before they had moved with their main Body, and Pattent Government, which were fully Furnished with a Pastor and Teacher, worthy *Higgison* and *Skelton*, and all Materials for Compleating of a Church of Christ, according to Divine Institution: Who safely Arriving according to their predeterminate Design of Inlargement of Christ's Kingdom, and His Majesty of *England's* Dominion: Firstly, they set up their Standards,

[1] Suff. Reg. of Deeds, Bk. 2, p. 172. [2] Mass. Hist. Coll., Vol. XXXIV., p. 289.

Dethroning Satan, they cast him out of Heaven; which beyond times memorial, he had in the Natives Consciences, and by Turf and Twig they took possession of this large Continent, and set up the first Church in these parts in a place they then called *Salem;* at which Convention the Testimony which the Lord of all the Earth bore unto it is wonderfully memorable by a Saving Work upon a Gentleman of Quality, who afterwards was the Chieftain and Flower of *New England's* Militia, and an Eminent Instrument both in Church and Commonwealth; he being the younger Brother of the House of an Honorable Extract, his Ambition exceeding what he could expect at home, Rambled hither: Before one Stone was laid in this Structure, or our Van-Currier's Arrival, he was no debauchee, but of a Jocund Temper, and one of the Merry Mounts Society, who chose rather to Dance about a *May Pole,* .... than to hear a good sermon; who hearing of this Meeting, though above Twenty Miles distant from it, and desirous to see the Mode and Novel of a Churches Gathering; with great studiousness, he applyed himself to be at it; where beholding their orderly procedure, and their method of standing forth, to declare the Work of God upon their Souls, being pricked to the Heart, he sprung forth among them, desirous to be one of the Society, who though otherwise well acomplished, yet divinely illiterate, was then convinced and judged before all; the secrets of his heart being made manifest, fell down and Worshipped God, to their astonishment, saying, *That God was in them of a Truth;* the Verity hereof, as long since it hath been affirmed by old Planters, so by his own Manuscript, found after his Death it's confirmed; he about that time Lamenting his Christian Estate, which evidenceth that it ought to be said of that Sion, *This man was Born there.*"

He lived for a time in Charlestown, and represented that place in the General Court, in 1632. He afterwards removed to Boston; and, it having been decided, in the spring of 1645, to make war on the Narragansetts, the "command-in-chief was given to him."

Capt. Edward Johnson said of him: "He is a man of a resolute spirit, bold as a lion, being wholly tutor'd up in N. E. Discipline, very generous and forward to promote all military matters; his Forts are well contrived, strong and in good repair, his great artillery well mounted, and cleanly kept," etc. "He was frequently a deputy to the General Court, and was advanced to the magistracy in 1650." He was Captain of the Ancient and Honorable Artillery Company, and one of the "charter members."

In 1643, the Governor being unable to render la Tour the assistance he requested to enable him to dispossess D'Aulney of the territory which he claimed on the eastern coast, Major-Gen. Gibbons and Thomas Hawkins furnished him with four ships and 68 men; Major-Gen. Gibbons loosing £500 by him, by which loss, Winthrop says, "he was quite undone." Palfrey says "he was not so undone but that the next year he was sending a new ship of about one hundred tons to Virginia for tobacco." He lost by this venture £200, "the ship being forced on shore from her anchor and much of the goods spoiled." Winthrop, in writing about it, says "the Lord was still pleased to afflict us in our shipping."

Winthrop gives an account of a perilous voyage made by Major-Gen. Edward Gibbons:

> The pinnace started for the "Bermuda, but by contrary tempests was kept from hence and forced to bear up for the West Indies, and being in great distress arrived at Hispaniola, and not daring to go into any inhabited place there but to go ashore in obscure places and lived off turtle and hogs, &c. At last they were forced into a harbor where lay a French man-of-war with his prize, and had surely made prize of them also, but that the providence of God so disposed, as the captain, one Petefore, had lived at Pascataquack, and knew the merchant of our bark, one Mr. Gibbons[1] whereupon he used them courteously, and for such commodities as she carried furnished her with tallow hides &c., and sent home with her his prize, which he sold for a small price to be paid in New England. He brought home an aligarto, which he gave the governor."

[1] Edward Gibbons was a merchant, as well as Major-General.

Palfrey says that "some of the crew had prodigious experiences to relate which were appropriate grist for Cotton Mather's mill."[1]

Capt. Scarlett, the husband of Mary (Ellis) Scarlett, was killed at sea by the "blowing up of the great cabin, May 4, 1684." His will gives property consisting of a farm at Mystic, lands at Merrimac, an estate in New York, dwelling and warehouses, shops, bakehouse, wharves, barge, lighters, etc., in Boston, to his wife Mary while she lives, and afterwards it was to be divided between Freegrace Bendall, Hopefor Bendall, Mary Scarlett, Tamaszin Scarlett, Betty Scarlett, Jane Scarlett, his brother John Scarlett, Love Prout and John Freke, Jr.; his wife and brother John Scarlett to be executors. Donations to Harvard College and the society for "decayed" seamen were added; also legacies to the Second Church in Boston, and to the poor of his native town of Kerzey in Suffolk County, Eng.

Mather tells a remarkable story of "distressed people at sea happily meeting and helping one another," in which Capt. Scarlett is one of the principal actors:

"A ship whereof William Laiton was master bound from Piscataqua in New-England to Barbadoes, being two hundred and fifty leagues off the coast, sprang a leak; which notwithstanding their constant plying of the pump for fourteen hours together, so fill'd the vessel with water, that all the eight persons aboard betook themselves to their boat, with a good supply of bread for them there to live upon. The master would utter a strange perswasion, that they should meet with a ship at sea, whereby they should be reliev'd: But before they did so, they had so far spent their small supply of water, that they were come to the allowance of each man a spoonful a day. In this boat they continued upon the Atlantic Ocean for nineteen days together; after twelve of which they met with a storm which did much endanger their lives; but God preserv'd them. At the end of eighteen days a flying fish fell into their boat; and having with them an hook and line, they

[1] See Mather's "Magnalia," Vol. II., p. 297.

made use of that fish for bait whereby they caught a couple of dolfins. A ship then at sea, whereof Mr. Samuel Scarlet was commander apprehending a storm to be near, they suffer'd their vessel to drive before the wind, while they were fitting of the rigging to entertain that approaching storm; and by this means they met with a boat full of their distressed brethren. Captain Scarlet's vessel was then destitute of provissions: only they had water enough and to spare; For which cause the marrinors desir'd him that he would not go to take the men in, lest they should all die by famine. But the Captain was a man of too generous a charity to follow the selfish proposals thus made unto him. He reply'd It may be, these distress'd creatures are our own countrymen: Or however, they are distress'd creatures. I am resolved I will take them in, and I 'll trust in God, who is able to deliver us all. Nor was he a looser by this charitable resolution; for Captain Scarlet had the water which Laiton wanted and Laiton had the bread that Scarlet wanted: So they refresh'd one another, and in a few days arriv'd safe to New England. But it was remarked that the chief of the mariners who urg'd Captain Scarlet against his taking in these distress'd people, did afterwards in his distress at sea, perish without any to take him in. In another voyage he perish'd at sea and was never heard of." (Mather did not add that the good captain was killed at sea.)

The following account of the Ellis family was written by Mrs. Harriet (de Les Dernier) Prescott, the widow of William Pepperrell Prescott, and granddaughter of Dr. Edward and Mary (Willard) Ellis, at the request of her daughter:

You ask of me, my daughter, a written copy of what I know of your (our) progenitors in my own dear mother's line. I have been tardy, more perhaps than is mete, to attend to your request, but I have never for a moment been forgetful of it. It has seemed unavoidable till some late premonitions reminding me of the slight hold I have at this advanced period[1] on a much

[1] She was about seventy-nine years old.

longer term of life, and that if I have any work yet to do I must hasten to its accomplishment, for the night draweth near. I do not feel that what I shall be able to communicate will meet or gratify your expectations. Much that I have learned of my mother's family history is derived from occasional and incidental conversations between my aunt Deschamps and other members of the family and my mother; and that chiefly in those seasons of life when the subject of ancestral history has not much interest to the hearer, as in childhood or early youth. Doubtless many circumstances may have escaped my recollection, and possibly I may omit some that I still remember. However, there will enough remain to evince to you that, though there may be much to regret, there will be but little to make you ashamed of those from whom you spring.

I can not go much beyond my grandfather, Edward Ellis. He was of Welsh extraction, born in Boston. His ancestors were among the early emigrants to New England. He was born about the beginning of the last century. If he possessed any records of his family, they must have shared the fate of his books, papers and furniture which were destroyed by fire in his house, while he was absent on a voyage on business of importance.

I do not know if my grandfather received a collegiate education, but I am inclined to think it, from the fact that he went through a regular course of study for the medical profession under one of the most distinguished physicians of the time and place, whose name however I can not recall, and that he was early in life established in the practice of medicine and surgery in his native place, and in good and lucrative business as such.

Dr. Ellis was twice married; first to Mary Cuyler, a young widow lady, daughter of Daniel Willard of Boston, and widow of a young West Indian planter, of the island of Barbadoes, if I remember rightly, who came to Boston in pursuit of health, and boarded in her mother's house.

Mrs. Willard, my great-grandmother, had been left a widow, with a large family of children, of whom my grandmother was the eldest daughter. Attracted by her great beauty, Mr. Cuyler prevailed on her mother to consent to her marrying him immediately, though she was little more than a child, promising not to return to the island without her permission, or to take his young wife away without her consent.

He was a young man of agreeable manners and good temper, and Mrs. Willard, who had no other means of providing for her family but those accruing from the business of the boarding-house, probably reasoned that she ought not to refuse so eligible a provision for her daughter, consented, and they were united. These promises, however, he failed to fulfill. He was summoned suddenly by the death of his father to return to his island home, and would not be prevailed upon to leave his young wife with her mother, but solemnly pledged himself to bring her back as soon as he should be able to settle the business devolving on him by his father's death, and have made the necessary arrangements for his future residence in New England. But if indeed he was sincere in this promise, he was not permitted to fulfill it. On arriving at the place in which his mother resided, he did not take his young wife to that mother; but, telling her he must prepare her to hear of his marriage, as he had never given her any intimation of it, he bore his wife to a plantation of his own in the mountains, and left her in charge of his slaves until he should come back to take her to his mother and friends. A longer period of time than she had anticipated would be required, rolled on, heavily enough to the poor girl in her remote and lonely situation. Whether her husband had feared to communicate to his mother the rash step he had taken, and put off from day to day and week to week his information, or had entered again into the gaieties and dissipations of the city or town, she did not know; he wrote her sometimes, it is true, but said nothing in his letters of removing her from her solitude. But it appeared that he had done something towards it at last.

Mr. Cuyler joined on one occasion in the races, was thrown from his horse, and instantly killed. The information of this sad event was suddenly borne to his wife in all its horrible details, and the shock occasioned the premature birth of her child. It appeared that young Cuyler had told his mother of his marriage; for, on that lady's hearing that her unknown daughter had given birth to a male child, she dispatched a favorite slave with orders to bring mother and child to her residence as soon as the former should be able to travel. She was, however, so ill that it was many weeks before she left her bed; and as she had not been able to attend to her child herself, it was given to a healthy young negress who had lately become a mother also, to nurse. When she became sufficiently restored to her former health to bear the journey, she was taken to the home of her mother-in-law. There all was so strange, so ungenial, separated from the child she had borne, but whom, being unable to nurse, she had hardly seen, she thought of her distant home and the kind mother she had so thoughtlessly bidden adieu to, little more than a year since. At length, seeing her pining and distress, her mother-in-law consented to her returning to her own mother; but the child must be left; it was heir to a great estate, and must be reared to manhood, if permitted to live, among his own people. But she should hear of his welfare and progress. He should be told of her, and, when able, should be directed to communicate with her himself. This was all; she was not urged to stay, but knew she would be made welcome; but it would never be home. So she returned, on the first ship that left the island, to the arms and hearts of her mother and family. Her husband's mother was true to her word. She improved every opportunity that offered to inform her of the welfare of her child; and to remit sums of money to her until her marriage with Dr. Ellis. I know nothing more of my grandmother's connection with the family of Mr. Cuyler, except that I have a vague idea of having heard that her son did not live beyond the period of childhood. She was still young when she married Dr. Ellis. They had three daughters: Maria, Sarah, and Elizabeth. My grandmother did not enjoy good health after the birth of the latter. She died in the prime of life, during the absence of her husband at the siege of Louisburg on the island of Cape Breton.

My grandfather received the appointment, made by Gov. Shirley, of Surgeon-General to the troops furnished by Massachusetts for that expedition; and when the news arrived that Gen. Pepperrell had succeeded in reducing that hitherto impregnable fortress, my grandmother lay dead in her house. When my grandfather was about to leave home to join the troops, he consigned his family to the care of his brother-in-law, Thomas Kilby. This gentleman was a widower with two motherless children. He had married my grandfather's sister, Sarah Ellis. The descendants of Mr. Kilby still live in Boston. After my grandmother's death, Mr. Kilby let the house to a Mrs. Haliburton, who agreed to board him and my grandfather's family, consisting of his three young daughters, and two orphan children of my grandmother's sister, who had married a Mr. Hope, a wealthy banker of Amsterdam, and had died within a few hours of her husband, leaving two children to her sister's care, though not long since married to Doctor Ellis. Mrs. Haliburton had four children of her own, and two young women dependent upon her,—one the daughter of her late husband by a former wife, the other the daughter of that wife by a former husband. Mrs. Haliburton had been left with but small means, and was glad to add to them by taking the house and boarding the family to whom it belonged. She was, as I have heard, a smart, sensible, capable woman, well calculated to have the care and training of young people at that day.

My grandfather did not return immediately that the expedition was successfully accomplished, but remained some time at Louisburg. He formed acquaintance with several gentlemen, among whom was Mr. Deschamps, who was King's Solicitor, at Halifax, Nova Scotia; and unwilling perhaps to encounter the home that had lost its chief ornament and was now so utterly changed; knowing, too, that his good brother-in-law would supply his place in the care of his children; and being entitled to a "grant of land" in the Province of Nova Scotia, he decided to go thither. He had also taken the restitution claim for the children of Mr. Hope, for the property it was known that gentleman died possessed of. After some time, however, he reached home, and while preparing to embark for Holland with his nephew Henry Hope, Mrs. Haliburton became his wife. He then embarked for Holland, had a safe if not a speedy passage, and succeeded in having young Hope acknowledged by his grandmother, then at the head of the house (as was then the custom in Amsterdam). But though he had no difficulty in obtaining the acknowledgment of the lad by his grandmother, it was necessary to have certificates of the marriage of his parents, of his own baptism, and of the death of his father, before he could succeed him, either as it regarded his property, or his place in the establishment of which his father had been the head and of which he subsequently became. It was while my grandfather was absent on this business, that his house was destroyed by fire, communicated by a neighboring barn. The fire broke out in the night, and the family narrowly escaped with life and what garments they could lay hold of. When my grandfather returned to procure the documents mentioned above, he found his family removed to another part of New England; his wife having decided to avail herself of an offer made her by a friend to go to a distant city and take a house called in those days a Coffee House, the present inhabitant of which, having made his fortune in the establishment, wished to retire from business. Mrs. Ellis was of a strong mind, an enterprising disposition, and of much energy of character; but she had a family of eleven persons, many too young to provide for themselves; her husband was far away, and the fire rendered them houseless, and she had little or no means of providing them bread. I hardly need add that she had closed with the offer and removed with her family to Newport, Rhode Island. There Dr. Ellis found his family, and here I may as well add a sketch of my grandfather's character. He was of a mild and easy temper, of social and agreeable manners, and of good moral character. I can not say if he had made a profession of religion, but I think I have heard that he constantly attended church and observed family prayers and had a reverence for religious things and religious people. He was about to return to Holland with the certificates, and to take his niece to her father's friends and the noble fortune and high position that awaited her; his family were comfortably established, his wife admirably calculated for the business; so he left things as they were, and resumed his voyage, which he accomplished successfully for all parties. Crossing the ocean in those days was not the pleasure excursion it has come to be in our time. These voyages consumed much time. During that time, his eldest daughter, though very young, was married to an officer in the British Army, who had come over to join his regiment, then stationed at Newport, and had taken his residence at the house of which Mrs. Ellis was the mistress. He became enamored of my aunt

Maria, who was said to be exceedingly lovely in person, mind and manners; and though several years older, succeeded in obtaining her hand, and they were married, and he took passage for himself and wife and her sister Sarah, whom she had prevailed upon to go with her, to Halifax, Nova Scotia.

On my grandfather's return from his second voyage to Holland, which had been unexpectedly prolonged by the increase in the business which occasioned it, he followed his daughter to Nova Scotia, removing his family thither. He never, however, resumed the practice of his profession. He disposed of his wild lands, and purchased a farm in a small, newly-settled village, situated on one of the arms of a river called by the English, who succeeded to the "hunted French," the Avon. My grandfather named the village in which was his property, after the town he had lately inhabited, Newport. There Mrs. Ellis died; and my grandfather, at the request of his nephew, Henry Hope, once more crossed the seas to visit him at his then residence in Amsterdam. He returned no more. He died there, at the age of seventy. Mr. Hope, in gratitude for his exertions in his behalf, had given him a pension of fifty pounds sterling per annum. This annuity Mr. Hope, in after years, bestowed upon my dear mother, increasing it to a hundred pounds yearly, with an injunction to draw at any time that her necessities required for any additional; and, at his death, he bequeathed her two hundred pounds sterling per annum during her life, and to her two daughters, Harriet Prescott and Anna Maria Titcomb, five hundred pounds sterling each, on her death.

Mr. Hope died, I think, in the year 1811; my mother, in 1817.

Mr. Hope resided in London for some time previous to his death. His only sister, Harriet Hope, had married a wealthy merchant of that city,—once, I believe, a partner in the house of which Mr. Hope was the head; at any rate, he was an intimate and long-tried friend.

Now, my daughter, I have reached the generation immediately preceding myself. I have said that my aunt married a Captain in the British Army. His name was Watmough. She had four sons. She died in the prime of her days. Her husband, immediately after her death, having orders to depart from Halifax for another station, left his sons in the care of his wife's family. One of these motherless boys soon followed the mother. The eldest, named John, my grandfather took, aud when about fourteen obtained an ensign's commission in the British Army for him. This poor child was killed by a chance shot on the field of battle, when in the performance of some duty. He had been promoted for some reason or other to a lieutenancy. He was said to be a noble boy, of a daring though amiable disposition, active and ambitious. Edward Ellis, the second son, was taken by Judge Deschamps, the husband of my aunt Sarah. He pleaded to be permitted to enter the British Navy. His uncle had intended him for his own profession, but finally yielded to the entreaties of his protegee. Captain Watmough had procured for his son Edward a midshipman's warrant while he was yet a child, sending him at the same time a miniature uniform of an officer of that rank. The ship to which he was attached was soon in active service in the war of the American Revolution, and he soon rose to the rank of Lieutenant. In some engagement with the enemy, whether French or American I do not now remember, in which he had lost one hand and two fingers of the other, he had behaved most gallantly, and in the returns of the War Department was so highly spoken of, together with a young friend of his, and so warmly recommended for promotion that they were both appointed to the command, each, of a sloop-of-war, and ordered to the West India Station. Lord Sandwich, then at the head of the Admirality, on presenting them with their letters of appointment, presented them — my cousin with a fine pair of silver-mounted pistols, and Mr. Robinson, his friend, with a valuable silver-hilted sword.

The vessel commanded by Capt. Watmough reached the station first, and when Capt. Robinson came, he immediately came on board his friend's vessel to greet and to congratulate him. Of course the presents they had from Lord Sandwich as testimonials of his appreciation of their gallant conduct, were spoken of, and the pistols were taken down from where they hung in the cabin of my cousin's vessel, for examination, just as his servant entering exclaimed, "Have a care, sir, they are loaded." The words were not finished when the pistol went off, the charge lodging in my cousin's breast. He only lived long enough to clear his friend from intentional mischief, and closed his eyes in death. Capt. Robinson never recovered entirely from the shock of having destroyed his friend, his reason only partially resuming its sway. He died in early manhood.

I well remember the grief of my aunt and mother when the news of the death of my cousin Edward reached them. He was an excellent young man, of a lively, spirited, yet agreeable temper, refined and cultivated manners, intelligent, generous, kind-hearted, and a universal favorite. This sketch of his character is, of course, from hearsay, not merely from his nearer friends, but from many others who knew him well and loved him and mourned his early death.

James Horatio, the youngest of my aunt Watmough's sons, was taken by my dear mother, and lived with her as her own child until he had attained his fourteenth year; when my mother having been left a widow, her husband having died at Cape Town, I think, on the coast of Guinea, Mr. Hope begged to have the boy transferred to his guardianship, saying he would educate and do for him as for a son of his own, if he had one, alleging his great affection for his cousin

Maria as the motive for his desire to do all he could for one, at least, of her sons, the other having been provided for by Government. My mother, seeing the advantages to the boy so far above what she could have given him, and finding an opportunity with a friend of her late husband, sent James to Mr. Hope. Mr. Hope fulfilled his promises, giving his new ward a thorough mercantile education in addition to the usual academic course, intending to take him into the firm,—a large banking establishment, etc. This, however, was not done, as young Watmough wished to visit his native land, which he did, coming in one of Mr. Hope's ships, or one which he employed in some of the branches of his extensive mercantile pursuits. He landed at Halifax, N. S., where he remained a few months. He then, the war with the colonies having closed or being nearly at an end, went to Boston, and thence to Philadelphia, where he became acquainted with a young lady to whose family he had brought letters of introduction. To this lady he paid his addresses, and succeeded in obtaining her hand. Mr. Hope enabled him to enter into partnership with a house in one of the West India Islands—Cape Francais. At the birth of his first boy, who was baptized Henry Hope, Mr. Hope settled a large amount of money, —many thousands of pounds sterling,—on the boy, the parents to draw the interest during their lives. Mr. Watmough purchased a fine tract of land, on which he built a splendid house, to which he gave the name of Hope Lodge. It was a few miles distant from the city. Here he resided with his family for some years. His son, Henry Hope, died young.

My cousin James was in Cape Francais when the insurrection broke out in that place, and with his partner, a Monsieur Forbes, escaped from the massacre, almost by miracle. Fortunately, Madam Forbes with her family had previously gone to Philadelphia to spend a few months. My cousin, I think, did not go back to Cape Francais, but fixed his residence in Philadelphia. He visited my sister Dean at Newport, I think, in the summer of 1791, with his wife and her sister, Miss Carmick, and, on going back to Philadelphia, took my sister Anna Maria with him on a visit.

I do not know the precise time of his death, but he left four children. His eldest daughter Maria married a lawyer named Reed. The second, when I last heard particularly of the family, was unmarried. His son John, a remarkably handsome, elegant and talented young man, when about seventeen, came on to visit me, with my brother Dean who had come to get his daughter, Anna Watmough Dean (named for my cousin's wife). She had been with me twelve or fourteen months, and was called home to make necessary preparations to go to Philadelphia with young Watmough, who had been sent by his parents to accompany her on her journey. Mr. and Mrs. Watmough had been very urgent in their request to have Anna visit them, but her father had objected to her going alone so far as it was then thought. This young man entered the army soon after, when the war of 1812 broke out between England and the United States. He behaved gallantly; and at the close of the war, he left the army with the title of Colonel, and a wound from which he never entirely recovered. He entered warmly into politics, and subsequently was elected State Senator. He was, in the words of our good friend, Col. Watson, a noble fellow; and if he realized in a small degree the promise of his early youth, he was a man to be proud of as a relation.

There was another son, Edmund, I think, younger than his brother. He had a taste for the fine arts, wrote finely, and, if he lived, is probably in some degree an artist. I heard nothing of the family for several years after my cousin died, and, as I said before, do not know when that event occurred. I saw an account of the election of Mr. John Watmough in a paper, and, believing there was no other family of the name in the country, I applied to Col. Watson, who gave me the information above written.

One thing more, and I pass from the Watmoughs. Among the presents that my kind-hearted and generous cousin James made his friends and associates, was a large silver caster of eight cut glass bottles, a rich brocade silk dress, and a plain apple green silk dress to my aunt Deschamps; a library of three hundred books finely "bound and gilt," chiefly "in calf," which contained all the standard English classics; a silk dress of the same piece as that for my aunt above mentioned, and a rich India China dress; several dresses to ladies of his acquaintance, of rich and expensive brocade lutestring; and about five hundred acres of land, which he inherited in right of his father, to my sister Anna Maria and myself.[1] Besides these presents to the members of his family, he presented many valuable and expensive articles to almost every person with whom he was brought into companionship.

My grandfather's second daughter, Sarah, while on a visit to her sister Watmough, in Halifax, became acquainted with Isaac Deschamps, Esq., an Englishman, then King's Attorney for the Province of Nova Scotia. To this gentleman she was married. He was a widower with one son, who was then seven years old, and, at the time of his father's second marriage, was with an uncle in London, where he was educated. Mr. Deschamps was some years his wife's senior; but he was a man whom to know was to honor and respect,—to know well, was to love sincerely and affectionately.

[1] The land was in Falmouth (in Acadia), N. S., about fifteen miles from Grand Pré, and on the opposite side of the river Avon from Windsor, in the most fertile part of the country. A few years ago, I visited Windsor, to see if it were possible to claim the land. I found by the old records in Windsor, that the land was given in trust to a resident of Windsor, who had sold most of it,—reserving, in all instances, the gypsum quarries, which he afterwards sold for a trifle and immediately bought back for himself.

They had no children, yet both were fond of children, and, though they never absolutely adopted any but Edward Watmough, my aunt had children always in her house, and loved to have them about her. On recalling to my recollection all the people I can remember, I think I can say with truth that my aunt Deschamps was the most fortunate and happy person I have ever known. She was uncommonly handsome, had a great flow of animal spirits, was sensible and of quick wit and warm heart, and was charitable, benevolent and affectionate. She had almost uninterrupted health, and enough of worldly wealth for all reasonable desires or expenditure. A few years after their marriage, my uncle was appointed Judge of the Supreme Judicial Court, and soon after removed from Halifax to Windsor, a garrison town situated on a river which my uncle named the Avon. The Indian cognomen I have forgotten. It was about forty-five miles inland from Halifax. There they continued to reside during the residue of their lives. Of hospitable dispositions, polite and agreeable manners, of easy fortunes, they were surrounded by a numerous circle of friends and acquaintances, who loved and honored them; while the humble classes,—among whom they dwelt, many of whom largely shared their bounty as well as their sympathy in the welfare or afflictions to which, in common with all born of woman, they were subject,—loved, respected and prayed for them.

"Peace was within their house, and plenteousness within their gates." Nine years before her death, my good aunt Deschamps became a confirmed invalid, in consequence of an incurable internal disease that inflicted much pain, often reducing her to great exhaustion, which she bore with patience and resignation. She died at the age of sixty-two years, in the hope of the "resurrection of the just." My good uncle survived her little more than two years, when he also went to the "great assembly of good men made perfect."

He was seventy-nine. He died of apoplexy, after seven days' illness. He was noble-spirited, open-hearted, benevolent and hospitable. He made a will dividing what property he died possessed of, after his debts were paid, between his two granddaughters and his wife's two orphan nieces, my sister and myself.

Elizabeth was the youngest of my grandfather's family, my own dear mother. She was twice married; first to Capt. Peter Jacob Dordin, commanding and owning a ship in the Holland trade, involving voyages to the coast of Guinea for ivory, gold, and what was considered at that time neither sinful nor shameful,—slaves. With this gentleman she lived many years, having many children, only two of whom lived over the period of early childhood. Capt. Dordin was born on the "high seas" as the phrase runs, of Dutch parents. His parents died during his childhood,—not, if I remember rightly, leaving much if any property. I have but reminiscences of his early life; but recollect hearing that the sea, as it was his birthplace, was also his home. He was regularly bred to the sea, going through all the grades until he reached the command and ownership of a ship, a stanch sea-boat, and became wealthy. He was an excellent husband, and a firm, stanch friend. I have heard him spoken of, by many who knew him, as sensible, enterprising and intelligent. He was, for a time, in Mr. Hope's employ; and I have heard both my aunt and mother say that, through him, he became acquainted with my mother's family, he bringing letters to my grandfather from that gentleman. Capt. Dordin died at Cape Town, on the coast of Guinea.

When my mother had been five years a widow, she went with her two children, Elizabeth, five or six years old, and Peter Jacob, a year or two younger, to visit my aunt Deschamps. She was married very young, and was still young and handsome, and of sprightly and agreeable manners. There she became acquainted with Peter Francis Christian de Les Dernier, born in Halifax, of Swiss parents; bred a merchant and already (although only just having attained his majority) commencing business as such in the town of Windsor. They became acquainted, of course, as he was a great favorite at the house of my uncle Deschamps, and while there, were mutually attracted. However, my mother, when her visit was finished, returned to Newport, R. I., where she had hitherto dwelt. There my father found her, and they were married. They had four daughters. I was the second, my sister Maria the youngest, and only we two lived to attain maturity. We were born in Windsor, Nova Scotia, and baptized by an English clergyman by the name of Burnett, then rector of the parish church,—an inconsiderable, unpretending edifice, standing on a little eminence, about a mile from the village. This little church is endeared to my memory by many associations. There I first raised my voice in responses of our beautiful and excellent liturgy; there, repeated the catechism,—not to him who, "made a member of Christ," had gone to his reward, among the just made perfect, for he was, they told me, a good man; but to his successor, a grave, dignified, reserved and silent man, Dr. William Ellis, an Irishman. And there, too, kneeling on the bare floor round a little altar, covered only by the white communion cloth, I received the emblems of our Lord's death, from the hands of the last named minister. I well remember with what feelings I, in my childhood, used to meet Dr. Ellis at my father's house, or in that of my good uncle and aunt. He had a full, deep-toned voice, and a solemnity of manner that made a deep impression on me; and the delight his notice of me gave me, has never entirely faded from my memory, or from my heart.

Of my grandfather's second wife, I need say but little. She made a good wife, and was generally considered to be a good mother to his children; that is, she was careful that they should learn all good housewifery, and be careful, industrious and exceedingly neat. She held, as I have heard, a "tight rein" over them,—showing no partiality to her own children, of whom she had five by her former husband.[1] The eldest son studied the profession of law, and practiced many years in Windsor, N. S. His son William was also a lawyer, and became one of the Associate Judges of the Supreme Court. Another of her sons was Captain of a merchantman that sailed out of Portsmouth, N. H. One of his sons was cashier of the Rockingham Bank, in that place. Her other son,—a wild, headstrong boy, as I have heard,—left home at an early age, and was seen or heard from no more. Her first-born daughter married, first, a Capt. Hamilton of Portsmouth; subsequently, while on a visit to her brother George, she married Jacob Sha, Esq., father of the late James, Jacob, and several other sons anddaughters.

HARRIET PRESCOTT.

Thomas Chandler Haliburton, M. P., ex-colonel, judge, politician, and well-known as the author of "Sam Slick," was a descendant of Mrs. Ellis by her first husband.

The following is from an old tombstone in Doncaster, England:

"Yf gud turn dun, gud turn require,
Then prey for me, Robert Ellius, esquer,
Who, when I was 30 wyntar and one,
Was Alderman of thys town.
And hafeying lifed full long
Now ley undere yis ston.
I deyd y^e 11 of Avril, Anno 1402."

---

[1] "Jany 2, 171$\frac{5}{6}$ Capt. Holberton died at sea."—*Judge Sewall's Diary.* This may possibly have been the former husband of Mrs. Ellis.

PEMBERTON.

JAMES PEMBERTON came to New England in 1646. He settled first in Newbury, Mass., but soon removed to Boston. He lived on Pemberton Hill, "a spur of Beacon Hill which now marks a level of about eighteen feet below the original hill, it having been cut down in 1835."[1] "It was first called Cotton Hill[2] (so called as lâte as 1733) from the residence of Rev. John Cotton, and subsequently Pemberton Hill, from James Pemberton, a later resident at the north end of what is now Pemberton Square."[3]

Mr. Pemberton was made freeman in 1648. He was a brewer, and his place of business was probably at the corner of Dock Square and Wing's Lane, as that was called Pemberton's Corner. His name appears in the list of names appended to the New England Merchants' Memorial to the London Board of Trade.

He was one of the founders of the Old South Church in Boston. His wife Sarah was also one of the founders. They had eight children, viz.: James; Joseph; Thomas; Benjamin; Mary; Jonathan; Ebenezer; and Elizabeth, who married Dr. Robert, son of Dr. Edward and Sarah (Blott) Ellis of Boston.

Mr. Pemberton died Oct. 10, 1696.

Mrs. Pemberton was buried May 26, 1700.[4]

---

[1] Tradition says a kind of Golgotha was found there; and Mather relates that "three hundred skull bones were found there, in his youth."

[2] "In the time of Gov. Andros, this was the best part of Boston."

[3] "Drake's History of Boston."

[4] "May 26. Mrs. Sarah Pemberton buried. Bearers: Sewall, Sergeant, Walley, Checkly, Hill, Williams."—*Judge Sewall's Diary.*

Mr. Pemberton's will was made Feb. 12, 1695. The following is a copy of a part of it:

"Imprimis, I will that all the Debts that I justly owe to any manner of person or persons whatsoever shall be well and truly paid or ordained to be paid in convenient time next after my decease by my Executrix and Executor hereafter named.

"Item After my debts and funeral expenses are satisfied and paid I do hereby give and bequeath unto my beloved Wife Sarah Pemberton, the use benefit and improvement of my whole Estate both real and personal during the term of her continuing my widow.

"Item I do hereby give and bequeath unto my son Ebenezer Pemberton absolutely for his own use and behoof my negro boy Harry and all such plate bedding, books and other things which he has now in his own custody at Harvard College Cambridge Together with one hundred pounds to be paid him out of my Estate within two years next after my Wife's decease. And I do ordain and appoint that my son Ebenezer Pemberton shall have and receive such maintainance out of the improvement of my Estate (as he now hath) until he shall be in Some Settled way whereby to procure him a comfortable subsistance.

"Item I do freely give and bequeath unto my Daughter Mary Pemberton for her proper use and behoof the Sum of three score lbs. to be paid her out of my Estate within two years next after my s[d] Wifes decease. And I do ordain and appoint that my s[d] daughter Mary Shall have her Living in my house (as she now hath) until division of my estate be made among my Children as hereinafter in and by this my Will is expressed.

"Item I do hereby give unto my son John Pemberton of Md. five pounds to be laid out by him in a piece of plate. Item I do hereby order appoint and enjoin my s[d] Wife to show kindness out of my estate to my two Grandsons, James and George Pemberton, (Sons of my son Thomas Pemberton dec[d]) in such a way as to her shall seem meet without controul.

"Item After my s[d] Wife's decease and the before mentioned Legacies are paid, I do hereby will ordain and appoint that all my housing and lands and other Estate Shall be equally divided to and among my undernamed Children viz. John Joseph Benjamin and Jonathan Pemberton Elizabeth Ellis and Mary Pemberton part and part alike, to remain to them their heirs and assigns forever in Severalty..... Item my will is that if my son Ebenezer has cause to buy the housing and land I now live in after my wifes decease he have the same before another paying as much for it as any other will..... Item if it happens that my wife marries again then my will is that she shall only have the use and enjoyment of one third part of s[d] Estate during her life, the other two thirds being divided among my above mentioned children," etc.

His wife and son Ebenezer were appointed executrix and executor.

The following is from the old records at the State House, Boston:

"In the house of Representatives Nov[m] 9th 1711

"Resolved that the sum of Fifteen Pounds be allowed to Mr. James Pemberton in full for his extraordinary service in assisting the Commissary General, in forwarding the late exped[n] intended to Canada," etc.

Benjamin Pemberton is in the list of Esquires who subscribed to the first volume of Prince's Chronological History of New England.[1]

"The late Rev. Dr. Gray of Jamaica Plain, on page 8 of his half century sermon, published in 1842, has the following passage: '*The third or Jamaica Plain Parish, in Roxbury, had its origin in the piety of an amiable female. I refer to Mrs. Susanna, wife of Benjamin Pemberton. She was the daughter of Peter Faneuil.*' This is a mistake. Peter Faneuil was a bachelor. Mrs. Susanna Pemberton had not a drop of the Faneuil blood in her veins. Her nearest approximation consisted in the fact, that George Bethune, her brother, married Mary Faneuil, Peter's niece and the daughter of Benjamin Faneuil."[2]

---

[1] "Heraldic Journal." [2] "Sergeant's Dealings with the Dead."

The name of Robert Ellis was appended to the will of Ann Pollard, March 17, 1709–10. When the will was probated, Dec. 7, 1729,—the witness, Robert Ellis, being long since deceased,—Mr. George Pemberton (surgeon), who served his time with his brother-in-law Robert Ellis, testifies that he believes that the superscription to this will as a witness was written by him the said Ellis, etc.[1]

By the kindness of Mr. Samuel A. Drake, I have the following items:

"Last Saturday, died here, after a few days' illness, James Pemberton, Esq., aged 83, a gentleman well respected among us while living, and his death is much lamented. We hear the funeral is to be this afternoon.

"Boston News-Letter, Mar. 5, 1747."

"James Pemberton, Esq., late of Boston, deceased. Hannah Pemberton and Benjamin Coleman administrators.

"Weekly Letter, 16 April, 1747."

"On the 7th inst., died here, aged 46, that amiable, that virtuous, that completely accomplished lady Miss Mary Pemberton, second daughter of the late James Pemberton, Esq."

Boston paper, 15 Mar. 1764.

"Monday last the Rev. Ebenezer Pemberton was married to Miss Annie Powell, eldest daughter of the late John Powell, Esq., formerly a merchant of this town.

"Boston Chronicle, 20 June, 1768."

"On the 8th inst. died here after a languishing illness, in the 47th year of her age, Mrs. Anne Pemberton, the wife of Rev. Ebenezer Pemberton of this town, eldest daughter of John Powell, Esq., and niece of the late Lieut. Gov. Gen. Dammer. Boston Evening Post, 12 Mar. 1770."

"Benjamin Pemberton Esq. is appointed Naval Officer of this Province. New England Weekly Journal, 19 Apr. 1734."

---

[1] In "Sergeant's Dealings with the Dead," may be found the testimony of Dr. George Pemberton in regard to a duel fought by Benjamin Woodbridge (grandson of Rev. John) and Henry Philips, in which the former was killed.

"We hear a number of Dr. Pemberton's hearers left his meeting yesterday on account of his late conduct in reading the proclamation, one in particular who had attended there 40 years. Boston Gazette, 18 Mar. 1771."

"On Thursday the 15th inst. died greatly esteemed by all that knew her Mrs. Phebe Pemberton in the 82nd year of her age. Ibid."

In 1770, Samuel Pemberton was a Justice of the Peace. He was one of the seven who asked the Lieutenant-Governor to remove the British troops from Boston. His colleagues were Samuel Adams, Hancock, Warren, Phillips, Henshaw and Wm. Molineaux.

I am indebted to Henry Pemberton, Esq., of Philadelphia, for the following letters,—the first of which was probably written by a grandson of James Pemberton of Boston, and the second by a great-grandson:

"Maryland, June ye 23, 1703.

"To Israel Pemberton[1]

"Living with Saml Carpenter

"Merch^{t} in Phil^{a}

"Loving Cousin

"Israel Pemberton

"Thease may acquaint thee, that I have Gott safe whome after a tiresome and tedious Journey & to my Great Joy mett wth my Mother and Brothers In good health. The which was a great mercy, for I think I never saw such a sickly time In our partts In all my Life before. The Greater part of the young men are dead; some with the Small Pox & some with other Distemp^{rs} that was not usual hereaway, as paines in theire Stomaches & Sides & other Places, but now, through mercy I pray well over, wh^{ch} I pray God to Continue for it was not only troublesome to ye it kild but others.—So no more at present but kind Love & Respects to thyself &

[1] Israel Pemberton was only 18 years old at the date of this letter; his correspondent probably about his own age. The *writing* is beautifully executed.—*Henry Pemberton.*

Sister, remembering thy Master,[1] & thanks for thy kindness to us w^{n} In Philadelphia I remain with my Mother & Brothers

"In All Cander thy

"Cordiall & Affectionate Kinsman,

"James Pemberton.

"Pray lett me hear from thee when thee has such opportunity."

"Boston July 20th—1749

"To Ja^{s} Pemberton

"Phil^{a}

"S^{r}

"Agreeable to my promise while at Nantuckett I now write you. I arrived here the 4th instant, and have as you desired forwarded the pott of Spermacitae delivered me by our friend Coleman, who did his utmost to procure the best for you.

"I hope it will not be disagreeable to give you some account of our family, since by this means you will be able to know whether any relation subsists between us. My Great Grand Father *James Pemberton* left Wales about the year 1680 [this is undoubtedly a mistake, as he came in 1646—see p. 38], and came over to New England and had Six Sons and two Daughters. The names of his sons were James, Joseph, Thomas, Benjamin, Jonathan, and Ebenezer. James, his eldest son, inclining to the principles of the Quakers, left his father at about Nineteen years of age, went over to Maryland, there settled, and had several children. Some years after, he went over to London attended by one of his sons John, and died at one Thomas Bond's, a Quaker in Thomas St. London.

"Thomas, his third son, practiced Physick and Surgery in this town for many years. He had three sons and four Daughters; his sons were James, Thomas & George. James the eldest, was a merchant in this town for several years, and deceased about two years ago (his youngest son you lately saw at College). Thomas the second son (my Father) was bred to the sea and is still living. George the youngest, was a surgeon and practised here for many years; he deceased about ten

---

[1] Samuel Carpenter, a prominent merchant in Philadelphia, with whom Israel Pemberton was apprenticed.

years ago and left a Widow with one son Thomas (who is since dead) and two Daughters who are married here and alive.

"Benjamin, the fourth son of my Great Grand Father, was a Brewer. he died also and left a Widow with one son Benjamin, who was bred a Merchant, but is since Clerk of the Superior Court in this town.

"Ebenezer, who was the youngest son of my G^t Grand Father, was educated at the College in Cambridge, of which he was Tutor for some years, and was afterwards Minister of the old South Meeting House in this town. He likewise died and left a Widow with three sons (and a Daughter) Ebenezer, the Presbyterian Minister at N. York, John, and Samuel, whom you lately saw at this Island. You may also see by the inclosed Impression the Coat of Arms of the family.[1] If you should think it worth while to inform me relating to your family, I should take it as a favor.

"I hope this will find you much benefitted by your Journey, and I assure you it would give me great pleasure to hear of your welfare, and altho' our sentiments respecting Religion may not exactly correspond, yet I hope that will be no hindrance to my hearing from you. I am sir

"Y^r Most R. E. Servt

"Thos Pemberton Junr

"Please direct to me at

"Wm. Tyler's Esq. Merch^t

"In Boston"

Rev. Ebenezer Pemberton, son of James and Sarah Pemberton of Boston, was born in Boston, and baptized in the Old South Church, Feb. 11, 1671. He was graduated at Harvard College in 1691, and, after some years, was chosen fellow of the college.

From Quincy, we get a glimpse of the state of feeling then prevailing at the college. He says: "The sectarian controversies which at this period agitated

[1] The shield in the coat of arms enclosed in the letter was the same as that of the Pennsylvania Pembertons; but the crest was different, being a boar's head erect, couped.

the Province, the Corporation, and the College, were among the causes of the exclusion of Increase Mather.

"Thomas Brattle, William Brattle, John Leverett, Ebenezer Pemberton, and Benjamin Colman, were all graduates of the College, and, with the exception of Colman, had been connected with its government when Increase Mather presided. All were men distinguished for zeal in the cause of learning and religion, and highly esteemed by their contemporaries for moral worth and intellectual attainments. None of them were adherents to the rigid doctrines of the early established Congregational Church of New England, or concealed their preference of those milder and more liberal views of the Christian dispensation, which, after the charter of William and Mary had deprived the clergy of their civil power, began to be openly avowed. . . .

"From their proceedings it can not be doubted, that both the Mathers had determined to resist, with a strong hand, the tendency to deviate from 'the good old scriptural ways,' which, as they thought, was countenanced in the College and the community, by the Brattles, Leverett, and Pemberton; Colman being then in Europe. The agreement of these members of the College in religious sentiment was a subject of general notoriety. In 1697, Leverett and Pemberton were tutors, Thomas Brattle was Treasurer of the College, and William Brattle had just exchanged his office of tutor for that of pastor of the church in Cambridge. In the same year, Cotton Mather published his Life of Jonathan Mitchell. Availing himself of this occasion, President Mather wrote an Epistle Dedicatory for that work, addressed 'to the church in Cambridge and to the students in the College there.' In this Epistle, he enumerates the great lights Cambridge and the College had formerly enjoyed; and reminds them of the many countries and places, which, after possessing a faithful ministry, had become, through 'young profane mockers and scornful neuters, overgrown with thorns and nettles, so that the glory of the Lord had gradually departed.' 'Mercy forbid,' he adds, 'that such things should be verified in Cambridge.' . . . . The time, manner, and language of this publication could not but have been deeply offensive to the Brattles, Leverett, and Pemberton. Under the mask of advice, it was a reproof given to them before the students of the college and the world, with an evident design, in connexion with their known opinions, to load them with the reproach of degeneracy and apostacy." Soon afterward, Rev. Benjamin Colman was elected pastor of the new church in Brattle Square, which was founded by "an association of enlightened and pious Christians," led by Thomas Brattle. Mr. Colman says: "This invitation was accepted by me, and the more acceptable it was, by reason of the kind and encouraging letters, which accompanied it from my excellent friends, the Hon. John Leverett, the Rev. William Brattle, Ebenezer Pemberton, Simon Bradstreet and others."[1]

Mr. Pemberton was called to the pastoral office of the Old South Church, in Boston, as colleague with the Rev. Samuel Willard, and was ordained Aug. 8, 1700. He subsequently became the third pastor of that church.

Rev. Benjamin Wisner, in his "History of the Old South Church," says of him: "He was a man of eminent talents and great acquirements, and 'had the reputation of being as accomplished a preacher as this country ever produced.' 'He was,' says an intimate acquaintance well qualified to estimate his character, 'a hard student from his childhood; and, being blessed with brightness of mind, fervor of spirit, and strength of memory, he made wonderful dispatch. He was master of logic and oratory, in great perfection. The college never had a more accomplished tutor, nor one that

---

[1] "History of Harvard College," Vol. I., pp. 127–131. Quincy.

more applied himself to teach and watch over the morals of it.' His piety was of a decided character; producing, habitually, 'a strong conviction of the reality of things invisible and eternal,' and 'a zeal which flämed' in his Master's cause. His temperament was uncommonly ardent; which, when properly regulated, gave to his performances a peculiar energy and power; but which sometimes proved a great infirmity, —his passions, when suddenly excited, becoming impetuous and violent. Yet, 'when free from the excitement of any unpleasant circumstances,' it is said, 'he was mild and soft as one could wish.' In preparing for the pulpit, he usually made only hints, from which he enlarged with great readiness and propriety. His discourses were characterized by clearness of exhibition, and close and animated reasoning; they were remarkably practical, yet abounding in doctrinal truth; often pathetic; and commonly distinguished for pungency of application. His delivery was agreeable and peculiarly lively and vigorous. . . . . Of the few sermons which he wrote at length, but three or four were published by himself. An octavo volume, containing most of these and some not before printed, was published after his death. They are sermons of uncommon excellence,—'strong, argumentative, eloquent.' They are 'written,' says the late Dr. Elliot, 'in the best style, and would do honor to any preacher of the present age. They are wonderful compositions for the period.'

"Through life, Mr. Pemberton was a diligent student and a laborious minister. His constitution was always feeble; and during several of his last years, he was greatly afflicted with severe bodily pain; but, under weakness and suffering, continued to do much in his appropriate and loved employment."

Thomas Pemberton wrote of him: "He was of a strong genius, extensive learning, and a preacher of raised thoughts."

Dr. Sewall, his colleague, in his sermon occasioned by Mr. Pemberton's death, says: "It pleased God to furnish him with eminent gifts and endowments. And he is justly celebrated as a great scholar, an excellent Divine, and a good Christian.

"Might I presume to look upon myself as a competent judge of learning and learned men, I would say he was a great proficient in the study of the liberal arts and sciences. He had a great natural capacity, a large and comprehensive genius; and, by hard study and great industry, had amassed a rich treasure of learning. I suppose few in these corners of the earth have been better acquainted with books and men. He read much, and had an excellent faculty of digesting what he read and making it his own. He had the powers of reasoning and arguing in an high degree. He was a great master of speech, and was very happy in imparting his sentiments to others. . . . . He was highly esteemed for the pertinency, fervency and copiousness of his expressions in prayer. His discourses were elaborated. The subjects of them were well chosen, the method was accurate, the style strong and masculine. They were excellently well suited to make his auditors wiser and better; and he delivered them with extraordinary fervour. . . . .

"It pleased God in his holy providence to exercise him with strong pains, and that of long continuance, under which he was enabled to express himself with a becoming submission and resignation to the sovereign disposal of God. And I look upon it to be truly wonderful, that under such frequent returns of distressing maladies, he was strengthened and spirited in so great a measure to perform his ministerial labours in the house of God. Herein God's power was observably magnified in him. It is a comfort and refreshment to us, that this bright lamp of the sanctuary went out at last in a sweet perfume; that I may borrow the phrase used by him in his excellent discourse on this subject, above a year ago. These were some of his last words: 'I thank God, who hath given me a good hope through Christ. Notwithstanding my many infirmities, both in public and private, through his grace, I have been enabled to be sincere and upright before Him. And I can now look for an house not made with hands, eternal in the heavens, when this house of my earthly tabernacle is dissolved. And this hope is built only upon the merits of Christ, who hath suffered so much for me; who died, and is risen again, and lives forever to make intercession for me. And upon this foundation is built my hope for myself, my family, my church, and the whole Israel of God. And I thank God, who hath enabled me in a dying hour, to express this my hope.'"

Mr. Pemberton married Mary, daughter of John and Mary (Atwater) Clarke. She survived him, and married Henry Loyed, the father of Dr. Loyed.

Mr. Pemberton died on the 13th of February, 1716–17, aged 45. He left three sons and one daughter. There is an account of his last sickness and death, in "Judge Samuel Sewall's Diary." Judge Sewall, in writing of the death of Rev. William Brattle, which occurred two days later, says: "I wish it be not portentous that Two such great men should fall in one week! *Deus avertat omen.*" In writing of the funeral, Judge Sewall says: "Mr. Pemberton is buried between 4 and 5 [Feb. 18th], in Mr. Willard's Tomb. Bearers, Mr. John Leverett, presid$^{t.}$ Dr. Cotton Mather; Mr. Wadsworth, Colman,[1] Mr. Sewall, Webb, Dr. Increase

[1] In a letter from Rev. John Cotton of Newton to his father Roland Cotton of Sandwich, is this extract: "Mr. White and I trudged thro' (there had just been a severe snow-storm) up to ye South where I knew Mr. Colman was to preach in ye forenoon, when he designed to give the separate characters of Mr. Pemb. [Rev. Ebenezer Pemberton] w^{c} was n't time for on ye lecture, which he did sweetly and well; telling how emulous he always was to excel; his candle envied, &c. Y^{t} when we saw him stand up how our expectations w^{r} always raised & y^{t} he always exceeded them & never deceived them."

Mather, Maj.-Gen[l.] Winthrop. Col. Hutchinson not there, by which means it fell to me to wait on his Excellency; 't was good going, a broad path being made. Col. Lynde of Charlestown was there.....' Col. Byfield and Councellour Cushing there, Mr. Thacher of Milton." There are more than one hundred and fifty references in the "Diary" to the Pembertons, most of them being to Rev. Ebenezer Pemberton.

In 1727, a volume of Mr. Pemberton's sermons was published in London, with a portrait of him prefixed, underneath which, appeared a coat of arms,—argent a chevron between three buckets sable.[1]

Quincy, in his "History of Harvard College," says: "In 1717, the Corporation lost two of its most valued members. Ebenezer Pemberton, senior pastor of the Old South Church in Boston, died on the 13th of February; and William Brattle, pastor of the church in Cambridge, on the 15th of that month. Brattle and Pemberton were both men in life beloved, and in death deeply lamented. 'A great part of the beauty of our Israel is fallen,' exclaims Colman, in a funeral sermon on the occasion. 'They were stars of the first magnitude. Providence set them at the head of the country for learning and usefulness. They were singular ornaments of it, pillars in the church of Christ here, and among the fathers of the college;' 'alike philosophers and divines,' 'faithful in their trusts,' 'distinguished for their judgment, and for their mutual friendship and affection.'"

Ebenezer Pemberton, D. D., son of Rev. Ebenezer Pemberton, for many years held a "conspicuous and honorable place" among the ministers of New York City, as pastor of the Presbyterian Church. During Whitefield's first visit to New York, he was the only clergyman in the city who invited him to his pulpit. Dr. Pemberton was, during the latter part of his life,

---

[1] "Heraldic Journal."

pastor of the New Brick Church in Middle Street, in Boston. It is said that his piety was of that fervid kind for which his father was remarkable, and that he drew crowded assemblages by his manner.

Ebenezer Pemberton, LL. D., a grandson of Rev. Ebenezer Pemberton, was a learned classical teacher of Boston. He served as tutor in his alma mater (Nassau Hall), was principal of Phillips Academy, Andover, Mass., and for a number of years was Primate of the "Boston Association of Teachers." He received honorary degrees from Harvard, Yale and Dartmouth Colleges. His degree of Doctor of Laws was conferred by Allegany College.

Drake says of him: "No instructor of youth was ever remembered with more vivid affection by his pupils." It is said that he was dignified and elegant in his appearance, his manner and utterance. His attitude, look, voice and gestures were those of the orator. He died in Boston, in 1835, aged 87 or 88.

Thomas Pemberton, the antiquary, a descendant of James and Sarah Pemberton, was born in Boston, in 1728. He possessed an extensive knowledge of historical facts, and it is said that his manuscript *Memoranda, Historical* and *Biographical*, make about fifteen volumes. He furnished many articles for the periodical works published in his native town, and contributed almost a ninth part of the collections of the Historical Society of Massachusetts, bequeathing to them all of his manuscript. He had prepared a "Mass. Chronology of the Eighteenth Century," containing the remarkable events of every year, biographical notices of eminent men, topographical delineations, accounts of the settlements of towns, etc. As a companion, he is said to have been facetious, inquisitive, entertaining and instructive. In his youth, he was distinguished among his acquaintance for poetic talents, and had a peculiar turn for epigram. "He frequently recited some that were elegant and pungent, which he declined printing or circulating." He never married, and, at his death, left his estate in legacies "which do honor to his memory and benevolence."

For the following account of the Pembertons of Pennsylvania, I am indebted to the kindness of Henry Pemberton, Esq., of Philadelphia. It is supposed that the Pembertons of Pennsylvania and the Pembertons of Boston were originally one family, which supposition is justified by the fact that James Pemberton, who was undoubtedly a grandson of James Pemberton of Boston, in his letter to the ancestor of Mr. Henry Pemberton (on pp. 42-3 of this chapter), addresses him as "Loving Cousin," and signs himself "thy Cordiall & Affectionate Kinsman."

The Pembertons of Pennsylvania are descended from an ancient family of that name in Lancashire, England. This branch of the family early became converts to the doctrines of the Friends or Quakers; and, in 1670, Phineas Pemberton, a young man of twenty, then an apprentice to John Abraham, a grocer in Manchester, was imprisoned in Lancaster Castle for refusing to take the oath of allegiance to the king, and for attending Quaker meetings. He married, in 1676-7, Phoebe, the only child of James Harrison, an active and zealous Friend who had frequently been imprisoned for his religious convictions. Phineas Pemberton, at the time of his marriage, was established as a grocer in Boulton-le-Moors, Lancashire, where he carried on an extensive trade with Dublin and other parts of Ireland. In 1681, James Harrison was appointed agent of William Penn, he having the entire management of his affairs in America. Mr. Harrison purchased large tracts of land in Pennsylvania, and with his wife and her mother who was over 80 years of age, together with his son-in-law, Phineas Pemberton, and the father of Phineas, Ralph Pemberton, aged 73, and seven servants, sailed from Liverpool in the ship "Submission," Sept. 5th, 1682, arriving in America the last of October. Mr. Harrison settled upon one of the tracts of land he had purchased, adjoining William Penn's Manor of Pennsburg, near the Falls of the Delaware River. He continued to be Mr. Penn's agent until his death. He took a prominent part in State affairs, being Speaker of the House of Provincial Representatives in 1682, and also member of the Governor's Council of 16, and of the first Assembly, being one of the committee of three to prepare the charter. He held, also, many other important offices.

Phineas Pemberton, after the death of his father-in-law, which occurred in 1687, continued in the confidential relation to William Penn thus begun. He was early appointed Register-General for Bucks County; Clerk of the Courts; member of the Assembly; Master of the Rolls; member of the Provincial Council; and one of the Council of State.

When William Penn left for England in 1701, Phineas Pemberton was a dying man, and Penn, writing to James Logan (the son-in-law of Phineas, who had succeeded Mr. Harrison as Penn's agent) says: "I am grieved at it; he hath not his fellow, and without him, this is a poor country indeed." On receiving notice of his death, Penn writes: "I mourn for Phineas Pemberton; the ablest as well as the best man in the Province."[1]

Ralph Pemberton, Phineas and Phoebe Pemberton, with several of their children, as well as James Harrison, with his wife and mother, are buried in the family graveyard laid out by Phineas on his plantation

---

[1] "Penn and Logan Correspondence," Vol. I., p. 55.

at the "Point," four miles below Trenton. No interments have been made for over 175 years, but it is kept in repair by a fund left in charge of the "Fall Yearly Meeting," to keep it, and the walls around it, in decent order forever.

Israel Pemberton, born in 1685, was the only son of Phineas Pemberton who reached manhood. He was brought up in the counting-house of Samuel Carpenter, an eminent merchant in Philadelphia. He early became an active and influential Friend, and held "divers high and honorable offices." He was for nineteen successive years a member of the General Assembly of Pennsylvania. In his younger years, he was one of the most considerable merchants of Philadelphia, and was "distinguished for the uprightness of his conduct and dealings," also for his hospitality.

Israel (Jr.), born in 1715, James, born in 1725, and John, born in 1727, the surviving children of the above, ever maintained the characteristics of their father and grandfather. They were all active merchants and zealous Friends, giving much of their time and money to philanthropic purposes, especially to the preservation of peace and good-will between the Indian tribes of Pennsylvania and the rapidly increasing white population. Their lives justified the remark made by Thomas Wescott: "By force of intellect, activity of mind, strong predisposition to take part in public affairs, integrity and intelligence, the Pemberton family for nearly a hundred years was the most prominent in Pennsylvania."[1]

Until the Revolution, the three brothers, and especially Israel, were at the head of all public affairs. The outbreak of the war and the approach of the English forces caused the Revolutionary party to look upon former members of the Quaker government as disaffected, if not hostile to them; and in 1777, Israel,

---

[1] "Historic Mansions of Philadelphia," p. 494.

James and John Pemberton, with many other prominent citizens, were exiled to Winchester, Virginia, and detained there upwards of eight months. The hardships of travel and of a life to which they were so unaccustomed, seriously injured their health. Israel Pemberton died soon after their return.

Israel was twice married. By his first wife, Sarah Kirkbride, he left one son and two daughters; one of whom married Samuel Pleasants; the other married Samuel Rhoads. The descendants of the above are represented by the families of Fox, Fisher, Norris, Emlen and Byrd of Virginia, and by prominent families of Philadelphia.

By the second marriage he left one son.

James,[1] the second brother, lived to be 87 years of age. He left no male descendant. One daughter married Dr. Parke; another married Anthony Morris, whose descendants are a well known family in Philadelphia.

John Pemberton, the youngest of the brothers, devoted the latter part of his life to preaching the doctrines of the Quakers. He traveled much abroad, and died in Westphalia, Germany. He left no children.

Joseph, the only son of Israel Jr. who left descendants, married Ann Galloway of Maryland, first cousin of the well-known Joseph Galloway the Loyalist.

Joseph Pemberton died at the age of 36, leaving a large family, of whom John Pemberton, born in 1783, was in 1812 the only male representative of the children of William Pemberton who was born in 1580.

John Pemberton married Rebecca, only child of John Clifford, and left a large family,—of whom James lives in Paris, France; John C. married a Miss Thompson of Norfolk, Va.; Anna C. married Dr. Hollingworth; Rebecca married Charles Newbold; Henry

---

[1] "He succeeded Franklin as President of the Society for the Abolition of Slavery."—*Drake.*

married, first, Caroline Hollingworth, and, second, Agnes Williams; Andrew died unmarried; Clifford married Helen A. Tryer.

Gen. John C. Pemberton, the second son of John and Rebecca Pemberton, is well-known as the Confederate General who held Vicksburg, finally surrendering to Grant in 1863.

Gen. Pemberton was graduated at West Point, in 1837. Entering the 4th Artillery, he served in the Florida war, and was Aid-de-Camp to Gen. Worth, during the Mexican war. He was brevetted Captain and Major for gallantry at Monterey, and at Molino del Rey, Sept. 8, 1847. He was distinguished also at Contreras and Churubusco, and at the capture of the City of Mexico where he was wounded. He resigned in 1861. He entered the Confederate service as a Colonel of Cavalry and Assistant Adjutant-General to Gen. Joe Johnson, and in 1862 was made a Brigadier-General. He was subsequently a Lieutenant-General. He commanded the army opposed to that of Gen. Grant in north-east Mississippi, and was defeated at Champion Hills, May 16, 1863. Intrusted with the command of Vicksburg, he made a gallant defense, but was compelled to surrender to Gen. Grant, July 4, 1863. He resigned his commission, and at the close of the war was inspector of artillery, commanding at Charleston. He died July 13, 1881.

The arms of this branch of the Pembertons are: "Argent, a chevron, sa. between three buckets of the second, hooped and handled or.; crest, a dragon's head, couped sa. erect."

The Pembertons have a very large collection of manuscript, containing many thousands of letters.

WILLARD.

It is uncertain whether the family of Willard is of Celtic or Teutonic origin, though the evidence in favor of the latter preponderates. Unless the name can be identified with the name Wluard or Wluuard, it can not be found in any of its orthographies, previous to the Conquest. At this point, there are found in Doomsday Book the Latin names Wielardus and Wilardus in connection with the tenancy of certain land.

In the south-westerly part of Kent, within a few miles of the borders of Sussex, in the hundred of Brenchley and Horsmonden, in the lathe of Aylesford, lies the quiet and retired parish of Horsmonden.[1] Here lived in the latter part of the sixteenth century, Richard Willard. "The parentage of Richard," says Mr. Joseph Willard in the "Willard Memoir," from which the following account is taken, "has not been ascertained beyond all question. The absence of registers previous to the Reformation shuts out investigation." Richard Willard married Catherine —— who died at Horsmonden, March, 1597–8. His second wife was Margery ——, who died at Horsmonden, December, 1608. His third wife was Joan Morebread, who survived him but a few days. His children were: Mary, Thomas, Elizabeth, Richard, Margery, Simon, Catherine, Edward, John and George.

Richard Willard died at Horsmonden, February, 1617. In his will, which was proved March 14, 1616–17, he makes special provision for the "virtuous

[1] No one of the name or family of Willard remains at Horsmonden, where, as well as at Brenchley, they at one time formed a considerable part of the population.

bringing up of his children." He left all of his real estate to the three children of the second marriage, viz.: Margery, Simon and Catherine. To Simon he gave the lands called the "Hooks," the messuage and lands purchased of "Evenden and Paynter," and the lands and tenements called "Weesbines." To Margery and Catherine he gave the messuage, barn, close, two gardens and orchards, bought of "Wood." Mrs. Willard had a life interest in a part of the estate.

Simon, son of Richard and Margery Willard, was born at Horsmonden, probably in the early part of the year 1605, as he was baptized in the church at that place, April 7, 1605, by Edward Alchine, Rector. He married Mary, daughter of Henry and Jane (Feylde) Sharpe, of Horsmonden.

In April, 1634, Capt. Simon Willard, with his wife and one or two children, his sister Margery and her husband, Capt. Dolour Davis, embarked from England for New England, arriving at Boston about the middle of the month of May, after a short and very prosperous voyage. The name of the vessel is unknown, but there is on the files at Hartford, Conn., the deposition of a Mrs. Elizabeth Bacon, who states that she arrived in New England in the month of May, 1634, and that Samuel Greenhill "was reputed, by those who were well acquainted with him in the ship, a man of considerable estate, and was accordingly entertained in the ship with Mr. Willard and Mr. Pantry, and Mr. Crayfoote, and others of good account."

Capt. Willard settled in Cambridge, Mass. From the Proprietors' Record, we learn that he had one hundred acres on the Brighton side of Charles River, adjoining the land owned by his brother-in-law, Capt. Davis. He engaged in the purchase and exportation of furs, dealing extensively with the Indians of the interior.

At the time of his arrival the inhabitants of Cambridge were complaining of "straightness for want of land, especially meadow," and it may have been owing to this fact that he soon decided to leave Cambridge, and in company with others, to found a new plantation at Musketaquid. In September, 1635, a grant of land six miles square, was made by the General Court, Winthrop says, to "Mr. Buckly and [Simon Willard] merchant, and about twelve more families." The place was named Concord. Rev. Peter Bulkeley, with whom Mr. Willard was associated, was a man "of great learning, and large heart, 'of noble family,' 'possessed of wealth,' and distinguished as a divine. He arrived in Cambridge early in the summer of 1635, and to him Willard attached himself with affectionate regard."

The following is from Capt. Edward Johnson's account of their removal:

"Upon some inquiry of the Indians, who lived to the north west of the Bay, one Captaine Simon Willard being acquainted with them by reason of his trade, became a chiefe instrument in erecting this town: the land they purchase of the Indians, and with much difficulties traveling through unknowne woods, and through watery scrampes [swamps], they discover the fitnesse of the place, sometimes passing through the thickets, where their hands are forced to make way for their bodies passage, and their feete clambering over the crossed trees, which when they missed they sunke into an uncertaine bottome in water, and wade up to the knees, tumbling sometimes higher and sometimes lower; wearied with this toile they at end of this, meete with a scorching plaine, yet not so plaine but that the ragged bushes scratch their legs fouly. . . . . Their farther hardship is to travell, sometimes they know not whither, bewildred indeed without sight of sun, their compasse miscarrying in crowding through the bushes. They sadley search up and down for a known way,—the Indians paths being not above one foot broad, so that a man may travell many dayes and never find one. . . . . Thus this poore people populate this howling desert, marching manfully on (the Lord assisting) through the greatest difficulties and sorest labors that ever any with such weake means have done."

Soon after Capt. Willard's arrival in Concord, he and Maj.-Gen. Gibbons, with some twenty men under their control, were sent by Gov. Winthrop to Connecticut, with instructions "to take possession of the place and to raise some buildings."

Upon the organization of the town of Concord, Capt. Willard was chosen Clerk of Writs, and was continued in that office by annual election for nineteen years. The second year he was appointed Surveyor of Arms, having been a Captain in England. His first military commission in the colony was that of Lieutenant-Commandant. He was afterwards made Captain, and in 1653, was chosen Major of Middlesex, second in rank only to the Commander-in-Chief of the forces of the colony. The next year he was placed in command of an expedition against a tribe of the Narraganset Indians. At the earliest election made by the town, he was chosen a Representative to the General Court, and was re-elected fifteen times.

In 1654, he was placed by the freemen of the colony in a "more distinguished, responsible, and widely useful position, as assistant, or member of the higher branch of the Legislature, which office he held continuously till his death."

This embraced a very critical period in the history of the colony,—the earnest and exciting controversy with the Commissioners of Charles II. "The Commissioners were clothed with large powers, some of which were wholly inconsistent with the charter, while others were especially offensive to the people of Massachusetts, who had enjoyed so much actual liberty under its provisions." The Commissioners having perused the "Booke of the Generall Lawes and Libertjes," proposed, in the name of the King, no less than twenty-six alterations and additions. Gov. Bellingham, Major Willard and Messrs. Collins and Fisher were appointed a committee to peruse the Commissioners' exceptions to the laws of the colony. "The

Commissioners met," says Mr. Joseph Willard, "with a spirit as decided as their own,—a spirit that would not submit to any infringement of the patent, and hardly willing to stop even at that point. Thence arose a long and earnest controversy, which ended in the Commissioners being baffled at all points; and they left the country in a very angry frame of mind, with abundant threats of Royal indignation."

The Commissioners, having been authorized by the King "to hear and determine complaints and appeals in all cases, as well military, as criminal and civil," gave notice to the General Court, that on a certain day, they should sit as his majesty's Commissioners to hear and determine the cause of Thomas Deane and others against the Governor and company, "and," say they, "we do expect you will by your attorney answer to the complaint." They did answer, but not as the Commissioners intended. When the day for meeting came, they published a long declaration by sound of trumpet, declaring the proposed trial inconsistent with the maintenance of the laws and authority, and summoned Thomas Deane to appear and make good his charges. The Commissioners express unfeigned surprise, that, in a case wherein the Governor and company are impleaded, they should assume to themselves the hearing; "it being," say they, "unheard of and contrary to all the laws of christendom, that the same persons should be judges and parties." The General Court sent loyal addresses to the King, with a ship-load of masts for his navy, of which he stood much in need, "and the colony had rest for a time."

Major Willard resided in Concord twenty-five years, and was a "leading and valued citizen." His mansion house was afterwards owned by Dr. Joseph Lee, "who, being a strong tory, was imprisoned during the Revolutionary war, and his house was taken by the patriots and used for a time as a boarding-house for Harvard students, when the College in 1775 was removed to Concord, by order of the Provincial Congress, as the College buildings at Cambridge were needed for the use of the soldiers of the American army.[1] The house was burned some years ago.

Major Willard removed from Concord to Lancaster, Mass., "being importuned by the inhabitants to come and instruct them in municipal affairs. When the place was destroyed by the Indians, he removed to Groton, and remained there until that place was destroyed by the Indians, when he removed to Charlestown, Mass.

He was employed by the government in various transactions with the Indians, and was associated with Apostle Eliot, and Major Gookins, in their friendly missions. When a company was formed to encourage the trade in furs with the Indians, he was intrusted with the superintendence. He was chosen by the Indians about Concord "to record, and keep in writing," what they had generally agreed upon, touching their religious and civil government. Passaconaway, chief sachem of the Merrimac, requested that the Apostle Eliot and Capt. Willard would live near his people to teach them.

During the thirty-seven years that Major Willard was a member of the General Court, he was constantly engaged in the public service. "The records of the General Court and other archives show a large aggregate of assiduous and valuable labor." "He was much sought after to settle vexed questions of the boundaries of towns, to arbitrate in controversies on the administration of the internal affairs of towns, and to settle disputed claims." He was one of the committee chosen by the General Court to consider the subject of supplies. This resulted in a law requiring "that all hands not necessarily employed in

---

[1] "Concord Guide Book." G. B. Bartlett.

other occasions, as women, boys and girls," should "spin according to their skill and ability."

The office of surveyor was of very considerable importance in the early days of the colony, and Major Willard possessing the qualifications required for it, was frequently called upon for its exercise.

For years, Massachusetts had laid claim to the Province of New Hampshire, under the provision of her charter which granted on the north all of the lands which extended three miles north of the Merrimac; and, in 1652, when she was preparing to ward off the attack of Mason's heirs, and establish her claim to a wider jurisdiction, Major Willard and Captain Edward Johnson were appointed Commissioners to find out the most northerly part of Merrimac River. An interesting memorial of the survey still exists.

About forty-five years ago, in consequence of a dam having been thrown across the head of the weirs at the point where Lake Winnipiseogee discharges its waters into the Upper Merrimac, a large rock was exposed to view, deeply embedded in the gravel, with its surface but little above the water. On this rock was the following inscription:

E J S W
WP JOHN
ENDICOT
GOV

This points back unerringly to the spot which the Commissioners in their return to the General Court, designate and establish as the north line of the patent. Endicott was then the Governor of the Colony of Massachusetts Bay, so his name was inscribed, with the abbreviation W. P., for Worshipful, together with the initials of Simon Willard and Edward Johnson. The rock is now called the Endicott Rock.

"When King Philip's war began, Major Willard was summoned from the court he was presiding over, at the advanced age of 70 years, to lead the Middlesex

Militia, and drive back the foe from the exposed towns of his district. This he did, and rapidly marched through the desert to Brookfield, just in time to relieve the garrison there." Bailies states, that "Major Willard so silently and skillfully managed his approach, that he was perceived by the garrison before he was discovered by the Indians."

Increase Mather says: "What a black appearance of death and ruin was before the poor people at Quaboag, when they were all cooped up in one unfortified house, and surrounded by a barbarous multitude of cruel Indians, who thirsted after their blood! But God by a strange providence sent Major Willard, who, with a small party of soldiers, came a few hours or minutes before it was too late; by which means, the remaining inhabitants of that place had their lives given them for a prey."

Hubbard, in his history of the war, gives abundant commendation to the Major, whom he entitles "that honoured person, that worthy patriot and experienced soldier." Mr. Sidney Willard says: "For more than forty years he was a frontier commander with inadequate forces under his command, engaged with an enemy whose modes of warfare were of a kind to occasion the utmost perplexity, and who by sudden surprises and simultaneous attacks on different places, were enabled to accomplish their fatal purpose."

Major Willard received a number of grants of land, making in all between four and five thousand acres, exclusive of his right to subsequent divisions in the lands of Lancaster. The towns of Acton, Stow, and a part of Groton, are on land that belonged to him. After his death, his six youngest children received a grant of one thousand acres in payment of money that was due Major Willard from the Indians. In 1686, a tract of land twelve miles square,—afterwards the township of Rutland,—was conveyed by the Indian proprietors to Henry and Benjamin, sons of Major Willard; Cyprian Stevens, his son-in-law; Joseph Rolandson, son of the former minister of Lancaster; and Joseph Foster of Billerica.

Major Willard married for his second wife, Elizabeth, daughter of Henry Dunster, of Balehoult, Lancashire, Eng. She was sister to President Dunster. She lived but six months after her marriage. His third wife was Mary Dunster, cousin to President Dunster. She survived him and married Deacon Noyes of Sudbury.

Major Willard died April 24, 1676. While presiding at court, he was seized with an epidemic cold of a very malignant type then prevailing in New England, and after a few days' illness, died in the seventy-second year of his age. He had the pleasure of knowing a short time before his death "that a grateful public still acknowledged the value of his faithful labors, when the official count of the votes placed him among the highest on the list of the proposed assistants for the political year beginning in May, 1676; in fact, heading all others with the exception of the Governor and Deputy-Governor."

Rev. Ebenezer Pemberton says of him: "He was a sage patriot in Israel whose wisdom assigned him a seat at the Council Board, and his military skill and martial spirit entitled him to the chief place in the field."

Rev. Horatio Wood of Lowell, Mass., says: "Mr. Willard was a stalwart Puritan of the elder day, a conscientious, religious man, possessing strong religious convictions, a devout, humble and earnest spirit. He was a man of sound and enlightened understanding, of discreet wisdom and of a brave and enduring spirit, not boastful, but possessing that true courage which belongs to a modest and generous nature, and is ready, at the call of duty, to sacrifice ease and comfort, yea, life itself, in defense of the public weal. Never was motto on coat of arms more characteristic than that of the Willard family in him and all of its prominent members, 'Gaudet patientia duris.'"[1]

Mr. Willard had seventeen children, viz.: Mary, born in England, married Joshua Edmonds; Elizabeth, died in infancy; Elizabeth, married Robert Blodd of Concord, Mass.; Dorothy, died in infancy, or early youth; Josiah, married Hannah, daughter of Thomas Hosmer, a distinguished citizen of Hartford, Conn.; Samuel (see account of Rev. Samuel); Sarah, married Nathaniel Howard, of Chelmsford, afterwards of Charlestown, Mass.; Abovehope, died at the age of seventeen years; Simon, married first Martha, daughter of Richard and Joanna Jacobs of Ipswich, second, Priscilla Buttolph (Simon was a Marshal of Essex after the overthrow of Gov. Andros, and in active service as commander of a military company in an expedition against the eastern Indians); Mary, married Cyprian, son of Col. Thomas Stevens, of London, Eng.; Henry married first Mary Lakin of Groton, Mass., second, Dorothy, widow of Samuel Cutler; John, married Mary, daughter of John Hayward, of Concord, Mass.; Daniel, (see account of Daniel); Joseph, married, but his wife's name is unknown (he was a sea-captain in the London trade, his residence being in London); Benjamin, married Sarah, daughter of Ensign John Lakin of Groton, Mass.; Hannah, married Capt. Thomas, son of Thomas and Esther Brintnall of Boston; Jonathan, married Mary, daughter of Major Thomas and Patience Browne of Sudbury, Mass.

Rev. Samuel Willard, son of Major Simon Willard, was born at Concord, Mass., Jan. 31, 1639–40. He was graduated at Harvard College in 1659, and in 1663, was ordained minister at Groton, Mass., where

[1] The coat of arms was: Argent on a chevron sable between three fish weels proper, five ermine spots. Crest, a griffin's head erased or.

he continued till the breaking up of that town by the Indians in 1676. He was installed, April 10, 1678, as colleague with the Rev. Thomas Thacher, the first minister of the Old South Church in Boston, and continued in connection with that church till his death.

The Rev. Ebenezer Pemberton, his colleague, says of him: "His Master committed to his Pastoral Care a Flock in a more obscure part of this Wilderness. But so great a Light was soon observed thro' the whole Land. And his Lord did not design to bury him in obscurity, but to place him in a more eminent station which he was qualified for. The Providence that occasioned his removal to this place was an awful judgment to the whole land; yet it was eventually a mercy in this respect, in that it made way for the translation of this bright star to a more conspicuous orb; where his influence was more extensive and beneficial, and in that it was a great blessing to this congregation, to this town, nay, to all New England."

On the 6th of September, 1701, Rev. Increase Mather having been excluded from the Presidency of Harvard College,—nominally on account of his refusal to reside there, but really for other reasons,—a resolve was drawn up by the House of Representatives, making the Rev. Samuel Willard President of Harvard College, with the title of Vice-President, as he also objected to giving up his parish and residing in Cambridge.

Quincy says: "Mr. Willard held the station of Vice-President more than six years, and until his death. His duties were not less arduous than those of his predecessors, and his fulfillment of them was equally punctual, laborious, and successful.[1] Under the influence of that modesty which was a predomi-

[1] Rev. Increase Mather feared that the glory of New England had departed, and that the College under direction of Rev. Samuel Willard would "become a nursery not of plants of renown, but, of degenerate plants, who will forsake those holy principles of truth," etc.

nant feature of his character, he was content with this comparatively inferior title. Our historians have found it difficult to account satisfactorily for this anomaly in the title of the executive of the College. "Pierce, with his characteristic sagacity, intimates, that it might have been an evasion. Such it unquestionably was, and resulted from the position in which the Legislature found themselves placed, between the vote they had passed, that the President should reside at Cambridge, and the determination of a majority to rid themselves of President Mather. That vote they were not willing to rescind in favor of Willard, after having for a series of years pertinaciously insisted upon it in relation to Mather. But Willard being as unwilling as Mather to accept the office on condition of residence, and as they could not agree on a third person, they resorted to the subterfuge of continuing Willard in the office he then held of Vice-President, and vesting him with the power and duties of President. Thus, without rescinding their former vote, or any apparent inconsistency, they permitted Willard, during his life, to occupy at the same time the office of superintendent of the College and that of pastor of a church in Boston; and to perform the duties of President under the title of Vice-President, by occasional visits, without actual residence at Cambridge. These were precisely the relations Mather was desirous and had offered to sustain; and on account apparently of their incompatibility, he had been excluded from office.

"Many circumstances united to render Willard, in the state of the religious and political parties of the time, far more generally acceptable than Mather. Both possessed the confidence of the prevailing Calvinistic sect; for they were equally learned and sound in the articles of faith by that sect deemed fundamental. But their writings and demeanor exhibited a remarkable contrast. Willard was quiet, retiring, phlegmatic and unpretending; Mather, restless, obtrusive, excitable, boastful of his public services, and complaining of neglect and ingratitude. The life of the former had been devoted to professional research and pastoral duties. His study was the scene of his private labors; his church the theater of his public action. These had constituted a sphere of usefulness, to which his ambition had been limited; which he did not quit until after repeated legislative applications, for one higher and wider, and then with reluctance.

"The life of the latter, on the contrary, had been one series of theological and political controversy. He was a partisan by profession; always harnessed, and ready, and restless for the onset; now courting the statesmen; now mingling with the multitude; exciting the clergy in the synod, and the congregation in the pulpit, and the people in the halls of popular assembly.

"Amid the agitations consequent on that insanity of the age, denominated 'the Salem witchcraft,' the conduct of Willard was marked by prudence, firmness, and courage. He neither yielded to the current, nor feared to cast the weight of his opinion publicly in opposition to the prevailing delusion; an independence the more remarkable and honorable, as Stoughton and Sewall, two of the Judges of the court of trial, men of great influence in the Province, both his personal friends, and the latter a principal member of his church, were deeply affected by the distemper of the times. His tongue and his pen were, notwithstanding, employed to bring back peace and reason to his country. Increase Mather, on the contrary, although he had co-operated in that excitement with far less zeal than his son Cotton, and his course had been more prudent, yet shared, in the event, a full proportion of that odium, which attached ultimately to all the clergy and politicians, who had countenanced the infatuation.

"After it had subsided, the circumspection of Willard, in that trying season, was remembered and honored, and he derived thence a weight of popularity, which President Mather had lost by his conduct during the excitement. The resulting general impressions concerning the character of each were, undoubtedly, among the causes of that preference, which the exclusion of Mather and the appointment of Willard by the Legislature indicate.

"The family connection, which subsisted between Mr. Willard and Joseph Dudley, who became, the very next year, by royal appointment, Governor of the Province, might also have had some effect, in fixing attention thus strongly on Mr. Willard. They had married sisters, the daughters of Edward Tyng, one of the earliest, wealthiest, and most influential families in the colony. The appointment of Dudley was anticipated; and the friends of the College could not deem it indifferent to its interests with the new Governor, whether he should find the President's chair filled by Mather, an active leader of that religious and political party, which had imprisoned him and Andros, with whom his name and character had been an unvaried theme of abuse, or by Willard, a brother-in-law, who enjoyed at once his private confidence and personal respect."[1]

The Rev. Benjamin Wisner says of Mr. Willard: "He was one of the most eminent of the ministers that have adorned the New England churches ..... His powers of mind were of a superior order. He had a copious fancy, and a quick and accurate perception; and in argument was profound and clear. His piety was consistent, devoted, self-denying and confiding. His learning was extensive and solid; especially in theology, which was his favorite study, and for his proficiency in which he was greatly celebrated..... In the strange proceedings in regard to witchcraft in

[1] "Hist. of Harvard Coll.," Vol. I., pp. 145–149. Josiah Quincy, LL.D.

1692, though three of the judges who condemned the persons executed for that crime were members of his church, and to express doubts of the guilt of the accused was to expose one's self to accusation and condemnation, he had the courage to express his decided disapprobation of the measures pursued, to use his influence to arrest them, and to aid some who were imprisoned awaiting their trial to escape from the colony. And he had the satisfaction soon to see a stop put to those unhappy proceedings, and the judicious part of the community come over to his opinion."

"It ought never to be forgotten," says the Rev. Ebenezer Pemberton, his colleague, "with what prudence, courage, and zeal, he appeared for the good of the people in that dark and mysterious season when we were assaulted from the invisible world, and how signally instrumental he was in discovering the cheats and delusions of Satan which threatened to stain our land with blood and to deluge it with all manner of woes."

Edward Randolph wrote to the Bishop of London, May 29, 1682: "We have in Boston one Mr. Willard, a minister, brother to Major Dudley, who is a moderate man and baptiseth those who are refused by the other churches, for which he is hated."

John Dunton, who visited Willard, writes: "He 's well furnished with Learning and solid notions, has a natural fluency and can say what he pleases."

Mr. Sidney Willard says: "There seems to have been a remarkable infusion of affectionate feeling into his sound orthodoxy, the orthodoxy of the day which he held in common with his brethren."

Mr. Pemberton, in the discourse occasioned by Mr. Willard's death, says of him: "He had a deep thought and penetrating sagacity to make a just estimate of things on sudden emergencies, which made him justly esteemed one of the wisest men of his order in our land. His natural genius and spirit seemed superior to all narrow and selfish interests, not governed by the rules of carnal policy, nor biased by private views; but appeared to be almost incapable to be under the commanding influence of any thing but what was great, good, and honorable."

"He had a native modesty which continued in his advanced years, seldom known in conjunction with gifts of so conspicuous an elevation, which might seem to some to veil the brightness of some of his public appearances, though in the opinion of others it was but a foil to his greater excellences."

"His sermons were all elaborate, acute, and judicious; the matter being always weighty, and his subjects well chosen, suited to the state of his flock, and every way adapted to make them wiser and better. His common discourses might have been pronounced with applause before an assembly of the greatest divines." "His style was masculine, not perplexed, but easy as well as strong." "His delivery was characterized by gravity, courage, zeal and prudence, and with tender solicitude for perishing souls. And when the matter required it no man could speak with greater pathos and pungency." "He knew how to be a son of thunder to the secure and hardened, and a son of consolation to the contrite and broken in spirit." "His public prayers were always pertinent and pathetical, animated with a spirit of devotion," and characterized by "an uncommon compass of thought." "His spirit was truly pacific, and could sacrifice every thing but duty for peace." "The duties of holiness he explained and enforced with the most powerful arguments and with an address suited to melt the rocky heart, bow the stubborn will, to humble the proudest sinner, and charm the deafest adder." "In him bountiful heaven was pleased to cause a conjunction of all those natural and acquired excellences which are necessary to constitute a *great man*, a *profound divine*, a very considerable scholar and an heavenly christian." Mr. Pemberton spoke of him as one "who had been for a long time the light, joy, and glory of the place," and whose death was "a severe blow to his country, his church, and regarded as a rebuke to the whole land."

It is said that Mr. Willard was grave and dignified in his bearing and pleasant in conversation. There is a portrait of him in Memorial Hall at Harvard College.

Mr. Willard married Abigail, daughter of Rev. John and Mary (Launce) Sherman, and granddaughter of Thomas Darcy, Earl of Rivers. They had six children. Mr. Willard married for his second wife, Eunice, daughter of Edward Tyng, Esq., of Boston. There were fourteen children by this marriage.

Mr. Willard died suddenly, Sept. 12, 1707. Judge Sewall gives the particulars of his sickness and death in his "Diary," he being present when his "dear Pastor expired." Judge Sewall says: "Mr. Willard is laid by his tutor, in my tomb, till a new one can be made. Bearers, Dr. Mather, Mr. Allen, Mr. Thomas Bridge, Mr. C. Mather, Mr. Wadsworth, Mr. Colman. Fellows and students of the College went before. Mr. Pemberton led Madam Willard. Gov. and his lady had Rings; Bearers, Scarfs and Rings."

Mr. Willard's publications were numerous,—more numerous, it is said, than those of any other divine in this country except Cotton Mather. His largest work, was "A Complete Body of Divinity," which was published nineteen years after his death. It was a folio, and the first folio printed in America. The preface is signed by Joseph Sewall and Thomas Prince, "two of the most eminent scholars and divines in the Province; and in recommending the work, they might well observe, 'We need only say, 'Tis Mr. Willard's.'"

Moses Coit Tyler says of this work: "In the year 1726, the men of books in New England noted with considerable exultation, as a sign of national progress, the issue from an American printing-press, of a huge folio volume,—the largest that had ever been printed in this country. It bore this well-deserved title, 'A Complete Body of Divinity.' Within its nine hundred and fourteen pages,—each page having two columns in small and compact type,—it held 'two hundred and fifty expository lectures on the Assembly's Shorter Catechism,' all written out and delivered in order by one busy man, during a period of nineteen years. That man was Samuel Willard, himself, like his book, a body of divinity; a man of inexpressible authority, in those days, throughout all the land. . . . .

"Nineteen years before his death he began to give at his own church, on Tuesday afternoons, once a month, an elaborate lecture on theology. His was a mind formed for theological method. He did not desire to impose upon himself or upon any one a slavish submission to a theological system; he only wished to get for himself and others the clearness and vigor and practical utility that come from putting one's most careful ideas into orderly combination. He was a theological drill-sergeant. He was also a truly great divine. In the lectures upon systematic theology, which he thus began in 1688, and continued unflinchingly till he died, his object was to move step by step around 'the whole circle of religion.' The fame of his lucid talks on these great themes soon flew abroad, and drew to him a large, permanent audience of the learned and unlearned; and after his death, theological students kept clamoring for the publication of these talks. In 1726 all such persons were gratified.

"'A Complete Body of Divinity' is a vast book, in all senses; by no one to be trifled with. Let us salute it with uncovered heads. The attempted perusal of all these nine hundred and fourteen double-columned pages, was, for many a theological scholar of the last century, a liberal education—and a training in every heroic and heavenly virtue. Along the pages of the venerable copy that I have used—the copy which Jeremiah Dummer, of the Middle Temple, London, sent over in 1727 as a gift to Yale College—I find fading memorials of the toil and aspiration, and triumph, with which numerous worthy young divines of the last age grappled with the task of reading the book through; but on the blank leaf at the end, are only two inscriptions of final victory: 'Lyman perlegit, 1742,' and 'Timothy Pitkin perlegit, A. D. 1765.' Doubtless both of these heroes have long since had their reward, and have entered into rest, which they sorely needed: and the others perished by the way.

"The thought and expression of this literary mammoth are lucid, firm, close. The author moves over the great spaces of his subject with a calm and commanding tread, as of one well assured both of himself and of the ground he walked on. His object seemed to be, not merely to enlighten the mind, but to elevate the character and the life; and whenever, in the discussion of a topic, he has finished the merely logical process, he advances at once to the practical bearings of it, and urges upon his hearers the deduction of a moral logic, always doing this earnestly, persuasively, and in a kind way. The whole effect is nutritious to brain and to moral sense; and the book might still serve to make men good Christians as well as good theologians—if only there were still left upon the earth the men capable of reading it."

Josiah, son of Rev. Samuel Willard, was for many years Secretary of the Province of Massachusetts Bay, and was affectionately called the Good Secretary. He was Judge of Probate, and one of the Executive Council for Suffolk. He had a large family of children, only one of whom left descendants,—Katherine, who married Henry, son of Rev. Henry Gibbs of Watertown. Mr. Gibbs was Librarian at Harvard College, Clerk of the General Court, Representative from Salem, and a merchant there.

Abigail, the eldest daughter of Rev. Samuel, married, first, Rev. Benjamin Estabrook of Lexington; second, Rev. Samuel Treat of Eastham, son of Gov. Robert Treat of Connecticut. Mr. Treat, having acquired a knowledge of the Indian dialects, applied himself to the instruction and civilization of the Indians in his vicinity, by preaching to them, and by the establishment of schools. He published a Confession of Faith, in the Nauset Indian language. For the period of half a century, he discharged the office of a faithful Christian pastor.

It is said that "Mr. Treat had a voice so loud that it could be heard at a great distance from the meeting house, even amidst the shrieks of hysterical women, and the winds that howled over the plains of Nauset; but there was no more music in it than in the discordant sounds with which it was mingled. An anecdote, which shows how much the excellence of his matter was injured by the badness of his voice, has been preserved.

"After his marriage with the daughter of Mr. Willard, he was sometimes invited by that gentleman to preach in his pulpit. Mr. Treat having preached one of his best discourses to the congregation of his father-in-law, in his usual unhappy manner, excited universal disgust; and several nice judges waited on Mr. Willard and begged that Mr. Treat, who was a worthy, pious man, it was true, but a wretched preacher, might never be invited into his pulpit again. To this request Mr. Willard made no reply; but he desired his son-in-law to lend him his discourse; which being left with him he delivered it, without alteration, to his people a few weeks after. The hearers were charmed; they flew to Mr. Willard and requested a copy for the press. 'See the difference,' they cried, 'between yourself and your son-in-law; you have preached a sermon on the same text as Mr. Treat's; and whilst his was contemptible, yours is excellent.' "[1]

---

[1] "Annals of the American Pulpit," Vol. I., pp. 185, 186. Sprague.

Robert Treat Paine, LL.D., a grandson of Rev. Samuel and Eunice Treat, was a distinguished lawyer, a member of the State Constitutional Convention, and one of the committee who prepared the draft of the Constitution; a Judge of the Supreme Court, Attorney-General of the Commonwealth of Massachusetts, and one of the signers of the Declaration of Independence. He was father of Robert Treat Paine, the poet.

Daniel, son of Major Simon and Mary (Dunster) Willard, was born in Concord, Mass., Dec. 29, 1658. He lived in Sudbury, and removed to Charlestown, where he married, Dec. 6, 1683, Hannah, daughter of Capt. John and Mehitable Cutler of that place.

Capt. John Cutler[1] was the eldest son of Deacon Robert Cutler, a distinguished citizen of Charlestown, who came from Suffolk County, Eng., to New England as early as 1636. Capt. John was a deacon and a member of the Ancient and Honorable Artillery Company. He went as captain in some expedition in King Philip's war, and represented Charlestown at the General Court. He married, first, Ann Woodmansey; second, Mehitable, daughter of Increase Nowell, and widow of William Hilton.

Increase Nowell,[2] the grandfather of Mrs. Willard,

---

[1] Major John, the eldest son of Capt. Cutler, was the father of Rev. Dr. Timothy Cutler, the most eminent divine of his time. He was President of Yale College, but upon becoming skeptical as to the validity of Congregational ordination, was dismissed. He went to England, and was ordained deacon, and priest, and received from Oxford University a degree of Doctor of Divinity. He became Rector of Christ Church in Boston, and remained there until his death in 1765. "He was," says President Styles, "a man of strong powers of mind. He spoke Latin with great fluency and dignity, and was one of the best Oriental scholars ever educated in this country."

[2] Samuel, the son of Increase Nowell, was a captain in King Philip's war, one of the assistants, and Treasurer of Harvard College, which position he resigned in order to go to England to act with Mather at Court in favor of the country.

came to New England in the fleet with Winthrop. He was chosen an assistant in England in 1629, and continued to hold the office until his death, in 1655. He was ruling elder and one of the founders of the first church in Boston; also the first church in Charlestown. He married Parnell Gray, daughter of Widow Catherine Coytemore, by her first husband.

Daniel and Hannah Willard had three daughters: Anna, who died in infancy; a second Anna, who married, first, Timothy LeFevre, second, John Bosworth; and Elizabeth, who married Phineas, son of Joseph and Sarah Rice.

Mrs. Willard died Feb. 22, 1690-1, aged 30 years.

Mr. Willard married, Jan. 4, 1692-3, Mary, daughter of Jonathan and Mary (Shove) Mills of Braintree, now Quincy (see account of the Mills family). Mr. Willard removed to Braintree, and was afterwards a resident of Boston, being in trade there.

There were ten children by this marriage.

Daniel, the eldest, married Abigail, daughter of Rev. Cotton Mather of Boston. Rev. Increase Mather, the father of Cotton Mather, was a son of Rev. Richard Mather, who was of an ancient family in Lowton, in the parish of Winwick, Lancashire, Eng. The mother of Cotton Mather was Mary, daughter of Rev. John Cotton of Boston, Eng., "the most distinguished divine that came from England the first age." "Cotton Mather came forward," Savage says, "with strange rapidity," entering Harvard College at the age of twelve, and at the age of eighteen received his degree of Master of Arts from the hand of his father who was then President. He began the same year to preach, and was ordained at the North Church in Boston, as his father's colleague. Sprague says that his learning was probably more varied and extensive than that of any other person in America. His publications amounted to three hundred and eighty-two, the largest and most celebrated of which was his "Magnalia Christi Americana." He was three times married: first, to Abigail, daughter of Col. John Phillips of Charlestown; second, to Mrs. Elizabeth Hubbard, daughter of Dr. John Clark of Boston; and third, to Mrs. George, daughter of Samuel Lee.

Daniel and Abigail (Mather) Willard had four daughters: Mary, Katherine, Abigail and Resign. Mrs. Willard died two days after the birth of the latter.

Daniel Willard married for his second wife Ann Thomas. There was one daughter by this marriage, Ann. He is described at one time as "ship chandler in Boston, in Hanover Street, near the Orange-tree;" at another, "merchant on the Long Wharf, Boston." He died in 1727, aged 34.

Mary, the eldest daughter of Daniel and Mary, was born at Boston, Nov. 16, 1695. She married, first, a West Indian planter by the name of Cuyler; second, Dr. Edward, son of Dr. Robert and Elizabeth (Pemberton) Ellis (see account of the Ellises).

Susannah, the second daughter, "is probably the same Susannah who married Matthias Cowdry."

Of William, the second son of Daniel and Mary, nothing further is known.

Sarah, the third daughter, died in infancy.

Mehitable, the fourth daughter, married John Baxter. "A descendant of this marriage was the wife of Lemuel Shattuck, Esq., of Boston."

Sarah, the youngest daughter of Daniel and Mary, married "(William?) Hope, a branch of the ancient family of Craighall, descended from Sir Thomas Hope of Kerse (see account of the Hopes).

Mr. Willard died Aug. 23, 1708.

Mrs. Willard married for her second husband, David Melvill, of an ancient Scotch house. His first wife was Mary, daughter of Rev. Samuel and Mary (Sherman) Willard, of Boston. While residing in Boston, a merchant, Mr. Melvill "received the freedom of the city of Glasgow." He resided in Newport, R. I., at one time, and descendants of his still live in that city. "He had a brother who was the ancestor of Major Thomas Melvill, one of the Boston 'tea party.'"

Among the descendants of Major Willard, may be mentioned Col. Return Jonathan Meigs, a distinguished officer in the Revolution, and his brother Josiah, tutor and Professor of Yale, and President of the University of Georgia; Capt. Josiah Willard of Salem; Samuel Willard, Colonel and Judge, of Lancaster, Mass.; Col. Josiah, commander at Fort Dummer, Brattleborough, Vt.; Rev. Willard Wheeler, Rector of St. Andrew's at Scituate; Capt. Phineas Stevens of Charlestown, N. H., who so bravely defended the fort there, with some thirty men, against the combined force of French and Indians, four hundred in number; Major Willard Moore, of Col. Dolittle's regiment at Bunker Hill; Col. Samuel Willard of Saybrook, a distinguished Speaker of the House of Representatives of Massachusetts; Rev. Joseph Willard of Rutland, who was killed by the Indians; Hon. Judge Willard of Saratoga, N. Y.; Rev. Samuel Willard of Biddeford, Me.; Rev. Dr. Joseph Willard, for many years President of Harvard College; Dr. Hosmer of Watertown, father of Harriet Hosmer, the sculptress; Dr. Nahum Willard of Worcester; Dr. Samuel Willard of Uxbridge; Col. Abijah Willard of Lancaster (he married Elizabeth, sister of Col. William Prescott of Bunker Hill memory); Rev. John Willard, D. D., of Stafford, Conn.; Col. Josiah Willard; Prof. Sidney Willard of Harvard College; and Joseph Willard of Cambridge, author of the "Willard Memoir" and a "History of Lancaster."

Major Simon Willard's younger brother, George, came to America also, and was living in Scituate, in Plymouth Colony, in 1638. He had three children:

Deborah, Daniel, and Joshua. Daniel married Esther (or Hester) Mathews, daughter, probably, of James Mathews of Yarmouth, where she was born.

Deborah married Paul Sears of Yarmouth, son of "Richard Sears, the Pilgrim, who was a son of John Bourchier Sears and Maria L. van Egmont. John was a lineal descendant of Richard Sears of Colchester, Eng., and Ann Bourchier Knyvet. Richard, the Pilgrim, was driven from his native land and sought refuge among the Pilgrims in Holland, and came with them to the New World in 1630. He settled in Plymouth, and married Dorothy Thatcher.

The descendants of Paul and Deborah (Willard) Sears are very numerous. Among them are Robert Sears, the extensive publisher at New York; Rev. Barnas Sears, formerly Professor of the Baptist Theological Seminary at Newton, Mass., now President of Brown University, and Secretary of the Board of Education; Rev. Daniel Sears of Louisiana; Rev. Edmund Hamilton Sears of Wayland, author of "Pictures of the Olden Time;" Phillip H. Sears, Esq., of Boston, counselor-at-law; Fitzhenry Homer, who married Nancy Bradford, daughter of Hon. James D. Wolf; and Mary B. Homer, who married Thomas Dixon, Knight of the Order of the Lily, and of the Order of the Netherlands Lion.

Among the descendants of Margery, the sister of Major Simon Willard, who married Capt. Dolour Davis, may be mentioned, Capt. Stephen Hall, a distinguished merchant in Boston; Rev. Dr. Gray of Jamaica Plain; Hon. George Eustis, Chief Justice of Louisiana; Gen. Eustis of the United States Army; Hon. Isaac Parker, Chief Justice of the Supreme Court of Massachusetts; Rev. Willard Hall of Westford, Mass.; and Hon. Willard Hall, Judge of the United States District Court.

DUNSTER.

THE name of Dunster is an ancient one in England, especially in Lancashire. It signifies a dweller upon a dun, or down, and is of Saxon origin. There is in Somersetshire, England, a market town and a castle by that name.

Henry Dunster, the first of the name in this country, and the first President of Harvard College, came from England to America in the year 1640. The only known reference to the place of his birth, is found in a letter of his own, dated Feb., 1648, and addressed to Ch. Ravius, Professor of Oriental languages in London. In this letter, he says: "*Ego enim Lancastrensis sum*" (for I am from Lancashire). A letter to President Dunster from his father Henrye Dunster, is still extant, and is dated "from Balehoult, this 20th of March, 1640." "Balehoult," says Mr. Samuel Dunster in his "Henry Dunster and his Descendants," is supposed to have been the name of a private gentleman's residence in Bury, Lancashire." This letter indicates that the father of Henry Dunster was a man of liberal education. In the letter, Mr. Dunster mentions three sons, Richard, Thomas, and Robert, and two or more daughters. Elizabeth, the only daughter mentioned by name in the letter, came to New England and married Major Simon, son of Richard and Margery Willard.

The date of Henry Dunster's birth is not known, but it is supposed to have been in 1610–12. As a child he is said to have been thoughtful, beyond his years. Dr. Chaplin, in his "Life of Henry Dunster," says: Even at the age of four or five, the "awakening which stirred the religious element of England arrested his attention. Upon hearing men scoff at a powerful and popular preacher, and at the great flocking after him, he enquired why men did so, and upon being told that it was to hear the word, he replied, 'Then if it be the word, why do men speak against it?'" "When he was about twelve years old," continues Dr. Chaplin, "he became deeply concerned as to his personal responsibility to God. 'The Lord gave me,' he relates, 'an attentive ear and a heart to understand preaching. The Lord showed me my sins, reconciliation by Christ, and the word was more sweet to me than all the world.' But after the first experience of delight in religious things, he was destined to pass many years of inward conflict. 'The greatest thing,' he says, 'which separated my soule from God was an inordinate desire of human learning.' He wisely concluded to meet the temptation and go to the University at Cambridge. He came out of the trial an humble and earnest Christian, not spoiled by learning and culture, but fitted thereby for the wide sphere of usefulness designed for him by Providence in after years in the New World." Henry was graduated at Magdalen College, A. B. in 1630, and A. M. in 1634. Samuel Dunster says: "The University here had, from an early period, a reputation for liberality of opinion far beyond that of her ancient rival, Oxford, and it is not at all surprising that so many of her graduates, who were driven from home by the then existing intolerance toward non-conformists, were found among the early settlers of New England. Among his contemporaries at Cambridge, were Jeremy Taylor and John Milton, Ralph Cudworth and John Pearson, John Harvard, and others, who became more or less distinguished. He was trained for the ministry, but it is questionable whether he ever took orders in the church; and after a few years spent in teaching he emigrated to this country, apparently, so far as we know, with no settled purpose. He was a man of retiring disposition, and although holding to the most positive conviction of duty, he was by nature opposed to controversy and strife; and so we may with propriety assume that he was influenced in his movements by a desire to avoid taking part in the angry scenes just then commencing in England, which culminated in the establishment of the protectorate under Cromwell and the execution of King Charles and some of his ministers."

He arrived in Boston toward the latter end of the summer of 1640, and for a short time he resided on "his own estate at the North East corner of Court Street and Washington Street." His reputation as a ripe scholar had evidently preceded him, for, "immediately upon his arrival he was waited on by the Governor, magistrates, elders and ministers" and asked, "by a sort of acclamation and general consent, to remove to Cambridge and assume the Presidency of the College." Johnson, in his "Wonder-Working Providence," says he was "fitted from the Lord for the work, and by those that have skill in that way, reported to be an able proficient in Hebrew, Greek and Latin languages." Prince speaks of him as "one of the greatest masters of the Oriental languages that hath been known in these ends of the earth." Quincy, Pierce and Eliot—the modern historians of Harvard College—have recorded their testimony to the purity and nobility of his character, and his great success in both the executive and teaching departments of the College. The College had been already established, but very little had been accomplished toward securing any plan of organization, and it was little else than an advanced school, Nathaniel Eaton being the master. Of him Cotton Mather says, "He was one fitter to be the master of a Bridewell than a College."

Soon after removing to Cambridge, he united with the church there on confession of faith. He frequently supplied the pulpit in Cambridge and the vicinity during his Presidency, and took a prominent part in founding the church at Woburn. He manifested great interest in the education and conversion of the Indians, and joined heartily with John Eliot and the Mayhews in this work. Lechford, the Boston lawyer, says of him in this connection: "He will, without doubt, prove an instrument of much good in this country, being a good scholar and having skill in the tongues. He will make it good that the way to instruct the Indians must be in their own language, not English." The second charter of the College, obtained in 1650 on his express petition, declares its object is to include "the education of the English and Indian youth of this country in knowledge and godliness."

Besides the business of instruction and discipline which largely devolved on him, he was charged with the administration of the College matters, even down to such particulars as the direction of the Commons, the keeping of the students' accounts (their bills being mostly paid in commodities), the construction of the College edifice and the President's house, the collection of his own salary, etc. There is a letter from him to Gov. Winthrop, in which he speaks of abatements he has suffered, from sixty to fifty pounds, from fifty to forty-five pounds, and from forty-five to thirty pounds, "which," says he, "is now my rent from the ferry." He goes on to say, "I was and am willing to descend to the lowest step if there can be nothing comfortable allowed." The requisites for admission into College, the details of the course of study, and the rules and precepts for the government of the students, were prepared by him, and Quincy says that the principles of education established by him were not materially changed during the whole of the seventeenth century. "Under him the College prospered, and he was found equal in all respects to the expectations which had been formed of him." "That which was before,"—says the historian Hubbard—"but at best a *schola illustria* grew to the statue and perfection of a College," and "soon acquired so high a reputation that in several instances youth of opulent families were sent over to receive their education in New England.

In addition to the College work of so diversified a character, he found time to correspond with learned men abroad, and to devote his personal attention to the supervision through the press of several publications. The first printing press in North America[1] was set up in Cambridge in 1639, "as an appendage of Harvard College," for it was considered too powerful an engine for good or evil to be intrusted in private hands, and accordingly for more than a hundred years it was kept under the supervision of the General Court. In 1641 it was put under President Dunster's management, and was transferred to the President's house, where it remained until 1659. Among its earlier issues, was "The whole Booke of Psalmes Faithfully Translated into English Metre." This book, now known as the "Bay Psalm Book," appeared in two editions,—1640 and 1647. The translation was made by three well-known ministers of the day,—Mather of Dorchester, and Eliot and Weld of Roxbury,—and it was intended to take the place of the Sternhold and Hopkins version, in which, as is well-known, the translation was often very inaccurate, while the versification, as Dr. Chaplin says, "was too rugged even for our not very fastidious fathers." The new version did not, however, says Neal, "satisfy the expectations of judicious men," and accordingly for further improvement it was committed to the President. Associated with him in the work of "revising and polishing," was Mr. Richard Lyon, "and the re-

[1] It was brought to America by the Rev. Josse or Joseph Glover, the first husband of Mr. Dunster's wife, who died on the passage over.

sult of their combined labors seems to have been, on the whole, very satisfactory, for in its new form the book passed through more than fifty editions. "The poetry," says Samuel Dunster, "it is true was a little rough and shaky, though a great improvement on the prior editions. The authors themselves seem to have had mild doubts as to the smoothness of the metre, for in their preface they say: 'If the verses are not always as elegant as some desire or expect, let them consider that God's altar needs not our polishing; we have respected rather a plain translation than to smooth our verses with the sweetness of any paraphrase. We have attended conscience rather than elegance, fidelity rather than ingenuity,' etc. The quaint Cotton Mather bears his testimony as follows: 'Now, though I heartily join with those gentlemen who wish that the *poetry* hereof were mended; yet must I confess that the Psalms have never yet seen a *translation* that I know of, nearer to the Hebrew *original*.'"

For some twelve or fourteen years, Mr. Dunster administered the affairs of the College with eminent success. "Indeed," says Samuel Dunster, "it is doubtful if in the early history of Harvard any one person ever had so large an influence in perpetuating her existence and shaping her policy as her first President." But, at this time, the public avowal on his part of sentiments of opposition to infant baptism,[1] created an intense excitement in the colony, and roused a violent spirit of opposition toward him. Says Eliot, one of the historians of Harvard: "The orthodox spirit of the whole colony was instantly

[1] The Rev. Mr. Mitchel, pastor of the church in Cambridge, was a particular friend of Mr. Dunster, yet denounced the views of the latter on infant baptism, from his pulpit. After coming from the famous interview he had with President Dunster on the subject of infant baptism, he wrote in his diary: "After I came from him, I had a strange experience. I found hurrying and pressing suggestions against peadobaptism. . . . . Yet, methought, it was not hard to discern they were from the Evil One."

aroused; and the strongest because involuntary testimony is borne to the intellectual power and moral influence of Dunster, by the alarm his defection excited, and the harsh measures dictated by that feeling, while his conscientiousness is attested by the meekness of his submission to the rebukes which were sternly administered."

The first public and official movement taken against him, was by the magistrates, who sent a letter to the ministers in the early part of the year 1653, directing them to make an examination of the whole matter as a basis for their future action. Upon this, a conference was held at Boston, Feb. 2d and 3d, 1653–4, at which were present nine leading ministers of Boston and vicinity, and two ruling elders, before whom Mr. Dunster defended his views. The conference labored with the "erroneous gentleman," and endeavored to convince him of his error. But having failed, as Cotton Mather says, "to expedite the entangled out of the briars," the General Court, in May following, passed a vote commending his case "to the serious consideration" of the Overseers of the College, and instructing them "not to admit or suffer any such to be continued in the office or place of teaching that have manifested themselves *unsound* in faith," etc. Mr. Dunster the next month, June 10, 1654, forwarded through the Overseers a letter of resignation, which was ungraciously accepted by the Court, and referred back to the Overseers, with an order to secure "some mete person to carry on the work of the College," in case he (Mr. Dunster) should persist in his resolution more than a month. "Here," says Samuel Dunster, "was an avenue of escape opened to him, for he could now retain his position at the cost of silence only.[1] . . . But he was thoroughly and conscientiously an honest man—

[1] The Rev. Mr. Chauncy, his successor, was known to hold the same opinion in regard to infant baptism as that held by Mr. Dunster, and was notified, in the tender to him of the position, that "it was expected

not, as too many are, honest only from motives of policy, and there was for him but one course to pursue."

Eleven days after his resignation, Mr. Dunster sent to the General Court a petition, wherein, without receding in the slightest particular from his avowed position, he invoked their merciful consideration of his circumstances. After expressing his hope that it might not be thought nor reported that he "cast off his place out of any froward morosity, foolish levity, or ungrateful despising, either of the Court's forbearance or the Overseers' amicable conferences," he makes three special requests: First, for an allowance in salary which had been commended to the Court by a committee thereof; second, to be permitted to remain in the President's house during the settlement of his accounts with the corporation; and third, to be allowed to continue in the colony, in the work of teaching or preaching, "or in any other laudable or liberal calling as God shall chalk out my way." "This appeal," says Quincy, "was treated in a heartless way, and the reply to the third request was equivalent to warning him out of the colony."

Notwithstanding this contemptuous treatment, six days later, he sent to the Court a brief paper of "Considerations," intended as a rejoinder to the reply of the Court to his second request, which had been dismissed "as most unreasonable." These considerations had reference to the material circumstances of himself and family, and to the necessity of his remaining at Cambridge in order to acquaint the incoming President with the administration of the College duties. "This paper," says Samuel Dunster, "which shows not only a positive conviction of the correctness of his position, but a most commendable spirit of submission, closes in these words: 'The whole trans-

---

and desired that he forbear to disseminate or publish any tenets concerning the necessity of immersion in baptism, and celebration of the Lord's supper at evening, or to oppose the received doctrines therein."

action of this business is such, which, in the process of time, when all things come to mature consideration, may very probably create grief on all sides; yours subsequent, as mine antecedent. I am not the man you take me to be. Neither, if you knew what I hold, and why, can I persuade myself that you would act, as I am at least tempted to think you do. But our times are in God's hands, with whom all sides hope, by grace in Christ, to find favor, which shall be my prayer for you, as for myself.' The simple, touching pathos of this appeal was not without effect, and he was allowed to remain till the following March—some three months—in the President's house."

Mr. Dunster was indicted by the grand jury, the presentment being "for disturbance of the ordinances of Christ on the Lord's day." He was tried, convicted and sentenced according to the ecclesiastical law, "to be publicly admonished, and give bond for his *good behavior*. A second time, some two years later—a child having been born to him—he was indicted by the grand jury and tried by the County Court, for practically the same offense, the presentment being "for not bringing his child to the holy ordinance of baptism."

Mr. Dunster removed to Scituate in the adjoining colony of Plymouth, which was much more tolerant in religious matters than Massachusetts Bay. Mr. Dean, in his history of the place, says: "We find notices of him the same autumn (1655) employed in the ministry, in which he continued nearly five years." His persecutions had already attracted the attention of the Baptists in the mother country, and on the 10th of July, 1656, he received from Mr. Edward Roberts, a leading member of that denomination in Dublin, a letter, urging him to make that place his home, and informing him that £50 had been granted by the Lord Deputy (Henry Cromwell, younger son of the Protector) for the transportation thither of himself and his family. This invitation he declined.

Mr. Dunster's first wife was Elizabeth, widow of the Rev. Josse (or Joseph) Glover. There were no children by this marriage. He married for his second wife Elizabeth ——, who appears to have been well educated and to have had a superior mind. Their children were: David, Dorothy, Henry, Jonathan and Elizabeth.

President Dunster died at Scituate, Feb. 27, 1659–60. In his will, which was dated Feb. 8, 1658, he directs that his body be interred in Cambridge, by his "lovinge wife" and other relations. He made special legacies to persons, who, through his life, had been his most unrelenting persecutors; also to a number of relatives and friends, among whom he mentions "my cousin Bowers," "my cousin fayth Dunster," "my sister Willard," and "sister Hills[1] and all her children born in this country."

The place of burial was in the old cemetery opposite the College grounds, a few rods north-west of the church now standing there.

---

[1] The wife of Capt. Hills of Malden, Mass., a gentleman of note, and Speaker of the General Court in the earliest years.

MILLS.

John Mills came to New England probably in the fleet with Winthrop, as among the members of the first church his name is number thirty-three, and his wife Susannah next. His daughters Joy and Recompense were baptized in October, 1630, and their names were the first on our church records.

He was admitted freeman March 6, 1632. He resided about ten years in Boston; then removed to Braintree (the part that is now Quincy), of which town he was Clerk in 1653. Forty-four acres of land at Mount Wollaston was granted him by the town of Boston, there being six persons in his family. He and his wife Susannah were recommended, Dec. 5, 1641, by the church in Boston to the church in Braintree.

Their children were Susannah, Joy, Recompense, John, Jonathan, James and Mary.

Mrs. Mills died Dec. 10, 1675, aged 80 years. Mr. Mills died in 1678. In his will, he speaks of having "now fallen into years." Judging from the language of ardent piety used in the introduction, he was an eminently good man. He mentions his son John, and his daughters Mary Hawkins and Susannah Davis. He recommends his son John to bring up one of his sons to the work of the ministry, which was, he says, "the employment of my predecessors to the third, if not the fourth generation."

Savage says: "The grandson, Edward, seems not to have obeyed the will of his ancestor, but perhaps the fourth generation was more regardful, as Jonathan, who graduated at Harvard College in 1723, was a minister."

John, the eldest, married Mary, sister to Rev. George Shove,[1] the third minister in Taunton. She is mentioned in "Marshall's Diary," as a "precious saint."

Their children were: Elizabeth; Sarah; John, married Hannah ——; Jonathan, married Mary, daughter of Edmund and Sarah Sheffield of Braintree; Edward, graduated at Harvard College in 1685; Susannah; Mary, married Daniel, son of Major Simon and Mary (Dunster) Willard of Boston; Nathaniel, married Mary Spear; a second Susannah, married Dea. Jonathan, son of John and Sarah (Thayer) Hayward.

Capt. John, the eldest son of John and Mary Mills, lived in that part of Old Braintree which still bears the name. He is mentioned in old records as "Capt. John Mills, gentleman." He was a man of integrity and worth, of intelligence, capacity and influence. He was selectman for many years, a Representative for five years, and was frequently placed on important committees.

Rev. Jonathan, the youngest son of Capt. John Mills, was graduated at Harvard College in 1723, and was ordained pastor of the church at Bellingham, being the first minister of that place. He lived in Boston many years, and was afterward installed pastor of the second church in Harwich. He married, first, Jemima Hayward; second, Hepzibah, daughter of Dea. Samuel White of Braintree, and widow of Benjamin French. Among the children of Rev. Jonathan and Jemima Mills, were: Jemima, who married Capt. Thomas Vinton; and Hannah, who married Capt. Sturgis,—William Sturgis, Esq., of Boston being a son of theirs.

---

[1] "Mr. George Shove was a principal light in those parts, and the death of the St. George at this time (1687) calls for special mourning." —*An early writer.*

KILBY.

John Kilby of Boston, Mass., was born about 1667. He married Rebecca Simpkins. They had twelve children, viz.: Elizabeth, John, Thomas, Sarah, Christopher, Richard, William, Katherine, Rebecca, a second Christopher, Nicholas and Ebenezer. Mr. Kilby was one of the founders of the Brattle Street Church. He died in 1722, and is buried in the Old Granary burying-ground.

Thomas, the second son, was born in Boston, and baptized Aug. 24, 1690-1. He was graduated in 1723, at Harvard College, Cambridge. He was a poet and a wit. We learn from the Mass. Hist. Coll., Vol. III., p. 300, that he published essays in prose and verse. Knapp, in his Biographical Sketches, gives us the following account of him: "Thomas Kilby wrote a poem of a satirical character against the Land Bank. The names he mentions are now mostly forgotten; but notwithstanding much of its point is lost by this circumstance, yet the production is read with pleasure at the present day. Kilby was a man of distinction,—an agent for the Province in England, Grand Master of Masons,—a scholar and a wit. He died in 1746."

The statement that Thomas Kilby was an agent for the Province in England is probably an error. The statement that he was Grand Master of Masons, is also an error, as the following account of his connection with the Masonic Lodge of Boston, very kindly furnished me by Sereno D. Nickerson, Recording Grand Secretary of the Grand Lodge in Massachusetts, shows:

"The name of Thomas Kilby first appears on the Masonic records, January 13, 1741, O. S., as proposed by Brother Hallowell as a candidate in the First Lodge in Boston, which met at the Royal Exchange Tavern, in King Street, then kept by Bro. Luke Vardy. The site was on the corner of the present State and Exchange Streets, and is now occupied by the Merchants' National Bank building. In those days Lodge meetings were always held in taverns, because those houses afforded the only rooms large enough to accommodate the brethren, and because refreshments were always provided. No charge was made for rent, the landlord being supposed to be sufficiently compensated by the profit on his bill for refreshments. The practice still prevails in some towns in Great Britain.

"On Feb. 10th, 1741, according to the record, as kept by Brother Peter Pelham, 'the Brethren balloted in the candidate, Thos. Kilby, Esq., who, attending, was introduced and made a Mason in due form.' He paid to the Treasurer £8, having previously deposited £2; and '23 pair of Gloves, at £4.15 per Doz.,' were furnished. Among the brethren present were Henry Price, Past Provincial Grand Master and the 'Father of Masonry in North America,' and Thomas Oxnard, then Deputy Grand Master, and afterward Grand Master.

"Brother Kilby at once became an active member of the Lodge, and was rarely absent from its meetings. On the 9th of June, 1742, he was appointed Junior Warden, and Senior Warden on the 22d of December following. On the 14th of March, 1743, he was appointed chairman of a committee to revise the By-Laws. On the 27th of July, 1743, and on the 28th of December in the same year, he was chosen chairman of the committee to settle the Treasurer's accounts at the usual semi-annual examination, and on the 9th of November of that year he 'was added to the committee for settling the accounts of the deceased Treasurer.' He was elected Master of the Lodge on the 26th of December, 1744, and presided at ten of the twelve meetings held during the ensuing six months. He was re-elected on the 26th of June, 1745, and presided on the 1st and 10th of July following. His name does not afterwards appear in the records of the First Lodge.

"On the 24th of June, 1743, Brother Kilby was appointed Senior Grand Warden by Grand Master Thomas Oxnard, and on the 27th of December of that year he was continued in office. On the 6th of March following (being 1743, O. S.), Grand Master Oxnard, having received from the Grand Master of England a deputation extending his authority over all North America, reappointed as Senior Grand Warden, Brother Thomas Kilby, who was then serving as the Senior Warden of the First Lodge in Boston. On the 26th of June next (1744, O. S.), he was again reappointed and served until December following, when he was elected Master of the First Lodge, as above stated.

"It is to be regretted that the Masonic records in those days were very meager, comprising little except a list of the names of the brethren present, the amount contributed by each for charity and dues; together with the 'Reckoning'—the last named item being always carefully noted."

Mrs. Hannah (Mather) Crocker says of Mr. Kilby: "Thomas Kilby was celebrated for keen wit and humour; he wrote poetry blended with wit called pretty good. He was contemporary wag with Christopher Minot, a man of keen wit. They were much caressed for their pleasant good wit and humour. They moved in the first circles."

Sargeant, in his "Dealings with the Dead," has the following: "Mr. [Thomas] Kilby being at one time in Maine or Nova Scotia, made a will for his amusement in which he left liberal sums (that he did not possess) to a number of religious, philanthropic and literary institutions;—his eyes, which were very good, to a blind relative—his body to a surgeon of his acquaintance, 'excepting as hereinafter excepted'—his sins he bequeathed to a worthy clergyman, 'as he appeared not to have any'—and the choice of his legs to Peter Faneuil." Mr. Faneuil, it is said, wore a very high-heeled shoe, which probably occasioned the considerate bequest of Mr. Kilby. It is also stated that a knowledge of the will coming to Mr. Faneuil, he was so much pleased with the humor of it, that, probably having a knowledge of the testator before, he sent for him and made him his agent at Canso.

Thomas Kilby was married Dec. 1, 1726, by Thomas Prince, to Sarah, daughter of Dr. Robert and Elizabeth (Pemberton) Ellis of Boston. Their children were: Sarah, Robert Ellis, Christopher and William Tyler. Mrs. Kilby died previous to 1745, as Mrs. Prescott, in her account of the Ellis family, states that she was not living at that time.

The following is from the "Boston News-Letter," Sept. 11, 1746: "We hear from Louisburg that on the 23d of last month died there Thomas Kilby, Esq., Commissary of the King's Troops at that place."

Sarah, the only daughter of Thomas and Sarah Kilby, was married by Rev. Joseph Sewall, Oct. 5, 1748, to Daniel Jones. Thomas Kilby Jones, their son, who married Sept. 21, 1782, Polly Morton, was a very wealthy, hospitable and popular merchant of Boston.

Gen. Thomas Kilby Smith, who was with Gen. Grant at the taking of Vicksburg, is a descendant of Thomas and Sarah Kilby.

Christopher,[1] the fifth son of John and Rebecca Kilby, was born in Boston, March 25, 1705. He was bred to commercial pursuits, and, in 1726, became a partner in business with the Hon. William Clark, a distinguished merchant of Boston who carried on an extensive trade with England and the West Indies.

---

[1] From the account of Christopher Kilby by Charles Tuttle, Esq.

The same year Mr. Kilby married Sarah, the eldest daughter of Mr. Clark.

In 1739, Mr. Kilby was a Representative to the General Court from Boston, and two years later was sent by the House as a special "agent to the court of Great Britain to represent to his majesty the great difficulties and distress the people of the Province labored under owing to the King having instructed Gov. Belcher to limit the issue of bills of credit to a period not exceeding in duration those current at the time of a new issue." "The Province," says Mr. Tuttle, "had always selected its ablest men to act as agents, the functions requiring ability, sagacity, prudence and a knowledge of public affairs." Mr. Kilby, then only thirty-four years of age, accepted the appointment, and was soon after chosen standing agent of the Province in England. The following year, Mr. Kilby and Robert Auchmuty, an eminent lawyer of Boston, were joint agents to prosecute the appeal before the King in Council in relation to the boundary line between Massachusetts and Rhode Island. Mr. Kilby continued for twenty-seven years to act as standing agent of the Province, performing many important services.

The Duke of Newcastle promised the governorship of New Jersey to Mr. Kilby, but the friends of Gov. Belcher persuaded the Duke to change his purpose at the last moment, and Gov. Belcher received the appointment.

While agent of Massachusetts, Mr. Kilby was a member of the firm of Sedgwick, Kilby & Barnard, of London. The business of the firm was extensive, especially with the American Colonies.

In 1756, England having declared war with France, John Campbell, fourth Earl of Loudoun, was appointed Commander-in-Chief of the King's forces in North America, and Governor of Virginia, and Kilby being appointed "agent victualler" of the army, they sailed from Portsmouth for New York. The Earl afterward came to Boston to meet the commissioners, and the Boston Gazette of Jan. 24, 1757, after speaking of the arrival of the Earl in Boston, adds: "At the same time, and in company with the Earl of Loudoun arrived Christopher Kilby, Esq., who went from here about 17 years ago as Agent for the Province at the Court of Great Britain: the warm affection he has discovered for his countrymen, and the signal services he has rendered this Province during that space has greatly endeared him to us."

Mr. Kilby remained in this country till the peace of 1763. He was in New York when the terrible fire occurred in Boston, in March, 1760. He sent two hundred pounds sterling to the sufferers, "a sum that was regarded as enormous at that time." "The district burnt over embraced both sides of 'Mackerel Lane,' so called. When this part of the town was re-built, and the lane widened and extended, it was called Kilby Street by common consent, in compliment to Mr. Kilby."

"On his return to England, he purchased a large estate in the parish of Dorking, county Surrey, where he built a curious edifice called the Priory, and several ornamental seats. His wife died April 12, 1739, leaving two daughters, Sarah and Katherine. A son, William, died young. He married for his second wife Martha ——, who survived him. There were no children by this marriage.

Mr. Kilby's daughter Katherine died, it appears, soon after her arrival in England, she having gone with her sister to be with her father. On Sarah, his surviving daughter, Mr. Kilby bestowed every advantage that wealth could command. In 1753 she was betrothed to Nathaniel, son of Capt. Nathaniel Cunningham, "a merchant of the greatest wealth of any in Boston." Capt. Cunningham's daughter Ruth married the celebrated patriot and orator, James Otis.

Nathaniel Cunningham died about two years and a half after his marriage, leaving two infant daughters, Susanna and Sarah. When the Earl of Loudoun visited Boston, there came with him his aid-de-camp, Capt. Gilbert McAdam, who was introduced by Mr. Kilby to his widowed daughter. They were married the next year. Capt. McAdam was of an ancient Ayrshire family, and uncle to John Loudoun McAdam, the inventor of macadamized roads.

Susanna and Sarah Cunningham were the special objects of Mr. Kilby's bounty and solicitude. Susanna was twice married. Her first husband was James Dalrymple[1] of Orangefield, Ayrshire, the friend and patron of Robert Burns. By this marriage she had one son, Charles Dalrymple, an officer of the British Army. Through subsequent marriages, first with John Henry Mills and afterwards with William Cunningham, both of Scotland, she is now represented in this country by her grandchildren,—Mrs. Frances Maria Spofford, wife of the late venerable Dr. Spofford of Newburyport, Mrs. Susannah Myers of Boston, Mary Frances, wife of Hon. John Cochran Park of Boston, and Capt. Thomas Cunningham of Somerville, Mass.

Her sister, Sarah Cunningham, married William Campbell of Ayrshire, and had two daughters, the eldest of whom, Elizabeth, married the seventh Duke of Argyle, grandfather of the Marquis of Lorne. Mr. Kilby died in October, 1771. He left an immense estate, which was divided among his seven grandchildren, after provision had been made for his wife.

The Kilby arms are: "Argent three bars azure, in chief as many amulets of the last. Crest, an ear of maize stripped open."

The Hon. William Clark, the father of Mrs. Kilby, was brother of the Hon. John Clark, for many years

[1] Of him Burns wrote: "I have met in Mr. Dalrymple of Orangefield, what Solomon emphatically calls 'a friend that sticketh closer than a brother.'"

Speaker of the House of Representatives, and grandson of Dr. John Clark, an eminent physician of Boston, who married Martha, a sister of Sir Richard Saltonstall, one of the Massachusetts Bay Company. William Clark was a merchant, and had a large estate. He was a member of the House and Provincial Council, and a "man of marked distinction in the affairs of the town." For him Clark Square and Wharf were named. He married Sarah, daughter of Robert Bronsdon, a merchant of Boston.

Mr. Clark resided in Garden Court, in the most elegant house in Boston, which, tradition says, he built with the intention of rivaling in splendor the far-famed Hutchinson house adjoining it. Drake says of it: "In all Colonial Boston we have not met with its peer." It was built of brick, three stories high, and contained twenty-six rooms. A spacious hall run through the center, from which arose a flight of stairs so broad and easy of ascent that Sir Henry Frankland, who lived there afterwards, used to ride his pony up and down with ease and safety. The parlors were ornamented with fluted columns, elaborately carved, and richly gilded pilasters and cornices. The walls were wainscoted and divided by wooden pilasters into compartments with panels, on each of which was painted armorial bearings, landscapes, or ruins. Similar panels in the wainscot were ornamented with various devices. The floor of the eastern parlor was laid in diamond-shaped figures, and had in the center a unique and curious tassellated design, consisting, it is said, of more than three hundred kinds of wood, which were beautifully interwoven around a shield bearing the family device—a bar with three white swans.

HOPE.

The surname of Hope is one of great antiquity in Scotland. John de Hope, the ancestor of the present family, came from France, it is said, in the retinue of Madalene, Queen of James V., in 1537. He settled in Scotland, and left a son, Edward, who was one of the most considerable inhabitants of Edinburgh in the reign of Queen Mary, and being a great promoter of the Reformation, was chosen one of the commissioners for the metropolis to the Parliament in 1560. He left a son, Henry, a very eminent merchant, who married a French lady, Jaqueline de Tott. Henry left a son Thomas and a son Henry.

Thomas, the eldest son, having distinguished himself in no small degree, entered upon the study of law, and made such rapid progress, he was at a very early age admitted to the bar.

In 1606, six ministers of the Church of Scotland denied that the King and his Council possessed any authority in ecclesiastical affairs, and were imprisoned in Blackwell for high treason. They were put upon trial before a jury consisting chiefly of landed gentlemen of the three Lothairs. As it was carefully promulgated that the King and the Court had openly expressed the highest displeasure against the ministers, and had declared that they would show no favor to any person that should appear in their behalf, none of the great lawyers chose to undertake their cause; even Sir Thomas Craig, procurator for the church, refused to be concerned in the affair; and Sir William Oliphant, who had at first promised to plead for them, sent word the day before, that he must decline. The ministers, thus abandoned, applied to Mr. Hope, who, pitying their cause, with the greatest cheerfulness and resolution undertook their defense; and, notwithstanding the reiterated endeavors of the Court to perplex and browbeat him, conducted the case in so masterly a manner that he made a deep impression on the jury. However, by an unlawful tampering with the jury (some of the lords of council having procured admittance to them after they were shut up), and they being assured that no harm was intended against the persons or goods of the accused, nine of the fifteen jurymen were induced to bring in a verdict of guilt, and the ministers were sentenced to banishment from the kingdom. Owing to the intrepidity, knowledge of the law and singular ability manifested by Mr. Hope, he became so greatly the favorite of the Presbyterians that they never afterwards undertook any important business without consulting him, and he was retained on almost every case brought by them into the courts of justice.

He acquired in a few years one of the most considerable fortunes ever made at the Scottish bar, which enabled him to purchase the lands of Grantown, Edmonston and Cauldcotts in Mid Lothian, Preston Grange in East Lothian, Kerse in Sherlingshore, Moreton in the Merse, Kennemouth, Arnedie, Craighall Ceres, Hillarvet and others in Fife.

"It was the policy of King Charles to heap honors and emoluments upon those who had most power to obstruct his designs; so he made the great Presbyterian barrister, King's Advocate in 1627, and created him Baronet of Nova Scotia, the following year. He also appointed him to be his commissioner to the General Assembly," "an honor never before or since bestowed on a commoner." The Royalists were so incensed at the appearance of an enemy instead of a friend, that they very generally absented themselves from the Assembly, and the field was therefore left clear to the Covenanters, who carried all before them. As the sanction of this body was necessary to their transactions, the credit of the whole, direct or indirect, lay with Sir Thomas Hope. He was also appointed one of the commissioners for managing the exchequer. Notwithstanding the King's efforts to win him over to his interests, he steadfastly adhered to his early friends, the Presbyterians, and aided them by his sagacious advice in all their plans for the maintenance of their religious privileges.

Sir Thomas left a very large family. From his eldest son, descend the Hopes of Craighall.

Sir John Hope of Hopetoun, his sixth son, a member of the Scottish bar, married Anne, only daughter and heir of Robert Foules of Leadhills, county Lamark, and acquired the valuable mines there. "He applied himself to mineralogy, and brought the art of mining to the highest perfection ever before known in Scotland. He was appointed Governor of the Mint, and a lord of Sessions. He married for his second wife, Lady Mary Keith, eldest daughter and one of the co-heirs of William, seventh Earl Marischal. By the first marriage, he had several children; by the second, an only surviving son, William of Balcomil, who was created a Baronet in 1698, having had previously the honor of Knighthood.

Sir John was succeeded by his eldest surviving son, John Hope, Esq., of Hopetoun, who took up his residence at the Castle of Niddry, the Barony of which he purchased of Lord Wintoun. He was a member of Parliament from Linlithgo. He married Margaret, eldest daughter of John, fourth Earl of Haddington, by whom he had a son, Charles, and a daughter, Elinor. The latter married Thomas, sixth Earl of Haddington.

Charles succeeded to the family estates, and was elevated to the peerage of Scotland, by the titles of Viscount Aithrie, Baron Hope, and Earl of Hopetoun. He married Henriette, only daughter of William

(Johnstons), first Marquis of Amandale, and had thirteen children.

Sir Charles was succeeded by his son Sir John, who married, first, Anne, daughter of James, fifth Earl of Finlator and Seafield; second, Jane, daughter of Robert Oliphant, Esq., of Rossie, county Perth; third, Lady Elizabeth Leslie, daughter of Alexander, fifth Earl of Leven and Melville. His children were: James, who succeeded him, and died without issue; Elizabeth, married Henry, Earl of Drumlanrig, eldest son of Charles, Duke of Queensburg; Henrietta; Sophia, married Charles, eighth Earl of Haddington; Jane, married first Viscount Melville, second Lord Wallace; John, married first, Elizabeth, daughter of the Hon. Charles Hope-Vere of Craighall, second Louisa Dorothea, daughter of Sir John Widderburn, Bart.; Charles, married Anne, daughter of George Finch Hatton, Esq.; and Alexander, married Georgiana, daughter of Charles Brown, Esq.

John, the second son, entered the British Army at the age of fifteen as a volunteer, and rose to the rank of Lieutenant-General. He served with great distinction under Sir Ralph Abercromby, and was severely wounded in Holland; also in Egypt, at the battle of Alexandria. He served under Sir John Moore, and acquired great distinction by his intrepid march, at the head of three thousand infantry and nine hundred cavalry, with a large park of artillery and ammunition, through an uncultivated country overrun by the enemy, from the Tagus to Salamanca, where he effected a junction with his Commander-in-Chief. He commanded the left wing at the battle of Corunna, and after Moore was killed and Sir David Baird was wounded, the chief command devolved upon him. He commanded the left wing of the British army at the battle of Nivelle, in which Soult was defeated,—and repulsed an attack of the French and took a large number of prisoners. His conduct on this occasion was warmly eulogized by the Duke of Wellington. After the British army entered France, Gen. Hope was instructed to invest Bayonne, and was wounded and taken prisoner in a sortie made by the garrison four days after the abdication of Napoleon He was made Deputy-Governor of Portsmouth, Member of Parliament, and Commander-in-Chief of the forces in Ireland. He received the thanks of both houses of Parliament, the order of the Bath, and was created a British peer with the title of Baron Niddry. After the death of his brother, who had been created a British peer, he succeeded to the title of Earl of Hopetoun—and the extensive estates of the family. Then it was, we are told, that his character shone in its fullest luster. "He exhibited thus a model as perfect, seemingly, as human nature could admit of." He died in 1823, "deeply and deservedly regretted." The esteem in which he was held has since his death been shown by the erection of three monuments to his memory, on as many hills; also by an equestrian statue placed in St. Andrew's Square, Edinburgh.

Sir Thomas Hope of Kerse, second son of Sir Thomas and Anne (Foules) Hope, was the father of two sons, —Alexander, created a Baronet in 1672, and Henry who founded the opulent family of Hope of Amsterdam, Holland.

A descendant of Henry Hope, supposed to have been named William, and said to have been a Scottish loyalist, came to New England, and married, about 1735, Sarah, daughter of Daniel and Mary (Mills) Willard of Boston. They had two children: Henry, born in 1736, in Braintree,—that part which is now Quincy; and Harriet (see account of the Ellises).

According to one account, Mr. and Mrs. Hope sailed for England, and were lost at sea; while, by another, they visited Holland by the way of the West Indies, and on the return voyage, Mr. Hope died and was buried at sea; and Mrs. Hope died before the arrival of the vessel at Martha's Vineyard, near Vineyard Haven, where she was buried. Their children were taken care of by Dr. Edward Ellis of Boston, who had married their mother's sister Mary. When Henry was about thirteen years of age, he was taken by Dr. Ellis to Amsterdam, to his father's family. When old enough, he was taken into the firm; and on the death of his uncle Adrian, the vast business of the concern devolved on him.

Some idea of the amount of business transacted by the house of Hope & Co., may be obtained from "Fifty Years in Two Hemispheres," by Vincent Nolte, in which he gives an account of the stupendous scheme of the Hopes for replenishing the treasuries of France and Spain, at a time when the resources of the former government had been drained by the gigantic operations of Napoleon, and those of Spain were exhausted by the war then going on between that country and England.

Spain had, in a treaty of alliance with France, made herself available for a yearly subsidy of a large amount, part of which had "fallen due without one single franc having been accessible." The treasures which were lying at the command of the Spanish government in Mexico, Peru, and elsewhere, but could not be reached on account of the war then going on, were the only resources Spain had to extricate her from the embarrassments that surrounded her. J. G. Ouvrard, who, by daring speculation had amassed a large fortune, had contracted to supply the necessities of the French treasury for the year 1804, and on him "Napoleon laid his hand to bring about the payment of this sum." Ouvrard repaired to Messrs. Hope & Co., who engaged to carry out his plan, with the stipulation that he should not interfere with the manner and way they might see fit to adopt to gain that object.

Two different methods were adopted to lift the immense hoardings of silver on deposit in Mexico, and transport it thence. One was to procure from the British government, notwithstanding the war with Spain, permission to transport the silver piastres from Vera Cruz to England; the other, to transmit them through the natural channels of trade, by dispatching consignments of goods from America, especially from the United States, to the ports of Europe. "The United States, which were at that time wholly in possession of the carrying trade, presented the most extensive field for the purchase of all kinds of colonial produce,—not only their own, such as cotton and tobacco, but also of each and every kind, such as coffee, sugar, pepper, &c.,—since the latter were regularly shipped thither without the least difficulty, on American account, and under protection of their neutral flag." But the war between England and the Continent "made the transport of such purchases, for the account of even the Messrs. Hope, almost impossible. Measures had, therefore, to be taken to give them the character of neutral property, not in appearance merely, but in reality; and this could be done only by stimulating the enterprising spirit of the American merchants to send shipments on their own account into Continental Europe."

"The whole combination," continues Mr. Nolte, "was a most excellent one," but Napoleon's dislike of anything mercantile, "united to a blind personal hatred for Ouvrard, sufficed to overthrow the most stupendous structure that ever the spirit of mercantile enterprise had begun to erect for the benefit of both kingdoms." Napoleon made a decree that all that Ouvrard had in the hands of Hope & Co., should remain under his direction. "This powerful house, which then stood at the head of the mercantile order throughout the world, and, in Holland, not only felt itself perfectly independent, but considered itself equal in financial matters to any potentate on earth, and entitled to occupy a similar footing with them, could not recognize that it was bound in any way by the imperial decree." Napoleon dictated a letter to Messrs. Hope & Co., which he forwarded by an officer of finance, who was very coolly received and returned without having accomplished anything. "Soon afterward, Napoleon thought it advisable to send the Baron Louis—afterwards Louis Philippe's first Minister of Finance—to Holland, to explore the ground and discover what resources Ouvrard might have there. Baron Louis presented himself to the Messrs. Hope, and disclosed the object of his visit. Mr. Labouchere [one of the firm], who received him, at once replied: 'Whether we have money in our hands for Mr. Ouvrard, or not, Baron, is not a matter for which we are obliged to render any account to you; and the inappropriateness of your present visit must have been apparent to yourself.'"

"Mr. Henry Hope," says Mr. Nolte, "when I first made his acquaintance had reached his seventieth year, and was somewhat deaf. He had never married. It was he who opened the way for the autocratic power of Russia under the Empress Catherine II., to the confidence of the then wealthiest capitalists in Europe, the Dutch, and thereby laid the foundation of Russian credit. Always treated by the Empress with great distinction, he had been honored by the gift from her own hand, of her portrait the full size of life. This picture occupied the place of honor in the superb gallery of paintings fitted up by him, in his palace 't' Huy ten Bosch' (now a royal pleasure palace), which he had built in the woods of Harlem. Upon his emigration to England, he had taken this splendid gallery, entirely composed of cabinet pieces, with him, and I had the pleasure of seeing it frequently in Cavendish Square. To the tone of a refined gentleman and man of the world, he united a certain amiable affability which spoke to and won every heart. The whole-souled cordiality with which he always met me, when I came to his dwelling in the city, or to his country seat, East Sheen, in the neighborhood of Richmond, has always remained fresh in my memory." "The larger part of his considerable fortune," five millions eight hundred thousand dollars, "which he had bequeathed to Henry, the eldest son of his niece Henrietta, passed at Henry's decease to Adrian, the second son, who left no heirs, but from whom it descended to Francis, the third son, born several years afterward. This third inheritor is the rich and well-known Mr. Hope now settled in Paris, and the only surviving member of that branch of the whole family."

It is said that one of the above mentioned gentlemen, probably the latter, owned and occupied a celebrated palace in Paris, built by a prince, whose name I do not recall; and that upon one occasion, hearing a young lady of his acquaintance express a liking for violets, he gave a dinner party in her honor, and had his immense dining-room, capable of seating three hundred persons, decked entirely with violets.

Mr. Hope relinquished business when the French invaded Holland, in 1794, having lived at Amsterdam thirty-four years, and settled in England. He died in London, Feb. 25, 1811.

"He was distinguished," says Mr. Joseph Willard, "for amenity of disposition, open-handed, unbounded liberality, sound and discriminating judgment, and a remarkable talent for business. He possessed also good literary accomplishments in English literature, and a taste for the fine arts, of which he was a munificent patron. His collection of paintings was very celebrated.

"As the great banker of his time united with his reputation as a sound sagacious man, and possessing attractive personal accomplishments, he drew to his instructive society the most noted persons in Europe.

'He was visited by all distinguished travelers, even by crowned heads. His acquaintance was courted by all ranks of people; at the Exchange, he was the chief object of attention; the men of business formed themselves around him; and foreign ministers pressed forward to speak with him on the financial concerns of their respective countries.' "

Harriet, the only sister of Henry Hope, married John Goddard, Esq., of Woodford Hall, Bedfordshire, England, and at her death left three daughters, of whom Henrietta, the eldest, married John, son of the Rev. John Williams of Cornwall. Mr. Williams' name was changed to Hope, by a royal patent signed by the Prince Regent, George IV. He succeeded Mr. Hope in the management of the Amsterdam house, and resided with him. After his death, his widow married Baron Dopff, a German officer of dragoons, and lived in Amsterdam. Mrs. Goddard's second daughter married John Langston, Esq., of Sanden House, Oxfordshire. The youngest daughter married Admiral Sir Charles Morrice Pole, Bart., K. C. B., of an ancient and honorable family residing in Pole, in the parish of Tiverton, which has been the seat of the family since the Norman Conquest.

The wife of the late Duke of Newcastle, is said to have been a descendant of Harriet (Hope) Goddard.

Thomas Hope, connoisseur, philosopher and novelist, was born in 1767. He was a member of the family of Hope of Amsterdam, and a member of the firm at the time Henry Hope (the younger) was at the head of it. At the age of eighteen he became his own master, when he started on an extensive tour to gratify his taste for architecture, which had been a passion with him from infancy. "After eight years' exploration of architectural models and remains in Europe, Asia and Africa, he settled in England; and being the possessor of a magnificent fortune, he enlarged his mansion in Duchess Street, Portland Place, London, adorning it with pictures, statues and furniture, selected and arranged with the greatest care and taste. He published in 1805 a handsome volume, 'Household Furniture,' enforcing with novel enthusiasm his views on what may be called the philosophy of furniture, and illustrated by drawings of the furniture of his own mansion. Somewhat ridiculed at the time, this work is now valued as having given an early impulse to the study and practice of decorative art in this country.

"In 1809 appeared his elaborate work on the 'Costumes of the Ancients' [which evinces great antiquarian lore]; and he also published a letter to F. Annesly, Esq., on the proposed designs for Downing College, Cambridge. In his devotion to art Mr. Hope did not neglect the artist class. He was the earliest patron of Thorwaldson; he encouraged the rising genius of Chantrey, and called into requisition the recognized skill of Flaxman. His seat, the Deepdene in Surrey, owed much to his picturesque taste. Mr. Hope was known only as a connoisseur and a munificent patron of art, when, in 1819, appeared anonymously, 'Anastasius, or Memoirs of a Modern Greek at the Close of the Eighteenth Century,' a sort of oriental Gil Blas. The quiet but intense power of its delineations of Eastern life and character, at once attracted general attention, and this, with the character of the hero, led critics to ascribe its authorship to Lord Byron.[1] That it was the work of the author of 'Household Furniture' was scoffingly denied, and an amusing expression of surprise when its authorship was avowed by Mr. Hope, was forced from Sidney Smith[2] in an appreciatory criticism of

---

[1] "Byron said he would have given his two most approved poems to have been the author of 'Anastasius.'"—*Biog. Dict.*, *Thomas.*

[2] "Mr. Hope will excuse us," says Sidney Smith, "but we could not help exclaiming, in reading it, Is this Mr. Thomas Hope?—is this the man of chairs and tables?—the Œdipus of coal-boxes?—he who medi-

'Anastasius' in the *Edinburgh Review*, the periodical in which Mr. Hope's furniture-enthusiasm had long before been ridiculed. Nothing more of Mr. Hope's was published until his death which occurred on the 3d of February, 1831. Soon after appeared his 'Essay on the Origin and Prospects of Man,' when it was made evident that the personage who had been considered a mere dilettante, was not only the author of one of the most striking novels of the time, but had brooded for years over the construction of a new system of the universe. The 'Origin and Prospects of Man' may be considered the parent of the celebrated Vestiges of Creation, in which it is frequently quoted and referred to. With Frederick Schlegel's Philosophy of Language, it formed the basis of one of the most remarkable of Carlyle's essays, that entitled Characteristics. Another posthumous work of Mr. Hope was the 'Historical Essay on Architecture,' published in 1835, and which has attained a popularity denied to its predecessor.

"Mr. Hope married, in 1807, Louisa, youngest daughter of the Honorable and most Reverend W. Beresford, Archbishop of Tuam (subsequently created Lord Decies), and left at his decease three sons surviving. Mrs. Hope afterward married Field-Marshal Viscount Beresford."[1]

Alexander James Beresford Hope, M. P., a son of Thomas and Louisa (Beresford) Hope, was an author and connoisseur. Among his works are an essay on "Newspapers and their Writers," and "The English Cathedral of the Nineteenth Century."

Mrs. John Farrar, in her "Recollections of Fifty Years," has the following account of Mr. and Mrs.

---

tated on muffincers and planned porkers? Where has he hidden all this eloquence and poetry up to this hour? The work before us places him in the highest list of eloquent writers and superior men."—*Biog. Dict., Thomas.*

[1] From Francis Espinasse's account of Thomas Hope.

Thomas Hope: "The most brilliant party that I was ever at in London, was given by Mrs. Thomas Hope, the daughter of the Archbishop of Tuam, and wife of the learned author of 'Anastasius,' a wealthy merchant of Amsterdam, resident in London. They lived in a corner house in Harley Street, at the west end of London, and it was large enough to contain fourteen rooms *en suite.* These were fitted up with great taste and judgment, according to the ideas of Mr. Hope, who had written a book on furniture and upholstery, and introduced into England the classical forms which have ever since been in use. This house was like a museum, for every room was fitted up in a different style. One was *à la Chinoise*, and fitted with curious and beautiful objects from China; another was in Persian style, full of Eastern magnificence. A Grecian hall, adorned with statuary, delighted the eye, and a French saloon, full of mirrors, with objects of *vertu*, marquetry and *omolu*, Sèvres porcelain and bronzes, claimed the attention of the visitor. The English apartment, emphatically so-called, was the banqueting hall, across one end of which was a long table filled with every delicacy of the season, and where you took refreshments whenever you pleased."

Mrs. Hope "was so diminutive in her person, and so handsome in her face, that she was called the pocket Venus. The Prince Regent requested her to allow him to have her full-length likeness in enamel, for his collection of beauties; and Mr. Bone, the celebrated painter in enamel, made a lovely picture of her. The night that I saw her, she received her company standing on a low stool, and was dressed in gold colored satin, trimmed with black velvet, and had on a superb set of diamonds.

"I went with some particular friends of the Hopes. We had dined at a house only a mile from Mr. Hope's, but it took us two hours to go that distance, in a line of carriages that extended all the way there, and was checked in its progress every time a carriage stopped to set down its company. Directions had been given in the morning papers for the course the carriages were to take, so as to avoid confusion. . . . After a few words with the exquisite little hostess, we sauntered slowly through the rooms, all of which were filled, but not crowded. We soon came to the large English drawing-room, where we felt the soft crush of aristocracy, and pressing gently through it, we came suddenly on an open space, in which a large, fat gentleman was bowing to a lady who was just introduced to him. It was the Prince Regent; I knew him by his bow, and we drew back so as not to intrude on the magic circle around royalty. . . .

"Mr. Hope when I knew him had not published his remarkable novel called 'Anastasius;' but when that appeared, his book on furniture was forgotten, and the public learned to appreciate him as a fine scholar and a good writer."

WATMOUGH.

Capt. Edward Watmough of the British Army, a captain in the Earl of Dumlanrig's regiment, married, Jan. 30, 1748-9, Maria, eldest daughter of Dr. Edward and Mary (Willard) Ellis of Boston. They had four sons: John; Edward Ellis; the name of the third is unknown), and James Horatio (see page 29). Mrs. Watmough died in the prime of her days. Capt. Watmough is buried in Halifax, N. S.

James Horatio was adopted by his mother's cousin, Henry Hope, then at the head of the eminent banking house of Hope & Co. in Amsterdam. It is said that it was the intention of Mr. Hope to make James his heir, and that he was very desirous that he should marry Henrietta Goddard, the eldest daughter of his only sister Harriet; but as James had only the affection of a friend for her, he could not comply with Mr. Hope's wishes, and so left him and came to his native land, Mr. Hope providing handsomely for him on his departure. It is said that he was a very elegant, accomplished man, speaking six languages with great fluency. That he was exceedingly open-hearted and generous, we know from Mrs. Prescott's account of him (page 30). He married Maria Carmick of Philadelphia. Their children were: Henry Hope, who died young; Maria Ellis; Margaretta; John Goddard; and Edward Carmick. Maria married Joseph Reed, Esq., a prominent lawyer of Philadelphia, and had nine children, only one of whom is now living, Miss Maria Reed of Brooklyn, N. Y.

Margaretta married Hon. John Sargeant, a celebrated lawyer of Philadelphia. They had nine children, four daughters, of whom Mrs. Gen. Meade, Mrs. Harrison Smith, Mrs. Cram and Miss Ellen Sargeant survive her.

Edward, the youngest, married Maria Chew Nicklin, a sister of the wife of Vice-President Dallas, and granddaughter of Benjamin Chew, Chief Justice of Pennsylvania. Mr. Watmough was a lawyer. He left one son, William Nicklin, and three daughters, the eldest of whom married Judge Thayer, and the second married Richard Gilpin.

William married Sarah Elizabeth, daughter of Joshua Ratoone and Eleanor Ann (Crook) Sands. Joshua R. Sands was Rear Admiral in the United States Navy.

William Watmough entered the United States Volunteer service in 1861, and was wounded in front of Richmond while serving on the staff of Gen. George G. Meade. He was commissioned in 1862 as disbursing officer in the United States Navy.

John Goddard, the eldest son of James H. Watmough, was educated until the age of twelve with a view to entering the banking-house of Hope & Co., in Amsterdam; but upon his father's death, which occurred at that time, the idea was abandoned. Before he had attained his eighteenth year, the second war of our independence had commenced, and young Watmough, upon receiving a lieutenant's commission in the 2d regiment of United States Artillery, started for the Niagara frontier. During the eventful period which followed, the regiment to which he belonged, was constantly engaged. For several weeks, not a day elapsed that it did not meet the enemy. The whole period was one protracted battle,—"always nobly fought and as often triumphantly won."

During the fifty days and upwards of cannonade and bombardment before the walls of Fort Erie, Lieut. Watmough and his gallant comrades, Williams and M'Donough, were stationed on the advance guard battery nearest the foe. On the 13th of August, Lieut. Watmough was wounded by a piece of shell, notwithstanding which he left the hospital and joined in the brilliant battle of the next day. During that battle, Drummond, who charged the battery to which Watmough belonged, effected a footing on the bastion with a column of one thousand men, and charged the defenders while in the act of reloading their guns. A personal conflict of great violence ensued, and continued for some time with alternate success. The intrepid Williams and M'Donough both fell, and upon Lieut. Watmough the command then devolved. The enemy kept pouring in their masses upon him; but, although weakened by the loss of blood, and by long continued exertion, he still maintained his ground, until at length overpowered by numbers, and having been again wounded, he was driven with his few remaining comrades to the edge of the parapet, and while there, encouraging his men to hold firm until assistance should arrive, was struck with the butt end of a musket, and thrown by the violence of the blow into the ditch. Here he lay surrounded by the killed and wounded of the enemy, and exposed to the fire of the other batteries; at length recovering, he collected strength sufficient to regain the entrance to the fort. He found the bastion in full possession of the enemy. On a neighboring block-house was an eighteen pound gun, from which a fatal fire might have been maintained on the conquered battery, had it not been deserted. With the assistance of a brave corporal named Faraquhar, Lieut. Watmough succeeded in gaining the block-house, and loading and discharging the gun upon the battery several times with terrible effect. This rendered the position of the enemy untenable, so they immediately directed their whole force against it; volley after volley being discharged at the spot from which Lieut. Watmough still continued with unabated ardor, and with terrible effect, to direct his fire. For a long time he escaped unhurt, but at length, while in the act of loading the piece to the muzzle for the sixth or seventh time, a musket ball struck him in the breast, and he fell. At the same moment the bastion of which the enemy had gained possession blew up,—and with it went all their hopes of victory. As Watmough lay upon the field, supposed to be mortally wounded, he was cheered by the news that the enemy had been repulsed at all points. "To the intrepidity and desperate perseverance of the heroic Watmough, the glorious result of this battle was in great part ascribed."

While lying in the hospital near Buffalo, and at that time unable to rise from his bed, the news of the disaster at Washington reached Watmough, with an exaggerated account of the capture of Baltimore and the probable march of the British on his native city. It was no time to wait to be cured. Permission was obtained to return to Philadelphia; a one-horse wagon was hired; the bed with its occupant, was placed in it, and the painful journey home was with difficulty accomplished.

On his arrival he was immediately attached to the staff of his old commander, Gen. Gaines, who, on the first advance of the British army on the road, had been ordered thither to assume the command.

"In spite of the orders of his physician and the earnest entreaties of his friends, Lieut. Watmough determined to accompany that gallant officer on his journey to the South, whither he had been ordered; and set out, in the middle of a most inclement winter, to cross the mountains, and descend the river to New Orleans. The ice in the Ohio prevented their progress by water, and the impediments in land traveling being numerous, young Watmough was delayed too long on the route to contribute his aid in the achievement of the glorious victory of the 8th of January."

On the first reduction of the army, in 1815, Lieut. Watmough was retained, and having received the Brevet promotion to which his gallant services and severe sufferings entitled him, he was offered, by his friend and commander, Gen. Gaines, an unlimited furlough, to enable him to heal his wounds, and recover from their painful and harrassing effects. The same letter, however, which conveyed this offer, spoke of a "speck of war which had just arisen on our southern border," among the Creek and Seminole Indians. "As may well be supposed, the wounds and the furlough were instantly forgotten, and he once more set out to encounter the toils and dangers of a wilderness campaign. From New Orleans he repaired to Augusta, Georgia, at which place the troops were ordered to concentrate. From Augusta he was sent by his general to the city of Charleston, with orders to expedite immediately the march of the gallant 4th regiment of infantry for the Indian Territory, and to equip a brigade of light artillery with all speed. "How promptly all this was accomplished will be at once seen, when the reader is informed, that on the same day that the 4th regiment encamped for the night, at Augusta, having proceeded thus far on its route to the Indian nation, a regular battery of field-pieces completely equipped for immediate service reached the same spot." In the winter of 1816, all prospect of active service having terminated, Col. Watmough resigned his commission, and retired to an estate left him by his father, a few miles from Philadelphia, called Hope Lodge. He married Ellen, daughter of Judge Coxe of Philadelphia. He remained at Hope Lodge ten years, and, upon the death of his wife removed to Philadelphia, where he had many offices of public trust conferred upon him. In 1830 he was sent by the third district as a Representative to the United States Congress, and was three times re-elected. While there he became acquainted with and married Mary Matilda, daughter of Stephen Pleasanton, Esq., a nephew of Hon. Cæsar Rodney, one of the signers of the Declaration of Independence. Mr. Pleasanton was formerly of Dover, Delaware, but came to Washington in the early days of the government, and remained there, in office, fifty years. He was honored by the friendship of President Monroe, who created for him the office of fifth Auditor of the Treasury. Mr. Pleasanton was instrumental in saving the public archives during the war of 1812, taking them to Leesburg, Va.

Mrs. Pleasanton was descended from an old English family, being a daughter of Judge Hopkins of Lancaster, Penn. She was a woman of excellent judgment, thoroughly conversant with politics. Her opinion was sought and referred to by the political leaders who frequented her house, which was a favorite resort, she being a leader in Washington society. Her daughter, Mrs. Watmough, retains very pleasant memories of Webster, Clay, Calhoun, Adams, and a host of others, they being young men and visitors at her father's house when she was a young girl.

Col. Watmough, at the expiration of his term of office, returned to Philadelphia, where he spent the remainder of his life. In Congress he exhibited "the same high sense of honor, the same noble devotion to the welfare of the people, the same disinterested and enthusiastic patriotism" that he had exhibited in the field. "His speeches were what he was himself,—able, exalted, fervent and patriotic." "Always ready, always fluent, forcible, convincing and eloquent." It is also said that he was equally exemplary in domestic life, and possessed a very lovely disposition. Twenty-one years, Col. Watmough suffered from the severe wound he received in battle, the pain being at times almost unbearable; but his love of country and sense of honor were so great, he bore this infliction with the greatest cheerfulness, and never was known to utter a word of complaint. The ball that entered his breast, having finally worked its way near to the surface, was removed. He died in November, 1861. Bishop Potter, who visited him during his last sickness, afterwards remarked, that he had "never met with a mind more pure and guileless."

Gen. Gaines wrote of him: "While a lieutenant of artillery, and scarcely arrived at the age of manhood, when first known to me, he was distinguished for the purity of his moral sentiments, the vigor of his military mind, and the untiring assiduity of his attention to his professional duties, nor have I ever known a man whose intrepidity or perseverance in battle, under previous severe wounds, was more praiseworthy.'"[1]

Col. Watmough's children by his first wife were: Edward Coxe, who died young; Mary Ellen; James Horatio; Pendleton Gaines; and Catherine. The children by his second wife were: John Goddard, Margaretta, Mary Williams, and Anne Caroline.

James H. was for many years Paymaster-General of the United States Navy, his residence being in Washington. He married Emeline G., daughter of George and Catherine (Muhlenberg) Sheaff of Philadelphia. Mrs. Sheaff was a daughter of Frederick Augustus Muhlenberg, first Speaker of the House of Representatives, and brother of Gen. Peter Gabriel Muhlenberg of Revolutionary fame. Dr. Henry Melchoir Muhlenberg, the father of Frederick and Peter, was the founder of Lutheranism in America. His wife was Anna, a daughter of Conrad Weiser, the Pennsylvania statesman and Indian diplomat of the colonial era.

Pendleton G. was a captain in the United States Navy, and nobly performed his duty during the late rebellion, resigning his commission when peace was restored to the country. He married Minnie M., daughter of George Merwin, and granddaughter of Rufus Wood, Governor of Ohio and Judge of the Superior Court of that State.

John G. married Carrie, daughter of Francis M. Drexel, an eminent banker of Philadelphia. He is a broker in that city.

---

[1] The account of John G. Watmough is taken chiefly from a pamphlet published by his friends.

MARTINE AND DE LES DERNIER.

The following account was written by Mrs. Harriet (de Les Dernier) Prescott, the widow of William Pepperell Prescott:

"My great grandparents were natives of Geneva, Switzerland.[1] My great-grandfather Martine was a clergyman of the Reformed Church. The patrimony he inherited consisted of a handsome chateau, with acres enough, under his own careful direction, for the support of his family, which (besides servants) consisted of his wife and two daughters. But after his death, which occurred when his eldest daughter was sixteen years of age and his youngest eight, things went so differently that, after a time, Madam Martine, my great-grandmother, deemed it expedient to open a school for young ladies; in which she was assisted by her elder daughter. Her husband had taken great care in the training of his daughter, and both mother and daughter had been carefully educated and possessed the accomplishments of that day.

"The daughter when very young was married to Monsieur Moses de Les Dernier of Geneva; a man of property and talents, a gentleman and educated. He took his bride to England, where they lived several years, in the west part of London. They subsequently emigrated to British North America.

"Madam Martine continued her school several years till the destruction of the chateau by fire. It was entirely consumed, one very stormy night; and, besides a trunk with not a very large amount of money,

---

[1] The Martines were Swiss-French, and said to be Huguenots.

but little of value was saved. Madam Martine survived the shock and exposure of the night but a few weeks, leaving Madelon, her youngest daughter, overwhelmed with grief, and alone in the world, as it were. As soon as tidings of her mother's death reached her, the daughter in London wrote to her sister to dispose of the property as best she could, and join her with all speed, as they were on the eve of embarking for Halifax, B. N. A., and enclosed an ample money draft, in case of need. Monsieur Gideon de Les Dernier, an uncle (but younger) of her sister's husband, on his way to go with them to America, was to be her escort.

"Owing to unavoidable delays, the winter of 1748 was nearly half through when they reached London, and Mademoiselle Martine had the great grief of learning that her sister and her husband had already sailed for America. They had waited as long as their completed arrangements and the advancing cold season would allow, and left with sorrowful reluctance.

"From her sister's recent home, Mademoiselle Martine was conducted to the house of Madam Cyresme, a French lady, near neighbor and friend of her sister's. She was ushered by a liveried servant into the presence of a middle-aged and lovely-looking person, who rose, and extending her hand, said in French: 'I am quite sure I have the pleasure of greeting Mademoiselle Martine, the sister of my friend.' The fortitude of my grandmother quite gave way under the warm welcome and friendliness of Madam Cyresme, who directly brought forward letters and directions left with her for my grandmother, and claimed her at once as her guest during her stay in London.

"My grandmother had been so wrapt in grief for the loss of her mother, and distress at the departure of her sister, she was taken quite by surprise by a declaration of love from her escort, Monsieur Gideon de Les Dernier. She had not thought of it at all, but his persistent pleadings, aided by those of Madam Cyresme, who had been quite won by the fascinating and gentlemanly stranger, were finally successful, and they were married in the Protestant Church where Madam Cyresme worshipped, in her presence and that of several other witnesses. As soon as the spring was sufficiently advanced, my grandparents bade adieu to their friends in London and embarked for British North America, reaching Halifax in due season, where they lived some time. There their first son, my father, Peter Francis Christian de Les Dernier, was born. They afterward followed her sister and husband to Windsor, Nova Scotia, where my grandfather bought a fine tract of land, with fruit and many other trees, and built a cottage in the Swiss style, covering much ground. In this sunny home the happy part of my grandmother's married life was spent, in the care and culture of her little family of five sons, and in the society of her friends at Windsor, and the families of the British officers stationed at Fort Edward.

"My grandmother's first great sorrow, after her marriage, was the death of her sister (she left no children); but later, many sorrows came. When these now United States broke out into rebellion against the mother country, my father and his brother Mark held fast in their allegiance to the British King, but my grandfather and his other sons joined the revolted Americans. My grandfather lost his property in Windsor. When my uncle Louis determined to go into active service, my grandparents accompanied him to Boston, Mass.

"After the war my uncle Louis was appointed collector of the port of what is now Lubec, and my grandparents went with him to the Province of Maine. My uncle John, the youngest son, was lost during the war. My uncles Frederick and Mark settled in Western New York and Canada.

"I had all this from my grandmother herself. My

grandmother has always been represented as a woman of superior mind, interesting in manners and conversation, and of great personal beauty. I saw her last in 1798; her complexion was then wonderfully fair, and her beautiful eyes still clear and expressive, but her form was bent. My grandfather, who interested me deeply, was tall and erect, but at this time thin and pale. He ever retained that ease and grace of manner for which he had been distinguished. I never saw my grandparents after 1798, but I received a letter from my grandmother, written in French. They died, not long after I parted with them, very nearly together."

After giving some particulars of the family that are given in the account of the Elises, Mrs. Prescott goes on to say: "My only brother," [he was her half brother] was sent to Holland to be educated under the care of my mother's cousin, Henry Hope, the well-known banker. My brother, a youth, was returning home for a vacation; the vessel had been long out; every one was impatient for land, and ambitious to be the first to descry it. My brother went aloft, a lurch of the vessel threw him into the sea, and he was drowned; a sorrow my mother never recovered from."

Martha Maria, a daughter of Moses de Les Dernier (probably by a second marriage, as Mrs. Prescott states that his first wife left no children), married Attorney-General Richard John Uniacke of Halifax, N. S. A son of hers, Judge Norman Uniacke of Halifax, married a granddaughter of Gideon and Madelon de Les Dernier. It is said that during a conversation Mrs. Norman Uniacke once had with Lamartine, the French statesman and author, the discovery was made that his family and the branch of the Martines that she was descended from was the same.

Louis Frederick, the son of Gideon and Madelon de Les Dernier, was government agent to the Indians in Maine, and was known throughout that region as the

"Good Louis." The following account is taken from the "Augusta Age," Jan. 29, 1842: "Louis Frederick de Les Dernier came to this country during the Revolution, and was at that time an officer in the army. In 1785 he resided at Moose Island (Eastport), and was first Naval Officer, and afterwards first Collector of the General Government for the Passamaquoddy District. During these times he was of much assistance to our people as an Indian interpreter. He remained Collector until 1811. He was a gentleman of excellent mind and pleasant manners. He died in 1841."

The following account of Hon. William de Les Dernier, his son, is taken from the same paper: William de Les Dernier at the age of nineteen obtained a lieutenant's commission, and used his little property, in connection with a few others, in raising a volunteer company for the war of 1812. Later, he became a captain of marines. "Our navy (feeble in numbers) was much assisted by a class of large privateers. The Mammoth of Portland was one of these. On board of this, Lieut. de Les Dernier entered as captain of marines. The Mammoth cruised for six months along the shores of England and Scotland and in the English Channel, and was not excelled by any of that class of vessels in usefulness. Manned by strong arms and brave hearts from our *own* good state, they bore the stars and stripes through the battle and the breeze aloft to victory. Although often engaged with vessels of superior force, they captured and destroyed fourteen square-rigged vessels,—one of these being freighted with arms and provisions (exceedingly valuable to our country). She was placed in charge of Lieut. de Les Dernier to bring home. For fourteen days his run was fair and prosperous; hope gladdened their souls, and the heart of young de Les Dernier beat strong with anticipated triumph. When off George's Bank they fell in with and were captured by an English frigate, carried to Halifax and imprisoned. Capt. de Les Dernier was ordered to England. To avoid this, if possible, he wrote to the King's Attorney-General, was answered, and his petition granted." "The state loaded him with honors, and the press eulogized his name."

Miss Emily de Les Dernier, the talented public reader and author, was a sister of Capt. William de Les Dernier.

DEAN.

"The name of Den, or Dene,[1] which is the ancient way of spelling what is now written Deane, makes its appearance in England soon after the introduction of surnames. It was apparently derived from the Saxon word den, or dene, a valley. From different modes of spelling the word dene or den have arisen two surnames, which at the present time are entirely distinct, viz., Deane and Denne." In the reign of Elizabeth, the letter a was introduced into the name so that Dene became Deane. There are in England four distinct families of Deanes, from which all the others are offshoots. "The first person of the name that we have any record of, was Robert de Den or de Dene, who was 'butler or sewer' to Edward the Confessor. He held estates in Normandy, as well as in England, and may have been one of the Norman favorites which this monarch called around him. From him he may have received estates in England of sufficiently greater importance than his Norman heritage, to induce him to assume their appellation. Confirmatory of this conjecture it may be remarked that this family was not deprived of their estates at the Conquest."

Another person of the name, early met with, is Sir William of Dene, who was, at the time of the Conquest, owner of Throwly in Kent, the seat of an ancient "priory of Priors Aliens," suppressed in 1415. "There were many distinguished knights by the name of Dene, who, though it is impossible to identify

[1] The following is from an account of the Deans, published by William Read Dean, Esq., together with information furnished by that gentleman.

them with any particular families, are fixed to counties by the valuable Roll of Knights, in the eighth year of the reign of Edward II."

From William Dean, Esq., of London, we learn that Walter Deane of South Chard, Somersetshire, Eng., who died in 1591, was the father of three children, William who died in 1634, Jane and Elinor. William had nine children, of whom John, Walter and Margaret emigrated to New England about 1637.

"They arrived," says the late Rev. Samuel Deane of Scituate, Mass., "at Boston first, stopped a year or nearly, at Dorchester, and then came with others to Taunton, Mass." They "took up their farms on the west bank of the river, about one mile from the center of the present village." Houses occupying the same lots as those erected by them, or nearly the exact sites, are at this day owned and occupied by descend ants of each. The road which passed their dwellings has been called Dean Street to this day. They took the freeman's oath, Dec. 4, 1638.

John, the eldest, was born about 1600. He married Alice ——. Their children were: John, Thomas, Israel, Isaac, Nathaniel, and Elizabeth. Mr. Dean was of the grand inquest from Taunton in 1640. He died about 1650. "The following extract from his will shows that he possessed the Puritan feeling in regard to religion: 'Item. My will is that these my Overseers with the Consent of my Wife shall in Case theer be no Settled ministry in Taunton, they shall have full power to sell either the whole or a part of these my Housings & Lands so as my children & Posterity may remove elswhere, where they may enjoy God in his Ordinances.' The inventory of his estate amounted to £334. 18s."

His wife survived him and was alive as late as 1688, as she is mentioned in a grant of the Plymouth Court, June 1st of that year.

"The following anecdote has been preserved by tradition: Mr. Deane being out alone on a hunting expedition at one time, perceived through the bushes some Indians cautiously approaching, evidently for the purpose of capturing or killing him. When they were but a short distance from him, the thought suddenly struck him of making it appear that he was in the company of others. This he did by exclaiming loudly, 'Rush on, boys, and we will have them,' at the same time firing his gun and rushing forward. The stratagem succeeded and the wild men of the woods scattered, permitting him to return home unmolested."

Walter, the brother of John, was born in 1615 or 16. He married Elizabeth, daughter of Richard Strong of Taunton, Eng., who came to New England with her brother, Elder John Strong, afterward of Northampton.

Walter Deane was deputy to the Plymouth Court in 1640, and selectman of Taunton. When the inhabitants of Taunton were invited by the people of the cape towns to come to them with their movable property for protection during Philip's war, Mr. Deane was one of the persons appointed to decline their invitation and return thanks for their kindness.

Walter and Elizabeth (Strong) Deane had three children, viz.: Joseph, Ezra and Benjamin.

Margaret Deane, the sister of John and Walter, married John Strong.

There is a tradition in the family that a younger brother came to this country later and settled in Connecticut, and that from him was descended Hon. Silas Deane, Commissioner to France in the time of the Revolution. This tradition is confirmed by a member of the family to which Hon. Silas Deane belonged.

Silas Dean, a successful merchant of Newport, R. I., was a son of Edward and Mary Dean of Taunton, Mass. Edward was a son of Seth, who was a son of Ezra, the latter being a son of Walter and Elizabeth (Strong) Deane.

Silas Dean married Elizabeth, daughter of Capt. Peter Jacob and Elizabeth (Ellis) Dordin. Their children were: Sarah Ellis, married Stephen Deblois[1] of Newport; Silas; Elizabeth, married William Tisdale of Taunton, Mass.; Mary F. Jones; Anna Watmough, married Joshua Sayer, a merchant of Newport, and a descendant of William Sayer who came from Deal, Eng., in 1742; Harriet Hope; Martha Duncan, married Lysander Washburn of Taunton, a descendant of Sir Godfrey Washburn of Gloucestershire, Eng.

Mr. Dean, after the death of his wife, married a second time.

---

[1] It is said that Stephen, Earl of Blois, afterward King of England, was the founder of the family of Blois in England. The family bore fleurs-de-lis in their arms.

PRESCOTT.

THE name of Prescott is of Saxon origin, and is composed by the contraction of the words "priest" and "cottage." It was given to a street and lane, or place, in the ancient city of London, and it is also the name of a market town in Lancashire. The first mention of the name in history is in a confirmation of a grant made by H. de Petershall, Treasurer to the King, concerning aqueducts of the city of London, the confirmation being addressed to Walter de Prescott, Vice Chancellor, and others.[1] Orders of knighthood were conferred upon some members of the family.

In 1638, John Prescott, having left England to avoid persecution on account of his religious convictions, landed at Barbadoes, where he became an owner of land. In 1640, he came to New England, and settled in Watertown, where he had large grants of land allotted him. He was the second son of Ralph and Ellen Prescott of Shevington in the parish of Standish, Lancashire, Eng. Ralph was the second son of Roger and Ellen (Shaw) Prescott of Shevington, and Roger was the second son of James and —— (Standish) Prescott of Shevington. The father of the wife of James Prescott was Roger Standish, Esq., of Standish. This branch of the family was originally from the town of Prescott. James Prescott was one of the gentlemen of Lancashire who were required by an order of Queen Elizabeth, dated August, 1564, to keep in readiness horsemen and armor.

James, his eldest son, for his bravery and military prowess and achievements, was created lord of the manor of Dryby in Lincolnshire, and had new arms

[1] "Fœdera," Vol. II., pp. 29, 30. Thomas Rymer.

granted to him. The arms of the family are,—Sable, a chevron between three owls, ar. Crest, a cubit arm, couped, erect, vested gu., cuff ermine, holding in the hand a pitch-pot (or hand-beacon), sa., fired ppr. This coat of arms is worn by the Prescotts of Theobald's Park, Hertfordshire, Barts., and by the ancient families of Lancashire and Yorkshire.

John Prescott was baptized in 1604–5. He married, Jan. 21, 1629, Mary Platts of Wygan, Lancashire. John Prescott sold his lands in Shevington, and removed into Yorkshire, residing for some time in Sowerby, in the parish of Halifax, where several of his children were born. Three years after his arrival in New England he was associated with Thomas King and others in the purchase of a tract of land for a township which was to be ten miles in length and eight in breadth. An act of incorporation was petitioned for by the inhabitants, and a request made that the town might receive the name of Prescott. The General Court objected, on the ground that it appeared too much like man-worship. The name of Lancaster was finally given to the town in honor of Mr. Prescott, that being the name of his native county.

Mr. Prescott at a very early day "became a leading spirit, and a prominent and influential man, as very many of his descendants have been in each and every subsequent generation." "He was a man of strict integrity and of great energy and perseverance." He took the oath of fidelity in 1652, and was admitted a freeman in 1669. In November, 1653, he received a grant of land of the inhabitants, on condition that he would build a "*corn-mill.*" He built the mill in season to commence grinding on the 23d of the next May, the stone being brought from England. The erection of a saw-mill soon followed.

It has been stated that he had served under Cromwell. He brought with him from England a coat of mail, armor and habiliments complete, with which he would clothe himself whenever he had difficulties with the Indians. He was a very strong, athletic man of a stern countenance, and it is said that upon such occasions he presented a very fierce and frightful appearance. The Indians at one time having stolen from him a horse, he put on his armor and pursued them. They were surprised that he should venture to pursue them alone, and a chief approached him with uplifted tomahawk. Mr. Prescott told him to strike, which he did, and finding that the blow made no impression on his cap, was greatly astonished, and asked Mr. Prescott to let him put it on and then to strike him on his head, as he had done on Mr. Prescott's head. The stroke settled it to the ears of the Indian, but being too small for him, the skin on both sides of his head was taken off. The Indians gave him his horse, supposing him to be a supernatural being.

The Indians set fire to his barn on one occasion, but he put on his armor, rushed out, and drove them off, and let out his horses and cattle from the burning stable. At another time they set fire to his mill, but armed *cap-a-pie*, he drove them off as before, and extinguished the fire. "They attacked his house. He had several muskets, but no one in the house, save his wife, to assist him. She loaded the guns and he discharged them with fatal effect. The contest continued for nearly half an hour, Mr. Prescott all the while giving orders as if to soldiers, so loud that the Indians could hear him. At length they withdrew, carrying off several of their dead and wounded."

The children of John and Mary (Platts) Prescott were: Mary, married Thomas Sawyer of Lancaster; Martha, married John Rugg; John, married Sarah —— of Lancaster; Sarah, married Richard Wheeler of Lancaster; Hannah, married John Rugg (her sister being dead); Lydia married Jonas Fairbanks of Lancaster; Jonathan; Joseph (?); Jonas, married Mary, daughter of John and Mary (Draper) Loker.

Capt. Jonathan, Mr. Prescott's second son, was born, it is supposed, about 1649. He settled in Lancaster, but in a few years removed to Concord, Mass., his house there being fortified as a garrison. He was a farmer and a man of energy and influence, and highly respected. He took a prominent part in the affairs of the town, representing it in the General Assembly for nine years. He was a captain of militia.

He married, first, Dorothy ——; second, Elizabeth, daughter of John Hoar, Esq., a lawyer of Concord; third, Rebecca, the widow of Hon. Peter Bulkeley, Jr., and daughter of Lieut. Joseph Wheeler; fourth, Ruth Brown. His children were: A child, who died the day of its birth; Jonathan, died at 10 years of age; Samuel, married Esther Wheeler and settled in Acton; Jonathan (Doct.), married Rebecca, only daughter of the Hon. Peter Bulkeley, Esq.; Elizabeth, married John Fowle of Woburn; Dorothy, married Edward, son of Gershom Bulkeley (Edward was a son of Rev. Peter Bulkeley); John, died in his 23d year; Mary, married John, son of John Miles (the first) of Concord; and Benjamin.

Benjamin, the third son of Capt. Jonathan and Elizabeth (Hoar) Prescott, was born Sept. 16, 1687. He was graduated from Harvard College in 1709, and was ordained over the church of the Second Precinct in Salem, now Peabody, where he officiated with fidelity and success for forty-five years. He married, first, Elizabeth, daughter of John Higginson, Esq., of Salem; second, Mercy, daughter of Rev. Henry Gibbs of Watertown; third, Mary, daughter of Hon. William Pepperrell, and sister to Sir William Pepperrell (her first husband was Hon. John Frost of New Castle, N. H., and her second Rev. Benjamin Colman, D. D., of Boston).

Mr. Prescott, upon retiring from his pastoral duties, entered into public life, where he exhibited the same uniform piety and virtue. "He was well versed in the laws, rights and interests of his country, and defended them with signal ability and devotedness." "Being endowed with strong reasoning powers, his pen was frequently employed in the defense of the rights of the people, more especially at the commencement of the controversy which led to the Revolution, and it is said that his writings were distinguished for their force and vivacity,—even when he had entered his ninetieth year, in which he was seized with a violent fever which soon terminated his existence.

His children were: Benjamin, (Harv. Coll., in 1736), married Rebecca, daughter of James and Martha (Lane) Minot; John, died in infancy; Hannah, married Capt. Daniel, son of Col. Daniel Eppes; Elizabeth, married William, son of John and Mary (Pepperrell) Frost; Sarah, died in infancy; Henry, died in infancy; and a second Henry.

Henry, the youngest son, was born July 25, 1737. He married Mary, daughter of Hon. Joseph and Dorothy (Pepperrell) Newmarch. Dorothy was a daughter of Hon. William Pepperrell (see account of the Pepperrells). She was a woman of great courage and firmness, mingled with vivacity, cheerfulness and ready wit. It is related of her that, when advised to leave New Castle on account of the expected invasion of the British troops in 1776, she declared she would not leave "until she could see the whites of the enemy's eyes." Mr. Prescott was a merchant, and it is related of him, that, having unbounded confidence in his country's honor, he never refused to exchange coin for continental money; and bundles of the worthless trash were stored in his garret, with which his children played.

Their children were: Mercy Gibbs, married her cousin Benjamin Frost; Joseph Newmarch, died young; Dorothy, died young; Benjamin, married, first, Abigail Long, second, Hannah, daughter of Jacob Sheafe, Esq., of Portsmouth, N. H.; Henry and Mary, twins, lived but a short time; Henry, married, first, Abigail Shannon, second, —— Newmarch; William Pepperrell; Andrew Watkins, who died young; and George Washington, married Mary Grafton of Salem.

Mr. Prescott died Sept. 10, 1816. Mrs. Prescott died in 1822.

William Pepperrell, the fifth son of Henry and Mary (Newmarch) Prescott, was born Oct. 19, 1769. He married Harriet, daughter of Peter Francis Christian and Elizabeth de Les Dernier. Mrs. de Les Dernier was the daughter of Dr. Edward Ellis of Boston, and widow of Capt. Peter J. Dordin (see account of the Ellises).

Mr. Prescott was for many years a successful merchant in New Castle, N. H., being also extensively engaged in navigation until the war of 1812, when his business was cut off, his prospects blighted and his fortune shipwrecked. Later in life, he was again a merchant. It is said of him "that he was an intelligent, enterprising business man, maintaining throughout a stainless reputation for uprightness, and integrity, and all the virtues that adorn the true gentleman."

Mrs. Prescott was a woman of great loveliness of character, and of unusual intelligence. She was very benevolent, and had strong religious convictions. In a letter to her daughter, she once wrote: "I early came to the conclusion that, in matters of religion, it is better to feel than to reason." "I was born, as it were, and brought up, as you know, in the Episcopal Church. As soon as I could articulate, my single-hearted, true-minded mother taught me the 'Lord's Prayer,' the Apostles' Creed and Church Catechism. She did not content herself with the *letter*, but impressed upon my mind the meaning, the spirit and the *authority* of each and all. On these, my daughter, rests the superstructure of all I believe and all I feel of religion,—as far as they are clearly traceable to the *gospel* of our Lord and

Saviour, Jesus Christ. That gospel is the perfection of philosophy, the interpreter of all revelation, the key to all contradictions in the physical and moral world. It is life, it is immortality."

Their children were: Elizabeth Ellis, married Charles Cotsworth Pinckney, son of Hon. Silas and Mary (Thornton) Benton (Mary Thornton was a daughter of Hon. Matthew Thornton, signer of the Declaration of Independence); Joseph Newmarch (Elizabeth and Joseph were twins); Mary Newmarch, married her mother's cousin, John de Les Dernier; William Henry; George Benjamin, who was lost at sea at about the age of 21 years; Harriet Goddard; Adeline Ann, died in childhood; and Catherine Fraser Watson, married George Little, son of Rev. William and Jane (Little) Montague (see account of the Montagues).

Mr. Prescott died May 30, 1831. Mrs. Prescott died Dec. 29, 1864, aged 89.

William H., the second son, served under Santa Ana, in 1833, against the usurpation of Spain. He was in six engagements, and received three wounds in one battle, fighting three hours after receiving a bullet in his thigh, and until he fainted from loss of blood. He was promoted to the command of a man-of-war. He was afterwards the commander, and part owner of a packet sailing between New Orleans and Vera Cruz, which left the latter place for Tampico, Feb. 13, 1835, and was wrecked during a terrible gale off that port, all on board perishing. He was 25 years of age.

Joseph N., eldest son of William and Harriet Prescott, was born Jan. 19, 1807. He married, Dec. 18, 1833, Sarah Jane, daughter of John and Anna L. (Hitchings) Bridges of Calais, Me. John Bridges was a descendant of Sir John Bridges of Nova Scotia. Their children were: Harriet Elizabeth, married Richard S., son of Dr. Richard S. and Frances (Lord, nee Mills) Spofford of Newburyport (see account of the Spoffords); Annie Livingston, died in infancy; Mary Newmarch; William Pepperrell, died in childhood; Catherine Montague, married Edward Augustus, son of Edward Strong and Charlotte Augusta (Chapman) Moseley of Newburyport; Otis Livingston (Harv. Coll. 1868); Edith Josephine, married Arthur St. Clare Richardson.

"Mr. Prescott was by nature and education adapted to a commercial life." He began business first in Boston, but removed to Calais, Me., where he became quite active in public and business life. In 1847, he went to the Pacific coast, and after a short stay in San Francisco, he settled in Oregon City, Or., and took a prominent part in the early history of the great north-western State. He was three times elected Mayor of Oregon City, and remained there in active business until stricken with paralysis, when he came to Newburyport to spend his declining years. Through a long illness he was a patient sufferer. He died in January, 1881.

Mary N. Prescott, while yet a school-girl, began writing for magazines, "her mother's quick perception upon one occasion having detected a 'composition' worthy of a wider hearing—which it quickly got." Her only book is "Matt's Folly," but her stories for the children's magazines would make a large and interesting volume. In the words of Mr. Woodman, in "Poet's Homes," "there is rare depth and tenderness in her verse." Her love and faith and trust in God "well up like clear springs through beautiful grasses," in "Listening," "The Golden-rod," "Why," "Winter" and "Spring-time."

Mrs. Prescott survives her husband. The following beautiful tribute to her was written by her daughter, Mrs. Harriet Prescott Spofford:

MOTHER MINE.

When by the ruddy fire I spelled,
  In one old volume and another,
Those ballads haunted by fair women,
  One of them always seemed my mother.

In storied song she dwelt, where dwell
  Strange things and sweet of eld and eerie,
The foam of Binnorie's bonny mill-dams,
  The bowing birks, the wells o' Wearie.

All the Queen's Maries did she know,
  The eldritch knight, the sisters seven,
The lad that lay upon the Lomonds
  And saw the perch play in Lochleven.

Burd Helen had those great gray eyes
  Their rays from shadowy lashes flinging;
That smile the winsome bride of Yarrow
  Before her tears were set to singing.

That mouth was just the mouth that kissed
  Sir Cradocke under the green wildwood;
Fair Rosamond was tall as she was,
  In those fixed fancies of my childhood.

And when she sang—ah, when she sang!
  Birds are less sweet, and flutes not clearer—
In ancient halls I saw the minstrel,
  And shapes long dead arose to hear her!

Darlings of song I 've heard since then,
  But no such voice as hers was, swelling
Like bell-notes on the winds of morning,
  All angelhood about it dwelling.

No more within those regions dim
  Of rich romance my thoughts would place her,
Her life itself is such a poem
  She does not need old names to grace her.

Long years have fled, but left her charm
  Smiling to see that years are fleeter,
Those ballads are as sweet as ever,
  But she is infinitely sweeter.

For love, that shines through all her ways,
  Hinders the stealthy hours from duty,
A soul divinely self-forgetful
  Has come to blossom in her beauty.

While the low brow, the silver curl,
The twilight glance, the perfect features,
The rose upon a creamy pallor,
Make her the loveliest of creatures.

Now with the glow that, on the face
Like moonlight on a flower, has found her,
With the tone's thrill, a faint remoteness,
Half like a halo hangs around her.

Half like a halo? Nay, indeed,
I never saw a picture painted—
Such holy work the years have rendered—
So like a woman that is sainted!

Among the descendants of John and Mary (Platts) Prescott, may be mentioned: Hon. Benjamin Prescott[1] of Groton, Mass., and his three sons, Hon. James, Dr. Oliver and Col. William of Bunker Hill fame; Hon. William, LL. D., the son of Col. William; William Hinckling, LL. D., the historian, son of the former; Judge James, Col. Charles, Hon. James, Dr. Abel, and Dr. Benjamin Prescott of Concord, Mass.; William M. Evarts, LL. D., of New York, Secretary of State, U. S.; Judge Ebenezer R. and Hon. George L. Hoar of Concord, Mass.; Professor Willard Gibbs of New Haven; J. Prescott and David Priestly Hall, eminent lawyers of New York City; Hon. Roger Sherman Baldwin of New Haven; Dr. John Prescott of Nova Scotia; Rev. William Lawrence of Lincoln and Rev. George Prescott, Rector of the chapel of the Good Shepherd, Boston.

Among those who have married descendants of John and Mary Prescott, may be mentioned: Hon. Roger Sherman, signer of the "Declaration of Independence;" Rev. David Hall, D. D., of Sutton, Mass.;

---

[1] Hon. Benjamin was a son of Jonas and Mary (Loker) Prescott, the youngest son of John and Mary (Platts) Prescott. He married Abigail, daughter of Hon. Thomas Oliver of Cambridge.

Rev. Daniel Chaplin of Groton; Hon. Timothy Bigelow; Dr. Lewis Sagre of New York; Hon. Jonathan Fay of Cambridge; Hon. Simeon Baldwin of New Haven; Rev. Jeremiah Day, LL. D., President of Yale College; Capt. Richard Wheatland of Salem; Rev. Samuel Andrews of Milford, Conn.; Henry Hotchkiss, Esq., of New Haven; Col. Samuel Edmonston Watson, U. S. Marine Corps; Henry G. Clark, M. D., of Boston; John B. Hooker, Esq., of Hartford, Conn.; Hon. Abbott Lawrence of Boston; Hon. James M. Bullock; and Benjamin DeWolf Fraser, M. D., of Windsor, N. S.[1]

---

[1] Taken principally from the "Prescott Memorial," by William Prescott, M. D.

TITCOMB.

William Titcomb came from Newbury, Berkshire, England, in 1634. "He had taken passage," we are told by Savage, "in the Mary and John, from London, the 24th of March, of the same year, but was casually deprived of the opportunity, and came next month in the Hercules." He settled in Quascacumquen, which was incorporated the following year as the town of Newbury,—so named in honor of the Rev. Thomas Parker, their first minister, who had preached for some time in Newbury, Eng., before coming to America. The name of William Titcomb is in the list of original proprietors who had grants of eighty acres or less. In 1670, the town granted to "William Titcomb and Amos Stickney the little pine swamp, to be their property, with skirts of the common, provided they make and maintain a sufficient fence about the hole for the safety of the cattle from time to time." The pine swamp is the tract of land on the south side of Oak Hill cemetery, and was, it appears, surrounded by the common.

William Titcomb was a farmer. He was made a freeman June 22, 1642. In 1646 he was chosen a selectman, and probably filled that office at other times, as his name appears in the list of selectmen of 1675–6, who were instructed by the Council to see about fortifying from Merrimac River to Charlestown River. At a general meeting of the freemen, he was chosen, with others "to be a committee for the towne to view the passages into Plum Island, and to inform the courte by way of petition concerning the righte the towne hath to the said island," etc.

In 1655, he was chosen Representative to the General Court.

In 1645, began a long and bitter controversy between the Rev. Thomas Parker and a part of the church, which was not finally settled till a short time before Mr. Parker's death which occurred in 1677. This was occasioned by the change which took place in the views of Mr. Parker concerning church government, he holding that the church should be governed by elders or presbyters, and not by consent and election as held by the Congregational body. We are told by Savage that the famous Cambridge platform erected by the synod in 1648, "was in great degree occasioned by the change of sentiment respecting church discipline, entertained by the ministers at Newbury, Mr. Parker and Mr. Noyes" (his colleague). Johnson, in his "Wonder Working Providence," says: "The teaching elders in this place [Newbury] have carried it very lovingly toward their people, *permitting them to assist in admitting of persons into church society, and in church censures, so long as they act regularly, but in case of maladministration they assume the power wholly to themselves.*"

Mr. Coffin, in his "History of Newbury," says: "A majority of the church demanded as a right, what Messrs. Parker and Noyes, in the language of Johnson, 'lovingly permitted' as a favor, and believing that the church in its corporate capacity had a right, and were therefore under a sacred obligation, to manage its own affairs, they contended most strenuously, and with untiring pertinacity, against their 'elders' assuming under any pretext, the power wholly to themselves." In 1669, the trouble had arisen to such a height, that an appeal to the civil authority was deemed necessary, the whole church and town being in a very "excited and unbrotherly state." The church was divided into two nearly equal parties; one being called Mr. Parker's party, and the other, Mr. Woodman's,—so called from Mr. Edward Woodman, "a man of talents, influence, firmness and decision."

William Titcomb appears to have taken a prominent part in the controversy, he being of the Woodman party. The following is from the old records:

"After sunset William Titcomb, Stephen[1] Titcomb, Stephen Greenleaf, Richard Bartlett, and Caleb Moody came with a message to Mr. Parker and told him they were sent from the church to give him notice that the church had chosen two ruling elders, namely, Mr. Dummer and Mr. Woodman, and they were to send to the two neighboring churches to join with them, to ordain them upon this day sevennight. Witnesses to the message of the church, captain Gerrish, Richard Knight, Nicholas Noyes, John Knight, senior, Mr. Woodbridge and Anthony Somerby.

"We whose names are here underwritten do consent to the writing, which do declare an act of the church laying Mr. Parker unto blame and suspending him from all official acts in the church."

There were forty-one signatures to the above document.

On the 19th of April, 1770, the ex-parte council, which had assembled Nov. 4th, 1669, met again at Newbury. The grievances of Mr. Parker and his party were presented the first day, and Mr. Woodman's twenty-six grievances were presented on the second day; another grievance being sent in by his party on the third day, signed by William Titcomb and Caleb Moody in the name of the rest.

On the fourth day "articles of accommodation" were drawn up and subscribed to by Mr. Parker and

---

[1] On an ancient family tree belonging to a descendant of William Titcomb, is the following statement: "Capt. William Titcomb was the only one of the name who emigrated to America." If this is correct, the name of Stephen Titcomb is an error, and should have been either Penuel, or Benaiah Titcomb. Savage mentions only William and his descendants.

the church, they binding themselves to abide by the platform of discipline established by the General Court and practiced by the churches of New England.

This second attempt of the council, to reconcile the conflicting opinions and harmonize the discordant feelings of both parties, we are told, was of no avail. "The truce was of short duration." Before the close of the year, the "articles of accommodation" appear to have been entirely forgotten by Mr. Parker's party, and the storm raged more fiercely than ever.

At the April term of the court held at Ipswich, in 1671, Mr. Parker's party entered a complaint, which called forth the following letter from Mr. Woodman's party:

"To the honored court at Ipswich April eighteenth, 1671:

"Concerning the seven queries put to the consideration of this court, they do involve so many within them that they are from us uncapable of an answer, neither do we know what use the court will make of them against us, seeing they come in as queries and not as charges. We ourselves could trouble the court with many queries, but at this time we shall forbear. In brief, we would humbly desire you to consider that most if not all, the particulars mentioned, are such, as will prove good or evil, as we shall appear to be a church regularly acting or not, for if we be a church of Christ according to order, then it is lawful for a brother to complain to the church against any brother that doth offend. Then secondly it is lawful for the church to hear and judge. Thirdly, then it is lawful for two brethren also to sign an act of the church as witnesses. Fourth, then it is lawful for them to send messengers to Mr. Parker, or whom it may concern. Fifth, then it is lawful for them to meet as a church together. Sixth, then it is lawful for them to elect a ruling elder or elders. But we hope your honored court will convict us that we have broken some standing law or laws, that were made by the general court before they blame us, for we do not account ourselves well dealt withal by the authors of those queries and declaration, whom we leave to the Lord.

"Lastly we do profess ourselves to be servants of God and

faithful subjects to the commonwealth, lovers of magistrates and ministers, and all the churches and people of the Lord, and do not willingly err from any rule of God, nor of the commonwealth, but we trust such, as shall be found faithful!

"We do therefore desire this court to consider whether it is not against all order, law or custom that complaint should be brought to a court against brethren, which from conscience of the rule of Christ do complain to a church against an offending brother, merely because they have complained, when the church hath heard the complaint and acquit the complainer, by owning the complaint to be duly proved, and sentenced the person complained against. So leaving what have been said to your wisdoms to be considered, and yourselves to the God of all wisdom to be directed, with our hearty prayers for you, we rest in the Lord to be commanded.

William Titcomb,
Caleb Moody,
Samuel Plumer,
Stephen Grenlefe,
Richard Bartlet."

At the trial, an able defense was presented by the Woodman party, in which they say: "We humbly present these lines in way of apology to declare the grounds of our late acting as a church to be regular, both by our ecclesiastical liberties, secondly by our late covenant and thirdly correspondent to scripture rule and example." As Mr. Woodman's party claimed to be *the* church, on the ground that they had a majority of the members, testimony was produced by Mr. Parker's party for the purpose of showing that Mr. Woodman's party did not embrace a majority of the members of the church, since it was questionable whether Mr. Richard Dummer had been transferred from the church in Roxbury to the church in Newbury; also that Stephen Sweet, another of Mr. Woodman's party, was an Anabaptist, having refused communion with the church at Newbury.

The decision of the court was made May 29, 1671, from which the following is taken:

"Complaint being made unto this court against Mr. Woodman, Mr. Dummer, William Titcomb and a party adhering to them as doth appear in three papers presented by Daniel Pierce and Richard Kent, the said Woodman and divers others complained of, were summoned at the session of this court in March last, where the several complaints and charges were read to the said parties then appearing, and their answers required thereunto, when the said Mr. Woodman among other things alleging that their accusations were many and heavy, and that they had many matters to charge upon Mr. Parker and those adhering to him, which they had neither time nor opportunity on the sudden to prepare, the court not willing to surprise them and desiring fully to understand the whole state of a case so extraordinary and of so high a nature, adjourned to the eighteenth of April, allowing them copies of the charges exhibited against them, and advising them to prepare their objections against Mr. Parker and those with him, and to acquaint him with the same that they also might be in readiness to make their defense at the adjournment, and the court might then clearly understand upon hearing the whole case and according to the merit thereof give judgment. The court meeting at the day aforesaid, after a full hearing it did appear that Mr. Woodman, Mr. Dummer, William Titcomb and others adhering to them, (not appearing to be the major part of the church at Newbury, although the major part of such as met together) have proceeded to admonish their pastor, Mr. Parker, and to suspend him from the exercise of his office, as appeareth by their act sent unto him the said Mr. Parker as signed by Mr. Dummer and Richard Thorlay.... They have alleged nothing but that they were the major part of the church, not charging, much less proving, any offense given by their reverend pastor, Mr. Parker, who for anything that doth appear is altogether innocent, though so exceedingly scandalized, reproached and wronged by Mr. Woodman his party. All which clearly and undeniably appearing by the papers pleas and evidences that are on file, the court as in duty bound being sensible of the dishonor to the name of God, to religion here established and also the disturbance of the peace, the scandalizing of a venerable, loving and pious pastor and an aged father, can not but judge the said Woodman, Mr. Dummer, and William Titcomb, the parties joining with them guilty of very great misdemeanors, though in different degrees, deserving severe punishment, yet being willing to exercise as much lenity as the case is capable of, or may stand with a meet testimony against such an offence, which we are bound in duty to God and our consciences to bear testimony against, do hereby adjudge the said Mr. Woodman and party adhering to him to pay the several fines underwritten with the charge of the witnesses and fees of court, and that they all stand committed till the said fines, charges and fees be satisfied and paid."

Edward Woodman was fined twenty nobles;[1] Richard Dummer, William Titcomb, Stephen Greenleaf, Richard Bartlett, and Richard Thorlay, four nobles each; and the rest of the party, one noble each.

The action of the court was not a final settlement of the affair, and "peace and quietness" were not restored to the church and town for several years.

William Titcomb married Joanna, daughter of Richard Bartlett, Sen., of Newbury (see account of the Bartletts). Their children were: Sarah, who married Thomas Treadwell (the second) of Ipswich; Hannah (she probably died young, as her father, in his will, mentions Sarah and Mary as his eldest daughters); Mary married John, son of John Poore of Newbury (see account of the Poores); Mellicent, died at 17 years of age; William, died at 11 years of age; Penuel, married Lydia, daughter of John Poore; and Benaiah, married Sarah Brown, probably a daughter of the first Richard; Mrs. Titcomb died June 28, 1653, the day of Benaiah's birth.

William Titcomb married, March 3, 1654, Mrs. Elizabeth Stevens, probably the widow of William Stevens. Her maiden name is supposed to have been Bitsfield.[2]

---

[1] A noble is six shillings and eight pence.

[2] Elizabeth Bitsfield's will, penned Sept. 23, 1669, gives to William Titcomb's children £5, to be equally divided amongst them and "to my daughter Elizabeth Titcomb £10."

The children of William and Elizabeth were: Elizabeth, married Samuel, son of Richard Bartlett, Jun.; Rebecca, married Nathaniel Treadwell (she was his second wife); Tirzah, married first, Thomas, son of Richard Bartlett, Jun., second, James, son of James Ordway; William, married Ann, daughter of William Cottle (William Cottle was a son of Edward of Salisbury, Mass.); Thomas, married Mary Dam; Lydia, married Jonathan Clark; and Ann.[1]

William Titcomb died Sept. 24, 1676. Judge Samuel Sewall, in his "Diary," says that he died "Sabbath day, after about a fortnight's sickness of the Fever and Ague," and "one week or thereabout lay regardless of any person and in great pain."

His will was made six days before his death. After giving legacies to eleven of his children, he says:

"I give to my loving and dear wife the third of all my lands for her use and benefit, with the third of my housing during her natural life, and then to return unto my heirs.

"Lastly, I do make and hereby apoynt my sonne Penuel Titcomb to be my Heir to enjoy all my land and housing and all my estate besides, whom I do hereby apoynt my holl and solle executor to reseve all my estate in lands and house goods and drafts whom I do order and apoynt by this my will to pay all my debts that I doe owe, and all the legacies that I have given according to the true intent of this my will, and that this is my last will and testament, having my perfect memory and understanding witness my hand.

"I add to what is above written before my signing here of, that in case my heir should decease without children all my land and housing should be possesed and enjoyed by my sonne Benia otherwise Benomena or by the next eldest surviving at the death

[1] It is not known whom Ann married, but there are some reasons for thinking it was Stephen Sawyer.

of my sonne Peneel whom I have apoynted my Heir by this as witness this my will as witness my hand in presence of Richard Bartlett, Sen., & Thomas Bartlett eighteenth day of September one thousand six hundred seventy & six. William Titcomb.

"Richard Bartlett.
"Thomas Bartlett."

The inventory of the estate amounted to £571. 2s.

Penuel, the eldest son of William and Joanna Bartlett Titcomb who reached manhood, was born Dec. 16, 1650. He remained a resident of Newbury, having a tract of land in that part of the town that was incorporated in 1764 as the town of Newburyport. The Newburyport and Georgetown Railroad depot stands on land said to have been formerly owned by him. As early as 1691, the inhabitants of this part of the town petitioned the General Court "to be established a people by themselves for the maintenance of the ministry among them," as many of them lived four, and some of them even seven miles from the "meeting-house." The town voted against granting their petition, so the following year they sent in another petition, with a proposition about calling a minister. The town again refusing to grant their petition, they proceeded to call a minister, Mr. Edward Tompson, without acquainting the minister, church or town with their proceedings in the affair. The town, upon learning the state of the case, manifested its disapproval; and Mr. Tompson was "warned not to preach," by the minister, Mr. Richardson. As Mr. Tompson continued to preach, the town sent a complaint to the General Court, which induced the west end people to send in a petition, in which they request the Governor and Council "to pity and help them," "to ease them of a heavy burden of travel on God's day." "We have been," say they, "endevoring these five years to have the public worship of God established among us on the Lord's day for reasons such as these. The bulk of us live four miles from the ould meeting-house, some six or seven. Our number is above three hundred. Few of us have horses, and if we could get to the ould meeting house, it is impossible it should receive us with them so that many [would] lay out of doors, the house is so little. Some of us have groaned under this burden this thirty years, some grown old, some sickly, and although we were favored with the liberty granted by king James the second and had erected an house to the worship of God on our own cost and charge, and acquainted the two next justices with our intent before we built the said house. A committee of five were appointed to come on the place, but before they had finished their work the governor arrived which caused them to desist. We complained to the governor, who granted us a protection from paying to the ould meeting house, then countermanded it. The town had a meeting—they intend to delude us by granting the half of a schoolmaster at some-times for one yeare. We believe our neighbors would be glad to see us quite tired out. We beg the honorable court to establish peace among us [by] a rational dividing line."

The following year, a committee, consisting of Joshua Brown, John Ordway, and Samuel Bartlett, petitioned to the General Court, "in behalf of the company, that as they had erected a meeting house, and supplied themselves with a minister yet nevertheless our distresses do continually grow upon us toward an unsupportable extremity, since the imprisoning of some of our number for their signifying our desire to enjoy the minister, whom we had formerly invited to preach in the meeting house which we built at our own cost and charge, and some of us have been fined for not delivering up the key of the said meeting house," etc.

Penuel Titcomb was one of the six who were served by the sheriff with a process and order of the court, strictly forbidding them and their associates proceeding in the work of their intended meeting-house, etc.; said persons being summoned to attend the fall session of the court. The manner in which the difficulty was finally overcome, by a part of the people of the west end becoming Episcopalians, is told in the following extract which was found among the papers of Mr. Nehemiah Bartlett, and was written many years ago:

"Our fathers did not regard what the court sent to them, but had raised said building and had got on to finish it. This honorable court sent on express to forbid us going on under any pretence whatever. Resolved Pipe-stave hill to be the place for the whole parish. Our people went to this court to show their grievances. No relief. *Met with a gentleman, Mr. [John] Bridger, churchman, telling a way to protect them, to come under the church of England he would protect them. Some being acquainted with the church complied.* Rev. Mr. Harris came and preached, went home, sent Mr. —— Lampton, chaplain of a station ship, some abiding with him, some went back to Pipe-stave hill, and so forth."

The Rev. Christopher Toppan, in a letter to Cotton Mather, Nov. 28, 1712, wrote: "Perceiving that some of the ceremonies were camels too big for them at first to swallow, he [Mr. Lampton] told them they should be left to their liberty as to kneeling at the sacrament baptising with the sign of the cross and so forth."

Penuel Titcomb married, Jan. 8, 1684, Lydia, daughter of John Poore of Newbury. Their children were: Sarah, who died young; a second Sarah, who married Isaac Bailey; William; John; and Joseph, who married Sarah Bachelder.

Penuel died Feb. 5, 1718. In his will, which was made Jan. 4, 1717–18, he leaves his estate, both real and personal, to his three sons, William, John and Joseph, his wife having a life interest in a third part of it. She also had all of the silver and household goods. To his daughter, Sarah Bailey, he bequeathed four pounds only, as she had already had her portion. His three sons were appointed executors, and his brothers Benaiah and William overseers.

William, the eldest son of Penuel, born April 8, 1687, married, first, Joanna Ordway; second, Apphia Rolfe. By his first wife he had one daughter, Elizabeth. There was also one daughter by the second wife, Dorothy, who married Thomas, son of Thomas Woodbridge, who was a grandson of Rev. John and Mercy (Dudley) Woodbridge. Mercy was a daughter of Gov. Thomas Dudley. Rev. John Woodbridge was a distinguished nonconformist minister, who came to New England from Stanton, Wiltshire, Eng., in company with his uncle, the Rev. Thomas Parker, in 1634. He was of the fourth generation from Rev. John Woodbridge, a follower of Wycliffe, born in 1493. It is said that in each generation there was a Rev. John Woodbridge. Rev. John W. Woodbridge of Andover was the sixth Rev. John, in the regular line of descent.

John, the second son of Penuel and Lydia Titcomb, was born in Newburyport, Sept. 24, 1689. He married, April 17, 1712, Lydia Morse, who died May 27, 1753. He married in December, 1753, Sarah Ilsley. His children were: John, died at 15 years of age; Paul; Samuel; Enoch, died at 10 years of age; Mary, married —— Pearson; and Joseph, married Elizabeth ——. John Titcomb died July 23, 1774.

A will made by John Titcomb, Apr. 23, 1773 was recently found, together with one made by his son Samuel, in the secret drawer of an old secretary. In this will are mentioned three children, Samuel, Mary Pearson and Joseph Titcomb. The latter received the principal part of his father's estate.

Samuel, the third son of John, was born Aug. 12, 1715. He resided in Newburyport, the place of his birth. He was a large land-owner, most of the square bounded by High, State, Green and Harris Streets belonging to him. It was called his town farm. He also had a farm in West Newbury, and another in Pelham, N. H. The produce of his farms he shipped to the West Indies, in exchange for coffee, sugar, etc. There is a street by the name of Titcomb in Newburyport, that was named for him. He was a man of good business capacity, thrifty and influential. His mansion house was on State Street, and was afterward sold by his son William to Mr. William Balch, who took it down in 1830.

Samuel Titcomb married, Sept. 2, 1740, Elizabeth Kingsbury. Their children were: John; Moses; Sarah, married Benjamin Bradford; William; Samuel; and Rebecca, who married Capt. John Buntin of Newburyport.

The following extracts are from the will found as above mentioned, which was dated Feb. 2, 1798:

"Imprimis I give to my beloved son John Titcomb one of my farms in Pelham which I purchased of Peirce and Gage as he, my second son, and my late son Moses divided it; also my Plumb Island meadow lot adjoining Plumb Island River, to him and his heirs and assigns forever. I give to my beloved son William Titcomb my dwelling house and barns in said Newburyport, with all the lands under and adjoining the same except ten rods on the northerly side of Mirriam Tracy's land adjoining High street; also two meadow lots on little Pine Island Creek, (formerly called Tufts lots) also my lot in Birches meadow and three and an half rights in the common pasture; also four acres of land in the plains in the fourth Parish in Newbury, the five last mentioned parcels being in Newbury in said county. Also three acres and seven rods of land in said Newburyport, bounded southwesterly by land of Samuel Sayers, northerly by land of Theodore Parsons, Esq., northwesterly by the road leading to the Westerdies (so called) also all my household goods, live stock and farming utensils, to him and his heirs and assigns forever.

"Item I give my beloved daughter Rebecca Buntin ten dollars only (having heretofore given her her full share of my estate) to her use and disposal forever.

"Item I give to my beloved grandson George Titcomb son of my late son Moses, the other moiety farm in Pelham, as it has been divided as above mentioned, to him and his heirs forever.

"Item I give to my beloved grandson Samuel Titcomb son of my late son Samuel Titcomb, fifteen acres of land in New Salem adjoining Pelham be the same more or less, also one hundred and sixty-one dollars and two thirds of a dollar," etc.

To his granddaughters, Sarah, daughter of his late son Moses, and Anne, daughter of his late son Samuel, he bequeathed legacies. As his wife was not mentioned in the will, she was probably not living at that time. John and William were appointed joint executors. His daughter Rebecca Buntin had received, for her dowry, a house and lot on the corner of High and State Streets in Newburyport. The estate is at the present time owned by Capt. John Buntin, a grandson of Rebecca and Capt. John Buntin.

John, the eldest son of Samuel and Elizabeth Titcomb, was born in Newburyport, Feb. 1, 1746. He married Elizabeth Pierson of that place. Their children were: Mary, married Enoch Jackman; Rebecca, died unmarried; Catherine, died unmarried; and Pierson. John Titcomb removed from Newburyport to Pelham, and cultivated the farm left him by his father's will. He died in 1838.

Pierson, the only son of John and Elizabeth Titcomb, was born Aug. 2, 1776. He entered the army in 1799, as a cadet in the 2d regiment of Artillerists and Engineers, and in 1801 received a first lieutenant's commission. He was stationed at the forts on the New England coast, being at all of them, at different times, between Fort Adams at Newport and the fort opposite Portland, those included. Of some of them he had the command.

He married Margaret Morrill of Newburyport. They

had one child, who died in infancy. The mother died soon after the death of the child.

While stationed at Fort Adams, Newport, R. I., Pierson Titcomb became acquainted with, and married Anne Maria, daughter of Peter Francis Christian and Elizabeth (Dordin, nee Ellis) de Les Dernier of that place (see account of the Ellises). The home of the de Les Derniers was on the corner of Prospect Hill Street and what is now Bellevue Avenue, a few rods from the old stone mill. The house, which was a large gambrel roofed building, was taken down a few years since. The estate is still owned by descendants of Mrs. de Les Dernier by her first marriage.

The children of Pierson and Anne Titcomb were: Edward Ellis, married Sarah, daughter of Rev. William and Jane (Little) Montague of Dedham, Mass. (see account of the Montagues); Edgar Morrill, married Rohan, daughter of John and Mary (Fox) Putnam (John was a descendant of Gen. Putnam); Elizabeth Dordin, married Hon. Thomas James Duncan, son of Martin and Letitia (Duncan) Fuller (see account of the Fullers); Margaret Morrill, married William, son of Lemuel[1] and Mollie (Gay) Whiting of Dedham, Mass.; Louis Frederick; Harriet Prescott, married Jonathan Whitney; Mary Dean, married Elbridge Gerry, son of Daniel and Mary (Chase) Ayer (see account of the Ayers); Silas Betton, married Mary Jane, daughter of Daniel and Mary L. King; Henry Hope, married Lucinda Gay; John Pierson, married Lavinia Smith; Adelaide Ann, married John Kirby, son of

---

[1] Lemuel was a son of Moses and Sarah (Gay) Whiting; Moses was a son of John and Abigail (White) Whiting; John was a son of Nathaniel and Joannah (Ellis) Whiting,—Joannah was a daughter of Joseph and Mary (Gay) Ellis; Nathaniel was a son of Timothy and Sarah Whiting; Timothy was a son of Nathaniel and Hannah (Dwight) Whiting,—Hannah was a daughter of John and Hannah Dwight of Dedham. Nathaniel Whiting had a grant of land in Lynn in 1638, but was of Dedham in 1641, and was a freeman in 1642. The grant of land he had in Dedham was inherited by William above mentioned.

Robert and Martha Jane (Noyes) Chase (see account of the Chases); and Robert Dinsmore, married Clarinda Dalton.

Louis Frederick, the third son of Pierson and Annie Titcomb, was born July 8, 1809. He married Sarah Bradley, daughter of Ezekiel and Elizabeh (Bradley) Dow (see account of the Dows). Their children were: Sarah Elizabeth; Frederick Augustus, married Etta, daughter of Samuel S. and Phebe J. (Baker) Parker; Charlotte Augusta; and Martha Jane. Mrs. Titcomb died in Springfield, Mass., Feb. 10, 1878, aged 60 years.

A few years after his marriage, Pierson Titcomb resigned his commission and purchased a farm in Pelham, N.H. He afterward owned a farm in Salem, N.H. There was a grist-mill on the place, and a building that he wished to convert into a carding-mill, but it stood on ground that was about twenty feet higher than the pond. He decided to cut a new channel for the brook, or a part of it, beginning at a place where the brook was on higher ground, at some distance from the pond. He invited his neighbors to what is called a bee. They came one afternoon, with their teams and shovels, and said to him: "We are perfectly willing to help you, but you never can make water run up hill." Before night, to their amazement, a fine stream of water was running through the channel they had dug. The neighbors, who so kindly helped him, were allowed to grind their farming tools for several years at a grind-stone in the mill, which was turned by water. He lived in Salem fifteen years, and until the water in the pond failed to carry his mills on account of an unusually dry season. He removed to Dedham, Mass. Later, he was a resident of Lowell, which place he represented in the Legislature in 1840. In 1845, or about that time, his son Louis Frederick purchased a farm in the charming town of Northfield, Mass., and not intending to live on it himself for some years, if ever, suggested that his father should reside there. So there they remained until just before the death of Mr. Titcomb, which occurred in Dedham, Dec. 11, 1855. Mrs. Titcomb afterwards resided with her daughter, Mrs. William Whiting of Dedham. She survived her husband but one year, dying at 81 years of age.

The following account of Lieut. Pierson Titcomb and his wife was written by Mrs. Elizabeth Betton, the daughter of Mrs. Wm. P. Prescott, Mrs. Titcomb's sister:

"My uncle Titcomb was an *exceedingly handsome* man—one whom people would turn and look at; dark hair, black eyes, a smooth, fair skin, with rich, brilliant color, a full, handsome mouth and fine teeth, regular and not too large features, an Adonis face, with a good figure above the average height and well-proportioned. He had the manners of a finished gentleman, and was a very popular man in society,—and society was very popular with him. I have heard my mother and others say, that the flatteries and attentions that he received from both old and young, were enough to turn the head of a young man with less principle. He had a fine voice, and played well on the violin, and had a very good knowledge of music, for those days. He led the choir in the church where he lived. He wrote for the local papers, at times. In politics, he was a Federalist. I think, but for this, he would have been prominent as a politician, he was so very popular a man; but office would not tempt him to deny his principles, and Democrats ruled in that day.

"My aunt was very beautiful, but in another way. She had large, lovely gray eyes, and a profusion of brown hair. Her features were regular and not large, and her complexion fair, with delicate color. She was about the medium height, and very graceful. The *sisters* were reckoned among the handsome women of Rhode Island and Nova Scotia. Both my uncle and aunt had sunny tempers. I have made many visits to them, some extending to months, and look back with admiration at the cheerful, quiet, uncomplaining, daily life. They were ever ready to sympathize with and promote any pleasure or adventure we young people chose to engage in; and at home, while we would sit round a table of an evening with our various employments, my uncle would read aloud from Shakespere, Walter Scott, or his own efforts. When we write or think of those we have loved who have passed into the silent land, the thoughts and the pen linger, loth to leave them to their quiet rest. We forget faults, we emblazon virtues and we embalm their memories."

The following lines were written with *indelible* ink, by Pierson Titcomb, upon a work-bag belonging to his wife:

"You request that I something would write,—
On what subject I'm puzzled to think.
Should it be in your praise, then I might
Use the whole of your 'permanent ink.'[1]

"Since that time when you gave your consent
That your fate with my own I should link,
Our days have been marked with content
Full as lasting as 'permanent ink.'

"Happy still on life's voyage we sail,
For at each other's foibles we wink,
And no tempests of passions prevail
To stain deeper than 'permanent ink.'

"When this voyage that with pleasure we took,
Shall be o'er and we feel we must sink,
May our names be enrolled in that Book,
That is written with 'permanent ink.'"

Joseph, the youngest son of Penuel and Lydia (Poore) Titcomb, was born in Newbury, July 27, 1700. He married Sarah, daughter of John Batchelder of Reading, Mass. Their children were: Abigail and Stephen. The year after Stephen's birth, Joseph Tit-

---

[1] She had a large bottle full.

comb died; and after some years, his widow married Samuel, son of John and Hannah (Fessenden) Sewall. They resided in York, Me.

Abigail, the daughter of Joseph and Sarah Titcomb, married Henry, son of Nicholas and Mehitable (Storer) Sewall (for an account of her children, see account of the Sewalls).

Stephen, son of Joseph and Sarah Titcomb, was born, Dec. 27, 1721. He removed from Newbury to Kennebunk, Me., where he built a log house that he garrisoned, the Indians still being troublesome. He was an active, energetic man; embarked freely in trade and other business, owned coasters, and became extensively engaged in ship building. He was a religious, patriotic man, taking, in the early days of the Revolution, a decided stand in favor of the rights of the colonies. Immediately on receiving notice of the battle of Lexington, he started at the head of twenty-two of his company for the place of conflict. He was chosen agent of the town to prosecute all who were inimical to the State or the United States. He was a captain of the militia in Kennebunk, and one of the selectmen. He was an active member of the Second Congregational Parish, having been a leader among the founders of the church, and for many years its treasurer and one of its assessors.

He married Abigail Stone. Their children were: Joseph, who died at the age of 21; Benjamin; Stephen; Sarah, married Daniel Mitchell; Abigail; Samuel and John. Stephen Titcomb died May 23, 1815.

Benjamin, the second son of Stephen, was born May 21, 1751. He married Mary Burnham. Their children were: Benjamin, married Mary Waterhouse; Hannah, probably died young; James; Joseph; and Hannah, married John Perkins. Benjamin Titcomb's second wife was Hannah Bragden. Their children were: Samuel, David, Abigail and Lydia. The third wife of Benjamin Titcomb was Nancy, daughter of Rev. Moses

Hemingway, D.D., and widow of Dr. Gates. Dr. Hemingway was a distinguished divine of Wells, Me.

Benjamin Titcomb removed to Alewife, where he had a large farm. He was for thirty years a selectman. He was a faithful member of the Christian church. He died Dec. 26, 1827.

James, the second son of Benjamin and Mary (Burnham) Titcomb, married Abigail Durrell. Their children were: Joseph; Lucy Wildes, died in infancy; George Payson; William; Lucy Wildes, married James M. Stone; James W.; and Abby.

Joseph, the eldest son of James and Abigail Titçomb, born Jan. 8, 1822, married Mary A. Wise. He resides in Kennebunk, and has been an extensive shipbuilder and owner. He was formerly President of the Ocean National Bank, was Bank Examiner, and has held other important offices of trust and honor. He has served for several years as a member of the State Senate, and has been twice nominated as the Democratic candidate for Governor of Maine. He is an efficient member of the Congregational Church, and a deacon of it. He has devoted much time to the genealogy of the Titcomb family, and has a large collection of facts relating to it.

Samuel Titcomb, son of Benjamin, born in 1769, married, but I have not learned the name of his wife. His children were: Timothy; Emerson, married, first, Mary Robinson, second, Eunice B. Robinson; Amasa, married Matilda Burns; Deborah, married Daniel Burns; Eunice, married —— Mitchell; Matilda; Mary, married Israel Hutchinson; and Eliza, married John Bailey.

Stephen, the third son of Stephen and Abigail Titcomb, was born in Kennebunk, Oct. 3, 1752. He removed to Brunswick, and in 1776 married Elizabeth Henry of Topsham. In May of the same year, he visited Sandy River (Farmington), Me., and took up a lot there, being the first settler in Sandy River Valley. He built a log cabin, and "in 1778 began his perilous journey of seventy miles through the forests from Topsham to Farmington, with a young wife and two young children,—one an infant. The last habitation on the route was where Redfield Corner now is,—a log cabin twenty-two miles short of their destination." Two years after, he built a substantial two-story frame house, in which he lived sixty years. He amassed a respectable fortune by farming. He was for many years a Justice of the Peace, and a Representative. He and his wife were for many years worthy members of the Methodist Episcopal Church.

Their children were: Joseph; Henry, married Anne Buckminster, daughter of Rev. Timothy and Sarah B. (Williams) Fuller (see account of the Fullers); Hannah; Stephen, married Nancy Haines; Lydia; Nancy; Betsey; and John, married Lydia Abbott.

Joseph, the eldest son of Stephen, married Mehitable Belcher. Their children were: Stephen; Henry, married Hannah Allen; John, married Catherine Merrill; Joseph, married Wendell Craig; Benjamin and Hiram.

Stephen, the eldest son of Joseph, was graduated at Bowdoin College, and ordained a Congregational minister. He married, first, Apphia Stanley; second, Harriet, daughter of Rev. Manning and Harriet C. Ellis.

Hannah, the eldest daughter of Joseph and Mehitable Titcomb, married William, son of William and Love (Coffin) Allen. William Allen was a descendant of James Allen, who came from England, and had by special grant the manor of Tisbury, Cape Cod. William Allen was a Justice of the Peace, Civil Justice of the Court of Common Pleas, and Clerk of the Courts.

Of Mrs. Allen, who died in 1859, it was said that "she was the dearly beloved, most worthy and cherished companion of her devoted husband for fifty-one years, and died deeply lamented."

They had four sons, and one daughter, Elizabeth,

who married John S. Abbott, an eminent lawyer of Maine, and at one time Attorney-General of the State. He now resides in Boston.

William, the eldest son of William and Hannah, was graduated at Bowdoin College with the highest honors of his class, and died three years later. Stephen was graduated at the same college, and was ordained a Methodist Episcopal minister. He resides in Augusta, and is Presiding Elder of that district. He married Rachel Sturdivant of Cumberland. Charles F., was also graduated at Bowdoin College, and was ordained a Methodist minister. He has been for several years President of the Agricultural College of Maine. He married Ruth S. Morse of Sutton, Mass. Albert B., the youngest son, is a student at law.

Samuel, son of Stephen and Abigail (Stone) Titcomb, was born in Kennebunk, May 27, 1758. He settled in Hallowell, Me. He was a surveyor of land, and in 1796 was appointed by the British government one of the two surveyors "to mark and establish the eastern line of the State from the ocean to the St. Croix River." The survey was accomplished in about three years, and the initials of his name are engraved upon the monument at the head of the river. He afterward settled in Augusta, and was the second postmaster of that town. He was a Representative to the General Court. Later, he removed to Belgrade, and, in company with John Pitts of that place, founded an academy, which was incorporated in 1834, by the name of the Titcomb Belgrade Academy.

Samuel Titcomb married Nancy Tiffany of Sidney. Their children were: Nancy, married Henry Clark; Samuel, died in childhood; David, died in childhood; Albert, married Mary R. Lander. Samuel Titcomb married for his second wife, Chloe Cummings of Augusta. They had one son, Samuel. Samuel Titcomb, Sen., died Sept. 18, 1849.

Samuel, his son, was born July 19, 1820. He was

graduated at the Harvard Law School in 1843, and began practice in Augusta. He was for many years Judge of the Municipal Court. He has been City Solicitor, a Representative to the Legislature, and was Mayor of Augusta in 1869–70. He is one of the Trustees of the Augusta Savings Bank, and a Director of the First National Bank. "He is a man of uprightness, sound judgment and benevolence." He married Julia A. Kimball.

Benaiah, the third son of William and Joanna (Bartlett) Titcomb, was born June 28, 1653. He took the oath of fidelity in 1678. He married Dec. 24, 1678, Sarah Brown, "probably a daughter of the first Richard Brown." Their children were: Benaiah; Josiah, married Martha Rolf; Edmund; Elizabeth, married Henry, son of John and Hannah (Fessenden) Sewall, —John Sewall was a son of Henry and Jane (Dummer) Sewall; Sarah; (Elizabeth and Sarah were twins); Joseph; Enoch; and Mary.

Among the old records at the State House, Boston, is the petition of Benaiah Titcomb, dated July 16, 1703, to the Governor and Council, in which he asks that the impost money may be abated on goods brought in his "Ketch," from the Island of Antigua to Newburyport, on account of the vessel having been taken by Guilliam La Fauche, a Frenchman, with a letter-of-marque, his vessel having twenty guns and fifty men. The son of Benaiah, who was supercargo and mate of said Ketch, was forced to buy the vessel of La Fauche at an extreme rate, the master, Robert Kimball, going to France as a hostage for the payment of said money. His petition was granted. The following items are from "Judge Sewall's Diary:"

"July 30, 1695, Jane sails for Newbury in Benayah Titcomb's Sloop, loosed from the wharf past ten, night before last."

"Nov. 10, 1707. I received a letter from Bro^r who

says Doct[r] Topan fell off Mr. Titcomb's Wharf last Tuesday, was found by it on Wednesday morn."

In 1683, an order having been passed by the Court of Assistants, making the ports of Boston and Salem the lawful ports for the lading and unlading of vessels, the following petition was sent in from Newbury:

"To the honored General Court now sitting in Boston, the humble petition of some in Newbury.

"We humbly crave the favour that your honors would be pleased to consider our little Zebulon, and to ease us of that charge, which at present we are forced unto, by our goeing to Salem to enter our vessels, and thereby are forced to stay at least two days, before we can unload, besides other charges, in going and coming. That some meet person might be appointed to receive the enter of all vessells, and to act and doe according as the law directs, in that case we shall be bound forever to pray for your honors. May fifteenth, 1683."

The signatures of Penuel, Benaiah and William Titcomb are among the eleven on the above document.

Gen. Jonathan Titcomb, son of Josiah and Martha (Rolf) Titcomb, was born Sept. 12, 1727. He was appointed a Brigadier-General in the Revolutionary war, and "manifested great zeal and activity in his country's cause throughout the war." He was with Gen. Sullivan at the battle of Rhode Island. Of this engagement, Lafayette is said to have remarked "that it was the best fought battle of the war." "In this battle were the Massachusetts troops under the command of Brigadiers Lovell and Titcomb, whose conduct was such as to win high praise."

The book of "Orders, Returns, &c.," of Gen. Jonathan Titcomb's Brigade, kept by Brigade Major Enoch Titcomb, is in the possession of the family of Mr. Moses Lord of Newburyport. It contains the following account of the retreat of the 28th of August, 1778: "Began to retreat this evening at 8 o'clock—the enemy pursued us the next morning and began to engage with our advanced corps—29th at 6 o'clock the fire kept increasing on both sides. Sometimes it was very severe, the enemy pushed hard to gain a hill upon our right, but by assistance of Gen. Lovell's Brigade of militia were obliged to turn their backs upon us and run, at four o'clock P. M., the action ended."

Gen. Titcomb was a member of the first General Court held in Boston after the evacuation by the British, and a member of the convention that framed the State Constitution. He was the first naval officer in Newburyport, receiving his appointment in 1784, from Washington. He was again appointed naval officer in 1790. In October, 1790, Gen. Washington visited Newburyport, and was met by the High Sheriff of the county of Essex, the Honorable Tristram Dalton, Esq., Major-General Titcomb and a number of other officers, as well as several gentlemen from that and neighboring towns. The following account of his departure is from his diary:

"Saturday, 31st, Oct.

"Left Newburyport a little after eight o'clock (first breakfasting with Mr. Dalton) and to avoid a wider ferry, more inconvenient boats, and a piece of heavy sand we crossed the river at Salisbury, two miles above, and near that further about; and in three miles came to the line which divides the State of Massachusetts from that of New Hampshire. Here I took leave of Mr. Dalton and many other private gentlemen:—also of Gen. Titcomb who had met me on the line between Middlesex and Essex Counties," etc.

Gen. Jonathan Titcomb married, May 9, 1751, Mary Dole. His second wife was Sarah Steadman. Their children were: Mary; Paul; and Benaiah.

Gen. Jonathan died March 10, 1817. He was buried with his first wife, in the Oak Hill cemetery, in Newburyport.

The children of his son Benaiah were: Paul, married Priscilla Kendall; John Hancock, married Vara Pearson; Mary Ann, married Pasley Goddard; Harriet, who probably died in infancy; and a second Harriet.

The children of Paul and Priscilla, were: Emeline; Priscilla; Benaiah; and Paul.

Enoch, the youngest son of Benaiah and Sarah (Brown) Titcomb, born April 1, 1695, had a son Richard, born in 1736, who was the father of Enoch, born in 1760. The children of Enoch were: Eleanor, married —— Johnson; Sarah, married Henry Wadleigh; Mehitable, married Insley Page; Anna, married Moses Gill; Miriam, unmarried; Benaiah, married Sally Locke; and Enoch.

The children of Benaiah and Sally Titcomb were: Lowell Locke; Charles Smith, married Frances Alice, daughter of James and Mary (Haywood) Greenhalgh; John Locke, married, first, —— ——, second, Catherine Smith; Smith, married Hannah, daughter of David Morrill.

Edmund, the third son of Benaiah and Sarah Titcomb, born Dec. 9, 1682, married Elizabeth Greenleaf. They had a son Edmund, who was born Mar. 26, 1710. He married Sarah Merrill, and resided in Falmouth, Me. He had a son Edmund, born May 20, 1736, who married, in 1752, Martha Sweet. Their children were: Elizabeth; Lydia, married Nathan Lord; Edmund, unmarried; Samuel, unmarried; Priscilla, married Joab Black; Moses, married Sarah Batchelder.

Edmund Titcomb married for his second wife, in 1770, Mary Whittier. Their children were: Samuel, married Maria Hinckley Batchelder; Benaiah, married Sarah Humphrey; and Enoch, married Hepsibah Stubbs.

William, the eldest son of William and Elizabeth (Stevens) Titcomb, was born Aug. 14, 1659. He is called Sergeant William in the Newbury records. He married, May 15, 1683, Ann, daughter of William Cottle (William Cottle was a son of Edward of Salisbury,

Mass.) Their children were Jedediah, married Elizabeth Boardman; Joanna, married Michael Hodge; Daniel; Sarah, married Dea. Moses, son of John and Priscilla (Hazen) Pearson of Rowley; Elias; Joseph, married Ann Smith; Benjamin (Joseph and Benjamin were twins); Moses, who died young; John; Mary; and a second Moses (Col.), married Miriam Currier. William died Feb. 4, 1740. His wife died Aug. 15, 1847.

The following items are from Coffin's "History of Newbury:"

"From the tax-book of William Titcomb, junior, I make the following extracts: 'This year [1716] the number of ratable polls in Newbury was six hundred and eighty-five, of which four hundred and thirty-seven were in the first parish, one hundred and ninety-six in the west parish, and fifty-two in the Falls parish. In August a valuation of the town's property was taken. Plough land and meadow were estimated at twelve shillings per acre, pasture land at six shillings. The whole valuation of property, real and personal, was nine thousand and sixty-two pounds and one shilling.'"

"Sept. 20th, [1721] the town chose Deacon Nathaniel Coffin, Ensign William Titcomb and Lieutenant Rolfe, to receive the town's part of the fifty thousand pounds, granted by Massachusetts, thirteenth of July, 1720, and let it out, on good security, in sums not less than ten pounds, nor more than thirty pounds, at five per centum, for no longer period than one year at a time. For the use of this money, the town was to pay the state four per centum. This was the famous 'land-bank' scheme, as it was called, which proved so injurious to the estates of so many individuals."

Daniel, the second son of William and Ann (Cottle) Titcomb of Newbury, married, Jan. 1, 1718–19, Ann Wingate, widow of Francis Drew. Their children were: Ann, probably the one who married Joseph Drew; William; Sarah, married —— Wingate; Mary, married, first, —— Tebbets, second, Edward Woodman; John; Elizabeth, married —— Plummer; Daniel; David; Abigail, married —— Libby; Enoch; and Benjamin. In a conveyance of land in Kingston from William Titcomb to his son Daniel, the latter is mentioned as his "loving and dutiful son." Daniel removed to Dover, N. H., and was received to the church in that place, March 10, 1728. Tradition says his farm was called the "Dame farm." He died in 1758 or 9. In his will he gives his dwelling-house to his son Daniel, land in Rochester to Benjamin, and to his other children from fifty to two hundred pounds (old tenor) apiece.

Col. John, the second son of Daniel and Ann Titcomb, was baptized June 12, 1726. He was a Captain in the French war. In 1756 and 1757, he had a company in Col. Nathaniel Meserve's regiment at Crown Point. At the siege of Louisburg, he was a Major, and subsequently a Lieutenant-Colonel. In the records he is spoken of as "that brave John Titcomb." It is said that the first chaise in Dover was owned by him. His wife was Sarah ——, of Newbury. It is said that she had for her dowry her weight in silver. Their children were: Elizabeth, Sarah, Samuel Waterhouse, Martha, John, a second Sarah, and William.

Col. John was not living when the Revolution began.

John, the second son of Col. John Titcomb, was baptized, Aug. 3, 1760. It is said that at the time of the battle of Bunker Hill, a company of fifty-nine men was raised in Dover, and one more being needed, John Titcomb, then only fourteen years old, though very tall and large, stepped into the ranks, and was received, but was kept for a time as a waiter on his uncle, Col. Benjamin Titcomb.

John, married Sarah, daughter of Capt. Samuel and Sarah (Wingate) Ham of Dover. Their children were: Elizabeth, married John Foss; Sarah, died young; Sarah, married —— Pardexter; George; Abigail, married George Pardexter; John; Samuel; Mary, married Jeremy Wingate; Lydia, married Isaac L. Folsom; Martha, married James C. Sewall; Jeremy H., married, first, Joanna W. Rollins, second, Charlotte Corson.

John Titcomb was the first man in Dover who ventured to wear an overcoat. His house stood where the old Dover Bank now stands. He died Aug. 9, 1816, from disease contracted while carrying supplies to the army in the war of 1812. His widow, after his death, removed to Farmington, N. H.

John, the second son of John and Sarah Titcomb, was apprenticed to his uncle, Capt. Samuel Ham of Portsmouth, and became an importer and wholesale dry goods dealer, in the days when Portsmouth was a rival of Boston. He married Sarah, daughter of Capt. Daniel Sweet of Portsmouth. Their children were: Charles John, who died at the age of twenty; George Alfred, who married Mary Lemist Lancaster, and is now living in Exeter, N. H.; and Samuel Ham, who married a lady in Tennessee, and was shot down in the streets of Nashville at the beginning of the rebellion, on account of his outspoken Union sentiments.

Mr. Titcomb died suddenly, when 32 years of age.

Col. Benjamin, the youngest son of Daniel and Ann (Wingate) Titcomb, was baptized, June 12, 1743. In 1775, he was a Captain in Col. Poor's regiment; and in 1777, he was Major in Col. Hale's regiment. From "Belknap's Diary" we learn that his company marched from Dover, the second day after the battle of Bunker Hill. Stearns, in his "History of Rindge," N. H., mentions him as the "gallant Benjamin Titcomb." He was severely wounded in three different battles, yet served through the war. The following is from the old records: "May 18, 1784. Paid Maj. Benjamin Titcomb, of Col. Reed's regiment, wounded in three different battles, for half-pay from Jan. 1, 1781, to Jan. 1, 1782, which is 12 months, £7. 10s.,—£90." He married Hannah, daughter of Isaac Hanson. Isaac was a son of Tobias Hanson, a Friend.

The children of Col. Benjamin and Hannah were: Daniel, died unmarried; Benjamin, married Polly Whitehouse; Joseph; Isaac, died unmarried; William, married Eunice Whitehouse; Susannah, married James Whitehouse; Nancy, married Ephraim Wentworth; Hannah, married Nicholas Peaslee; Sarah; and Betsey, who died young. Col. Benjamin died Jan. 28, 1793.

Joseph, the third son of Col. Benjamin, removed to Anson, Me. He was a Captain of militia. He married Dorcas Dinsmore. Their children were: Benjamin, married Fanny Moore; Hannah, married James Bryant; Thomas Dinsmore; Calvin, died unmarried; Ann, married Oscar Albee; Joseph, married Sally Titcomb; Sarah, married Hiram Chase; Stephen, married Jane Wolcott; and Paulenah, married Seth Hutchins.

Thomas D., the third son of Joseph and Dorcas, removed from Anson to Kingsbury, Me., when a young man, and bought a large tract of wild land which became one of the best farms in the town. He was frequently chosen a town officer, was town treasurer for many years, and is said to have been a noble man in the best sense of the word. He married Susan Briery, daughter of Samuel and Ruth (Briery) Campbell. Their children were: Calvin, who died in the army; Frances Ann, married Daniel, son of Daniel and Emeline (Fosse) Knowles; Thomas, married Alice Jane, daughter of Ichabod and Sarah (Watson) Rollins; Samuel Campbell, married Eva Esther, daughter of John and Esther (Kincaid) Rideout; Amasa Campbell; Dorcas Dinsmore; Joseph; Alvin; and Edith Abbie.

Capt. Joseph, the fourth son of William and Ann (Cottle) Titcomb, was born Mar. 30, 1698. He married Oct. 3, 1721, Ann Smith. Their children were: Sarah, married John Ropes of Salem; Henry; Mary, married —— Lowell; Benjamin; Oliver, married Anna Osgood; Joseph, married, first, Hannah Hale, second, —— Wyatt; John, died young; Anna; Elizabeth,

23

married Ebenezer Lowell; Eunice, married Jonathan Dole; John, married Sarah Titcomb; and Abigail. Capt. Joseph held many important offices in church and state.

Henry, the eldest son of Capt. Joseph Titcomb, married his cousin Mary Titcomb. Their children were: Enoch; Elizabeth; Mary; Lucy, married —— Thompson; Joseph; John Smith; Henry, married Abigail Whitmore; and John Berry. There is a street in Newburyport named Berry Street, for the latter.

Hon. Enoch, the eldest son of Henry and Mary Titcomb, was born Dec. 6, 1752. He resided in Newburyport, and was a merchant. For twenty-eight successive years, he was town treasurer. He was a notary public, justice of the peace, a member of the council that framed the State Constitution, and a member of the State Legislature during the early days of the State. He was also a State Senator for a long term of years. He was a Brigade-Major under Gen. Sullivan, during the campaign in Rhode Island. He was a deacon in the first Presbyterian Church, and is said to have been a devoted Christian, and a man of excellent judgment.

He married Ann, daughter of Ephraim and Mary Jones of Portland, Me. Their children were: George; Luther, married Sarah Teel; Francis, married Sally Dodd; Salina, married Greenleaf Dole; and Fanny, married Moses Lord of Newburyport. Mr. Lord was postmaster of that place from the year 1812 to 1840. His children possess many interesting old documents. They have a Titcomb coat of arms, on the back of which is written, "Brought from London in 1740 by Judge Sewall." The coat of arms is: He beareth or., a bend azure, between two foxes' heads, erazed gu. Crest, a dexter arm couped above the elbow, armed garnished or., the hand grasping a broken lance gu.

Hon. Enoch Titcomb died Aug. 13, 1814.

George, his second son, was for many years a teacher in Newburyport. He married Catherine Deblois, daughter of John and Margaret (Laughton) Tracy. John was a son of Patrick Tracy, a wealthy merchant of Newburyport. The latter was the father of Nathaniel Tracy, a very successful merchant of that place, who, during the Revolutionary war, equipped a number of privateers which inflicted immense damage upon British commerce. Wealth poured in upon him and he lived in great splendor. His benevolence and charities were commensurate with his other expenditures. He generously tendered assistance to his country, and his fortune, credit and counsels were freely bestowed, but finally his privateers were swept from the ocean, and the government lacking the means or inclination to repay his advances, he became, in 1786, bankrupt to the amount of millions. "Fortunately one of his estates had been secured to one of his children, and to this remnant of his vast possessions he repaired to brood in grief over his ruined fortunes and disappointed hopes. He survived but a short period, and became a victim to his sensibility." He owned the Cragie house in Cambridge, since owned by Henry Wordsworth Longfellow.

Henry, son of Henry and Mary Titcomb, born April 9, 1760, married Abigail Whitmore. Their children were: Henry, married Sarah, daughter of Micayah Lunt, Esq.; Abigail; Silas, married Hannah Moody, daughter of Enoch Sawyer; Joseph Moody, married Sarah Newman Wills of Newburyport.

Dea. Benjamin, the second son of Capt. Joseph, was an ensign at the siege of Louisburg, and afterwards settled in Portland. He was a blacksmith, his shop being on the breastwork from which Central Wharf has been extended. His house was on the corner of Plumb and Middle Streets, but after the war he lived opposite the custom house. The house is still standing. In 1769, he was chosen deacon of the First Church, and in 1780 was elected a Representative to the General Court. It is said that "he was a man of fine personal appearance, tall and well proportioned. He dressed well, wearing a full bottomed wig and small clothes,[1] and was a very worthy and influential citizen." He married Anne, a daughter of Dea. Moses and Sarah (Titcomb) Pearson of Farmington (now Portland).

Dea. Moses Pearson was a son of Jeremiah and Priscilla (Hazen) Pearson. Jeremiah was a son of John Pearson, who was of Rowley in 1643. "John Pearson set up the first fulling-mill in America." He was a Representative to the General Court, and a deacon. Moses Pearson bore a distinguished part in the early history of the city of Portland, being the first sheriff of Cumberland County, and for several years a Representative to the General Court. He was also a Judge of the Court of Common Pleas. He had the command of a company at the siege of Louisburg.

The children of Deacon Benjamin and Annie Titcomb were: Moses, Benjamin, Joseph, Anne, Andrew Phillips, Eunice, Elizabeth and Mary. Dea. Benjamin died Oct. 15, 1798. His wife survived him two years.

He left a valuable estate to his children, appraised at £10,000, which was increased to £12,000 by his wife's estate. Included in the estate, was a tract of three

---

[1] "In our town the persons who were distinguished by the cocked hat, the bush wig and the red cloak, the envied marks of distinction, were the Waldos, the Rev. Mr. Smith's family, Enoch Truman, Brigadier Preble, Alexander Ross, Stephen Longfellow, Dr. Coffin, Moses Pearson, Richard Codman, Benjamin Titcomb, William Tyng, Theophilus Bradbury, David Wyer, and perhaps some others. The fashionable color of clothes among this class was drab; the coats were made with large cuffs reaching to the elbows, and low collars. . . . Most of those above mentioned were engaged in trade, and the means of none were sufficiently ample to enable them to live without engaging in some employment. Still the pride of their caste was maintained, and although the cloak and perhaps the wig may have been laid aside in the dust and hurry of business, they were scrupulously retained when abroad."—*History of Portland*, page 776, by Wm. Willis.

acres of land, extending from Congress Street to the Back Cove, just below the meeting-house of the First church.

Moses, the eldest son, died in the West Indies, wealthy, and without issue.

Benjamin, the second son of Deacon Benjamin, after his education was finished, served an apprenticeship in the art of printing, and on the first day of January, 1785, "struck off," with his own hands, the first sheet ever printed in Maine. The name of his paper was the "Falmouth Gazette and Weekly Advertiser." About four years later, he left printing, and "with no other preparation than that which the grace of God gives," began to preach to the small Baptist society then recently gathered in Portland, the first meetings of which were held at his house. In 1804 he removed to Brunswick, Me., and became pastor of the Baptist Church which had been gathered at that place. He was elected a delegate to the convention that formed the Constitution of Maine, and at the request of Gen. Keey, opened the Convention with prayer. Not caring for political preferment, he afterwards declined office which was several times offered him. He was one of the original trustees of Waterville College, now Colby University, and took great interest in that institution. "He was a man of decision, strong in faith; a ready speaker, preaching without notes."

Rev. Benjamin married Mary, daughter of Rev. John Fairfield of Saco, Me. (He was the grandfather of Gov. Fairfield). Their children were: Benjamin; Mary E.; William; John Fairfield; Henry; Elizabeth Harris, who married Ephraim Brown; Eunice; Moses; Sarah Cleaves; Sophia Ann; Harriet Maria, who married Richard T. Dunlap; Harriet H.; and Henry.

Rev. Benjamin retired from the pulpit at the age of 83, after a forty years' ministry in Brunswick. He died Sept. 30, 1847.

Moses, son of Rev. Benjamin, was for thirty years

superintendent of the United States Senate Document Room.

William, the only son of Rev. Benjamin who married, was born March 17, 1850. He married Salome Delano. Their children were: William Henry, married Mary Crockett; Mary Ann, who died in infancy; Benjamin, married Anne Williams; Mary Ann, married Nathaniel Mayhew; Josiah W. M.; Helen Maria, married Anson D. Blunt; Sophia Ann; and Lucretia Hamlin, married George F. French.

Joseph, the third son of Dea. Benjamin, was an active shipmaster, and commanded a large privateer out of Portland during the Revolutionary war. He was for ten years one of the selectmen, and for nine years a Representative. He married Eunice, daughter of Ephraim Jones, by whom he had several children. The wife of the late Reuben Mitchell of Portland, was a daughter of his.

Anne, the eldest daughter of Dea. Benjamin, married Hon. Woodbury, son of John and Mary (Langdon) Storer. Mary Langdon was a daughter of John and Mary Dudley Langdon, and sister to Woodbury and Gov. John Langdon. John Storer, who was for many years a prominent man in the affairs of York County, was a son of Joseph and Hannah (Hills) Storer of Wells, Me. Joseph Storer was a Representative, and a man of energy and distinction in the Indian wars.

Hon. Woodbury Storer engaged very largely in commercial pursuits with his brother Ebenezer, in Portland. In 1788, Mrs. Storer died, leaving one son, Woodbury, and two daughters, Anne and Mary. By a second marriage with Margaret, daughter of James Boyd, Mr. Storer had a large family of children. Rev. John Parker Boyd Storer of Syracuse, N. Y.; Judge Bellamy Storer of Cincinnati; Robert Storer, a merchant of Boston, and Humphrey Storer, also of Boston, were sons of Mr. Storer by this marriage.

Woodbury, son of Woodbury and Ann (Titcomb)

Storer, became a lawyer, in whose hands, it is said, clients felt safe. "His life and practice cast no shade upon a career of uniform gentleness, moderation and useful endeavor." He married Mary, daughter of John Barrett of Boston, and a niece of Judge Barrett Potter of Portland.

Anne, the eldest daughter of Woodbury and Anne (Titcomb) Storer, married Judge Barrett Potter of Portland. Their children were: Eliza A.; Mary Storer; and Margaret Louise. Judge Potter was a member of the Executive Council in Massachusetts, and of the Senate in Maine. "Mrs. Potter was a lovely woman, but of frail and delicate organization." She died at the age of 40 years.

Mary Storer, their second daughter, married Henry Wordsworth Longfellow, the Poet (see account of Longfellow).

Margaret Louise, the youngest daughter, married Peter, son of Hon. Stephen and Harriet (Preble) Thacher. Mrs. Thacher was a woman of distinguished excellencies, a sister of the late Hon. William Pitt Preble. Hon. Stephen Thacher was a son of Rodolphos and Mary (Cone) Thacher; Rodolphos was a son of Peter and Abigail (Hibbard) Thacher; Peter was a son of Rev. Ralph and Ruth (Partridge) Thacher; Rev. Ralph being a son of Rev. Thomas Thacher, the first minister of the Old South Church in Boston, who was a son of Rev. Peter, Rector of St. Edmonds, Salisbury, England.

Rev. Thomas Thacher was distinguished, not only in the common academical studies, but in Hebrew, Syriac, and Arabic, in the first of which languages he composed a lexicon. As was not uncommon at that period, he studied for two professions, medicine and theology, in both of which he obtained a high reputation. He was the author of the first medical work published in Massachusetts. He was one of the most popular preachers in the Colony, and was greatly and deservedly esteemed. He married, first, Elizabeth, daughter of Rev. Ralph Partridge of Duxbury, Mass.; second, Margaret Sheaffe, widow of Henry Sheaffe, and daughter of Henry Webb, the benefactor of Harvard College. She was one of the founders of the Old South Church. The children of Rev. Thomas and Elizabeth were: Thomas, Ralph, Peter, Patience, and Elizabeth. Thomas was a merchant in Boston; Peter was the first minister in Milton; and Ralph was minister at Chilmark, Martha's Vineyard.

Peter Thacher, Esq., formerly a member of the bar of Knox County, is now practicing in Boston, his eldest son, Stephen, being a partner with him. Mary Potter, his eldest daughter, is the wife of Col. Thomas Wentworth Higginson of Cambridge.

Mary, the youngest daughter of Woodbury and Ann Storer, married William Goddard, a prominent merchant of Boston.

Andrew Phillips, the fourth son of Dea. Benjamin and Anne (Pearson) Titcomb, married Mary, daughter of Daniel Dole of Portland. The wife of Daniel was a daughter of Moses and Sarah (Titcomb) Pearson of Portland. Andrew left a large family of children, of whom Almira, the eldest daughter, married Judge Fitch of Portland, and had five daughters and one son. Her eldest daughter married Dr. Josiah Blake of Harrison; another married Samuel E. Perley; a third married Henry E. Perley; and the youngest married Henry Willis of Portland. Of her three sons, one is a physician in California, and another is a surgeon in the army.

Eunice, the second daughter of Dea. Benjamin and Anne, married Ebenezer, son of John and Mary (Langdon) Storer who was extensively engaged in business with his brother, Woodbury. Mr. Storer was an efficient officer in the army.

Oliver, the third son of Capt. Joseph and Ann (Smith) Titcomb, was born July 27, 1729. He married Anna

Osgood, about 1752. Their children were: Molly; Lois; Rhoda, died young; a second Rhoda; Moses; Sarah, died young; Betsey; Jonathan; a second Sarah; Ichabod; and Tabitha.

Oliver Titcomb resided at Amesbury, Mass. The old mansion which he built on School Street, Amesbury Mills, still stands.

Ichabod, the youngest son of Oliver, was born Nov. 24, 1768. He married Feb. 15, 1793, Hannah Gale. Their children were: Mary, Oliver, Dorothy, William, Susan, Ichabod, and Alfred.

The descendants of Ichabod and Hannah Titcomb are very numerous.

Ichabod, the youngest son of Ichabod, born June 21, 1804, married March 3, 1836, Hannah Matilda, daughter of Col. Daniel Moulton of West Newbury. Their children were: Silas Moulton, married Hannah Matilda Poore; Hannah Matilda, married Capt. George Carr Dow; Harriet; Mary; Ellen; Frank Pierce, married Emma S. Brooks; and George McClellan.

John Poor Titcomb of Byfield, Mass., a son of Silas M. and Hannah Titcomb, is collecting the genealogy of the Titcomb family for publication.

Col. Moses, youngest son of William and Ann (Cottle) Titcomb, was born June 19, 1700. He married Miriam Currier. Their daughter Miriam married Nicholas Tracy. Col. Moses was at the siege of Louisburg as Major of a regiment under Gen. Pepperrell. Upon his return from Louisburg, he was commissioned Colonel of a regiment that was in the battle of Lake George, where he was killed, Sept. 8, 1755. Coffin, in his "History of Newbury," says: "In the battle of Lake George, he commanded his regiment on the extreme right wing of General Johnson's line. He got behind a large pine tree about one rod distant from the end of the breastwork, where he could stand up and command his men, who were lying on the ground, and where he could have a better opportunity to use his own piece. Here he was insensibly flanked by a party of Indians, who crept around a large pine log across a swamp about eighty yards distant, and shot him. Colonel Titcomb and Lieutenant Baron stood behind the same tree, and both fell at the same fire."

Barry, the historian, in his account, says: "But one English officer was killed in the engagement—the gallant Titcomb, who had fought with such bravery at the battle of Louisburg, and whose name should be transmitted to posterity with honor."[1]

Hutchinson, in his account of the siege of Louisburg, says: "Major Titcomb's readiness to engage in the most hazardous part of the service, was acknowledged and applauded. He survived the siege, was Colonel of a regiment when General Johnson attacked Dieskau, and there lost his life in the service of his country. Of the five fascine batteries that were erected in the reduction of Louisburg, the last which was erected the 20th of May and called Titcomb's battery, [of which he had the command], having five forty-two pounders, did as great execution as any."

On the departure of Col. Moses Titcomb and his regiment for Lake George, a sermon was preached by the Rev. John Lowell of Newbury, from Deut. xx. 4. This sermon was afterwards published, and the following was the introduction to it:

"To Moses Titcomb, Esq.: Lieutenant-Colonel of the Militia in and about *Newbury*, and Colonel of a Regiment raised in the Province of the *Massachusetts-Bay* against the *French* at *Crown-Point*, &c.

"PERMIT me SIR to congratulate you upon your Increase of Honour in that new and great Trust, which your KING and Country is at this Day reposing in you.

"When in delivering the following Sermon, your Courage, Conduct and Success at the Siege of *Louis-*

[1] "History of Massachusetts," vol. II., p. 197.

burg were mentioned I had not the mean View of serving my self by flattering you, for could I have allowed *my self* in any such low Art with any; yet I knew too well *you* were above being influenced by it, and was sensible of the forwardness of your Mind to shew me proper kindness as your Minister without my Application. I then only honestly aimed at serving the Publick (as was my Duty) in encouraging those to proceed who were enlisted under your Command, by that among other Motives: And what I shall now add and publish, is not merely to pass a Compliment upon *Newbury*, where you drew your first Breath, and whose Esteem of you has been exprest in employing you in several Offices of Importance, particularly as their Representative at the General Court, and whose Interests have been your growing Care, with your rising Honours: This, tho' not an unworthy, is lower than my End: but my Design herein is to extend your Character as one of the Heroes of *New England*, (which, notwithstanding all your own Pains to have it forgotten, will always be *here* remembered) to *Great-Britain*, or as far as this mean Performance shall reach.

"Sir—That *Battery* which was projected and raised by you at *Cape-Breton*, and then called *Titcomb's* did great Execution (in the Opinion of the best Judges, and as the *French* own), in the Operations of the Siege; and perhaps without it, the important Fortress there, would not have been reduced, and so Peace not so soon and easily have been restored to *Europe:* If we consider your Services in this light, what a vast Expence of Blood, how many Millions of Money must we see you have saved: And what a great Blessing thro' the Favour of Heaven, have you herein had the Honour to be, not to this Country only, but to *Great-Britain* and Mankind!

"'Tis strange the printed Plans have not done you that Justice (especially those among ourselves) which the Manuscripts did, in distinguishing that Battery by your name.

"I hope for the Credit of our Country, and the future encouragement of the Brave, your Name, and this important Fact, will have an honorable Record in the Annals of *North-America*, which may derive Blessings upon your Posterity: However, you'll have the Satisfaction and Pleasure in your own Breast, which arise in good and great Minds from publick and noble Designs happily executed.

"SIR—Our Eyes are now again turned upon you, vested with an higher Character; And that with your greater Power, you may, by the Help of the LORD OF HOSTS, acquire a more illustrious Reputation, that you may recover our Rights, that you may again humble those who have encroached upon them, even *those French* to whom *you* with other brave *New England* Men have proved *superior;* that *you* may be saved in all Dangers and *all those with you*, thro' God's gracious Presence and Care, and (by the Will of God) be returned to us with Joy, being crowned with Victory, if obliged to contend, are the Wishes and Prayers of your Town and Country and all the faithful Subjects of King GEORGE, and Friends to these his Dominions, among which, none are more sincere, ardent, and constant than those of your

frequently and greatly obliged Pastor
and humble Servant
John Lowell."

Thomas, the youngest son of William and Elizabeth (Stevens) Titcomb, born Oct. 11, 1661, married Mary Dam, and had four daughters, viz.: Hannah; Judith; Mary; and Anne.[1]

---

[1] Many of the facts in the preceding account, relating to the Titcombs of Massachusetts, are from "Coffin's History of Newbury;" and many of those relating to the Titcombs of Maine, are from "Law, Lawyers and Courts of Maine."

BARTLETT.

Richard Bartlett, with his two sons and a daughter, and his brothers John and Thomas, came from England to New England as early as 1635. The three brothers were probably sons of Edmund Bartelot of Ernely, Sussex County, England, who was a descendant of Adam Bartelot, the esquire of Brian, a knight who came from Normandy to England with William the Conqueror. Richard, a descendant of Adam Bartelot and heir of the estate of Stopham, died in Tournay, France, in the year 1518, leaving four sons. William, the eldest, succeeded to his father's estate; and Edmund, another son, had a landed estate in Ernely. Edmund had three sons: Edmund, who succeeded to his estate; and Richard, John and Thomas, who left Ernely in 1634, or about that time, and are supposed to have come to America. A coat of arms belonging to the descendants of Richard, John and Thomas Bartlett, the emigrants to New England, is said by Sir Walter Bartelot of Stopham, the present representative of the Bartelots of Stopham, to be substantially the same as his coat of arms.

We learn from the Rev. C. J. Robinson of England, who has prepared and published a pamphlet from a history of the Bartelots in Sussex County, that "the name of Bartelot, or Bartlett, is of Norman origin," and "has been thought to be clearly a diminutive of Bartholomew. It is still current in Normandy as Berthelot," and exists in many Sussex parishes as Bartelot, Bartlet and Bartlett.

Thomas Bartlett settled in Watertown, and was known as Ensign Thomas. He had several daughters, but no sons. We are told by Coffin, that "Richard and John settled in Newby, Mass., at or around Bartlett's Cove, opposite Amesbury Ferry, where some of their descendants of the same name still reside." John was made a freeman in 1637. His wife's name was Joan, and they had one son, named John. John, Sen., died April 13, 1678. His wife Joan died Feb. 5, 1679. John, their son, married Sara, daughter of John Knight. Their children were: Gideon; and Mary, who died young.

Richard Bartlett, we are told, was a shoemaker. He appears to have taken part in the church controversy that agitated Newbury nearly thirty years, his name being one of five appended to the petitions sent to the General Court by the Woodman party (see account of William Titcomb, page 145). In the testimony concerning his last will and testament that was taken by William Titcomb, his son-in-law, husband of his daughter Joanna, and Anthony Somerby, about a month before his death, his sons Richard, Christopher and John are mentioned; also his daughter Joanna Titcomb, and her three daughters. He died May 23, 1647.

Richard Bartlett, Jun., we are told by Coffin, was a very intelligent man, and was a Representative to the General Court in 1679, '80, '81 and '84. He resided at first at Oldtown Hill, but afterwards moved to Bartlett's Cove. He married Abigail ——. Their children were: Samuel, Richard, Thomas, Abigail, John, Hannah and Rebecca. Richard Bartlett died in 1698, aged 77 years. His wife died March 3, 1687.

Samuel, son of Richard Bartlett, Jun., married Elizabeth, daughter of William and Elizabeth (Stevens) Titcomb of Newbury. Their children were: Elizabeth, Abigail, Samuel, Sara, Richard, Thomas, Tirzah and Elizabeth.

It is said that Samuel Bartlett was a staunch friend to liberty, a very facetious, but decided man. On the first intimation in Newbury of the difficulty at the time Gov. Andros was seized and confined, some of the people of Newbury started for Boston, Samuel Bartlett being one of them. He armed himself with a rusty sword minus the scabbard, mounted his horse, and rode with such speed, it is said, that his long sword, trailing on the ground, left as it came in contact with the stones in the road a stream of fire all of the way. He arrived in season to assist in imprisoning the Governor.

He was one of the six who were served by the sheriff with "a process and order of the court strictly forbidding them and their associates proceeding in the work of their intended meeting house and so forth said persons being summoned to attend the court," (see account of Penuel Titcomb, page 152). He died May 15, 1732. His wife died Aug. 26, 1690.

Richard, son of Richard, Jun., born Feb. 21, 1649, married Hannah Emery. Their children were: Hannah, Richard, John, Samuel, Daniel, Joseph, a second Samuel, Stephen, Thomas and Mary.

Thomas, son of Richard Bartlett, Jun., born Sept. 7, 1650, married Tirzah, daughter of William and Elizabeth (Stevens) Titcomb. Their children were: Elizabeth, who died young; and Tirzah. Thomas Bartlett died April 6, 1689.

Joseph, the fifth son of Richard and Hannah (Emery) Bartlett, was born Nov. 8, 1686. During the Indian depredations in Haverhill, he was impressed and sent with others from Newbury, to defend the inhabitants of that town. He was stationed at Capt. Simon Wainwright's house, and at the massacre of Aug. 29, 1708, was captured by the Indians and taken to Canada. The following extracts are from a published account of his captivity: "At first I was taken by the French, and was with them till this fight was over; during which an Indian came to me in great fury with his hatchet, I suppose to take away my life; but through the mercies of God, the French put him by; and so I was spared. I heard many bullets hum over my head as we marched away. After the fight was over the French gave me to the Indians—for the Indians killed their prisoners. How many were killed at the fight I do not know. I saw one Indian that had his thigh broken, whom two of them carried away to a pond of water, where I thought they put him in, but after a great while the French told me that another Indian staid with and took care of him, and in about three months he brought him to Montreal; but he was ever after lame. We traveled hard all that day till nearly sun-set when they camped for the night. They tied me down, and laid each side of me upon the strings; and so they did almost every subsequent night. The next morning they arose very early, and led me, my arms being tied behind me, and another squaw line about my neck. I was led by an Indian, who had a hatchet in his hand and a pistol in his girdle. In this manner I was led the most part of the way. They traveled hard the three first days. I had as yet eaten hardly anything, for they had little besides horse-meat; and carrying a heavy pack I was very much fatigued. Ascending a steep hill a little before we got to Winnipesocet pond, I was almost ready to give out; but, through the goodness and help of God, I was enabled to proceed this third day; but at night I was extremely faint. The Indians made a little water pottage without salt or sweetening, and gave me some to drink. I drank a little draught; and with the blessing of God it very much revived me, and proved the best cordial I ever took in my life. . . . Some of the Indians carried those who were sick upon their backs. Before we reached Montreal, we came to Capridia, a French fort, I think, about fifteen miles from Chamblee—where the Indians cut the hair from one side of my head—greased the remainder and my face, and painted the latter.

"We then went over the river to the governor,—where they examined and questioned me concerning the affairs of our land,—whether the English talked of invading Canada, or not. Afterwards we went to the seminary, that is, the priest-house, where we tarried that night. Next morning we set out for the Indians' fort, which the French called Sadrokelly, and which was about nine miles from Montreal. When they had proceeded about half way they made a stop, and marked a tree with the picture of a man's hand and some scalps. They then led me along a little farther to where there was a fire and about fifteen Indians and thirty boys. There they made a stop, and tied me for a short time; during which I believe they held a council whether to burn me or not. But God who hath the hearts of all in his hands, spared my life. The Indians that took me and the boys marched away, and left me with the others, who led me along a little way and permitted a squaw to cut off one of my little fingers, and another to strike me severely with a pole. Passing through a large company of Indians, we entered the fort, where they bound up my finger with plantain leaves, and gave me some roasted pompkin to eat. Here there came together a great company that filled the wigwam, which was nearly forty feet in length where they sung and danced a greater part of the night, as many at a time as could stand from one end of the wigwam to the other. In this manner they danced round their fires. They often invited me to dance; but I refused from time to time. However, they pulled me up, and I went around once with them. Next day they came together again with their scalps which they presented their squaws. One of them took me by the hand, and after a lengthy speech, gave me to an old squaw, who took me into another wigwam. Here, after a little crying and whimpering, she made me take off my Indian stockings and blanket, and gave me others; and she warmed some water and washed the red paint and grease from my face and hands. There was another family living in the same wigwam. An English woman, who belonged to one of the French nuns, came in and told me I need not fear, for I was given to this squaw, in lieu of one of her sons, whom the English had slain; and that I was to be master of the wigwam; but she being a papist, I placed little reliance on her assertions. The old squaw was very kind to me. I staid here about two weeks; and then went to another fort about eighteen miles distant."

He afterwards lived with the French, who endeavored to convert him to Catholicism. He finally escaped, and reached Newbury, after a captivity of four years. After his return, the General Court ordered that the sum of twenty pounds and fifteen shillings be allowed him, as he was in her majesty's service when captured. He settled on a farm in Newton, N. H. He was justice of the peace, and deacon of the church. He married, first, —— Tewksbury; second, —— Hoyt. He had four sons and six daughters, all by his second wife.

Josiah Bartlett, M. D., a son of Stephen, the seventh son of Richard and Hannah (Emery) Bartlett, was born in Amesbury, Mass., Nov. 21, 1729. After an imperfect medical education, he began the practice of medicine at Kingston, N. H., and soon became eminent by his success in treating a malignant throat disease which was fatal among children and very prevalent in the towns of New Hampshire. The method, hitherto, of treating this disease, was as a highly phlogistic complaint, but he was led from his own reason and observation to manage it differently. He made use of the Peruvian bark as an antidote and preventative, and his practice was very successful. In 1765, and annually until the Revolution, he was chosen to the Legislature. He was a member of the committee of safety, upon whom devolved for a time the whole executive government of the State, and on the organization of government by a Provincial Congress, of which he was a member, he was appointed a justice of the peace and Colonel of the 7th regiment. Being a delegate to Congress in 1775 and 1776, he was the first to give his vote for the Declaration of Independence, and its first signer after the President. He accompanied Gen. Stark to Bennington, as agent of the State to provide medicines and other necessaries for the New Hampshire troops. He was again a delegate to Congress He was appointed Chief Justice of the Court of Common Pleas in 1779, a Justice of the Superior Court in 1784, and Chief Justice in 1788. He was an active member of the convention called to adopt the Federal Constitution. He was for three years President of the State, and under the new Constitution, Governor. He was also President of the New Hampshire Medical Society, which he was chiefly instrumental in founding. He received an honorary degree of M. D., from Dartmouth College. He was always a patron of learning, and a friend to learned men. He married Mary, daughter of Deacon Joseph Bartlett. He died May 11, 1795. His son Josiah was a physician of extensive practice.

Hon. William Bartlett, a grandson of Thomas, the eighth son of Richard and Hannah (Emery) Bartlett, was born in Newburyport, Jan. 31, 1748. Having acquired great wealth by mercantile enterprise, he employed it in assisting the needy, and especially in advancing the cause of religion and morals. The temperance reformation, foreign missions, and the gratuitous education of young men for the ministry, were especial objects of his munificence. He gave $30,000 towards founding the Theological Seminary at Andover, Mass.; $25,000 to endow a professorship of sacred rhetoric; and contributed largely to the founding of another professorship. He built the chapel, which was named Bartlett Chapel in his honor; he also built one of the large halls, and two of the professors' houses. It is said that no small portion of the select and valuable library of that institution was given by him. At his death, he bequeathed $50,000 to the seminary. As a citizen of Newburyport, he is said to have been ever ready to devise and execute plans for its essential prosperity. In the First Presbyterian Church, where he worshiped, stands a beautiful and costly cenotaph, erected to the memory of Whitefield by him. Mr. Bartlett was, it is said, an uncompromising enemy to idleness and extravagance. "He was a man of iron frame as well as nerve, and lived to the advanced age of ninety-three."

Thomas Bartlett, a descendant of Samuel and Elizabeth (Titcomb) Bartlett, was a Lieutenant-Colonel under Gen. Stark at the surrender of Burgoyne, and in command of a regiment at West Point at the time of Arnold's defection. He was a member of the New Hampshire Legislature, Speaker of the House, and Judge of the Court of Common Pleas. He married Sarah, eldest daughter of Gen. Joseph Cilley, a patriot of the American Revolution. He died in 1805.

Among the descendants of Samuel and Elizabeth (Titcomb) Bartlett, were Gen. Bartlett of Nottingham, N. H., a Representative and Senator, and also Judge of the Court of Common Pleas; Hon. Josiah Bartlett of Lee, a lieutenant in the war of 1812-15, and a member of the Governor's Council; Hon. Ichabod Bartlett of Salisbury, an eminent lawyer; Hon. Josiah Bartlett of Amesbury, a distinguished physician, and a Colonel in the army; the three sons of the latter, who were eminent physicians; Hon. Samuel Bartlett, a physician of Kingston; and Hon. Bailey Bartlett of Haverhill, Mass. The latter was appointed by Gov. Hancock, sheriff of the county of Essex, which office he retained forty years, with the exception of a few months. He was elected in 1797 a member of the United States Congress, and served four years. His wife, who was a daughter of John White, Jun., of Haverhill, was distinguished for great personal beauty and piety. It is said that the memory of her benevolent character is still affectionately cherished by all who knew her. They had ten children. Their third son, Charles L. Bartlett, who married Mary Plummer, was the father of Gen. William F. Bartlett of the late civil war.

Gen. William Francis Bartlett was born at Haverhill, Mass., June 6, 1840. At the age of twenty-one, he left Harvard College to go to the seat of war as Captain in the Twentieth Regiment of Massachusetts Volunteers. In April, 1862, Capt. Bartlett was with his regiment at the outpost in front of Yorktown. While at the outer line, kneeling and examining the enemy through his field-glass, he received a wound from a sharp-shooter's rifle which cost him his leg. He was sent home, where he remained until the following November, when he again started for the seat of war as Colonel of the Forty-ninth Regiment. At the assault on Port Hudson, by Gen. Banks, Col. Bartlett was disabled by a ball from the enemy, which shattered his wrist. He was again sent North, where he remained until April, 1864, when he started for the South in command of the Fifty-second Regiment. The following June, he received the appointment of Brigadier-General of Volunteers. While storming the enemy's works at Petersburg, he was taken prisoner and carried to Libby Prison, where he remained until the last of September, suffering intensely a part of the time from a disease contracted in the army, and from which he never entirely recovered. In June of 1865, he again went to the seat of war in command of the Ninth Corps, where he remained until the end of the war.

In 1865, Gen. Bartlett married Mary Agnes, daughter of Col. Robert Pomeroy of Pittsfield, Mass. He died of consumption the 17th of December, 1876. He left six children.

Clement H. Hill thus wrote of him: "When the Forty-ninth Regt. Mass. Vols. passed through New

York, at its head rode a young man of only twenty-two years, tall, graceful and soldierly to such a degree that it seemed as if a year and a half of previous service had already moulded him into the ideal soldier. He wore one wooden leg, one arm was in splints, and a crutch was swung over his shoulder, but his conduct and bearing were those of a man whom nothing can daunt." "Frank Bartlett, as his friends were wont to call him, was all through a manly man." "Had his life been spared, he must have eventually been drawn into public life. He possessed capacity for leadership. He was a man of quiet, intense determination, and the charm of his presence was magnetic. He was just, honest, perfectly true and pefectly fearless. The few speeches, essays and letters that he has left us, are models of brevity, of strength and good honest English. That was almost Emersonian, when he said that he believed in administration that was above suspicion and not above investigation. When the history of the great Civil War is fully written out, there will be few names about which will gather so much of romantic interest and of tender regard as about that of this gallant young Massachusetts officer. He was the idol of young Harvard; perhaps we may say that the most of romance surrounded him of all the sons of Harvard, in the minds of young and old. In the re-union of 1874, Gen. Bartlett was Chief Marshal of the Harvard Committee. His staff was composed of twenty-four former officers. It was on this occasion that he made that short but most forcible and beautiful appeal for peace between the North and South. The effect was electric, and the audience fairly sprang from their seats, leaned toward him and gathered round him and cheered him again and again."

Gen. Bartlett was made Brevet-General at the close of the war. Gov. Andrew, it is said, pronounced him the most conspicuous soldier of the Gulf. When the war ended, he is said to have been the most conspicuous soldier of all whom Massachusetts sent to the field.

Lieut.-Col. Palfrey, in his "Life of Gen. Bartlett," says of him: "He was a born leader of the best men, and he had large endowments for controlling the worst. His patriotism was true patriotism, and his love of country embraced the whole country. He was tall and slender, his carriage conspicuous for its grace and dignity, and there was about him altogether a certain stately air which the New England men of this generation have rarely seen equaled. A share of composure and reserve was natural to him, but his manners were courteous and his smile engaging. His voice was deep, full-toned and powerful. Wherever he went, he was observed; and wherever he was known, he was admired and loved."

It is said that at the assault upon Port Hudson, Col. Bartlett was on horseback, the only mounted man in the field. He had to go that way or stay behind, and with his regiment he *would* go. A few days after this, Col. Walter Cutting being sent to the enemy under a flag of truce to ask permission to bury our dead, was asked by several Confederate officers, "Who was that man on horseback?" "*He* was," they continued, "a gallant fellow; a brave man; the bravest and most daring thing we have yet seen done in the war." After being told that it was Col. Bartlett, they said, "We thought him too brave a man to be killed, so told our men not to fire at him."

Prof. S. C. Bartlett of the Theological Seminary of Chicago, Ill., while in England, visited Col. Walter Bartelot, M. P., the present representative of the Bartelots of Stopham, Sussex County, England. The following extract is from an account sent by him to Mr. Levi Bartlett, author of the "Bartlett Family:"

"The estate is a large one, some 7000 or 8000 acres.

The house is a large three-story stone building, 150 feet or more long—quite an establishment. . . . A large amount of land about the residence is simply ornamental. The farming portion is on a large scale, and every thing well kept and in good condition.

"Col. Bartelot is satisfied that we came from some of the junior members of the family in former times."

"From London to Pullborough station by rail is two hours and fifteen minutes. The distance from the station to Col. Bartelot's mansion is about three-fourths of a mile. In going from the station to his residence, the river Arun is crossed by a stone bridge built by the family in 1300. From the front of the large stone mansion there is a beautiful outlook upon the South Downs and a fine range of hills; beyond them the ocean. On two hills in sight, the old Romans have left marks of their fortifications, and three or four miles away—South-east, a portion of the estate of the Earls of Arundel (Arundale) could be seen. Near the old Norman church built by the family in the thirteenth century, is an English yew tree, planted about the time the church was erected, which is from the ground seven and a half feet in diameter; there are also several large and aged cedars of Lebanon. On the stone floor of the church, are marble slabs with inlaid figures with a regular succession of Bartelots inscriptions, names and dates, from John Bartelot, who died in 1428, down to Col. George Bartelot, who died Nov. 28, 1872, aged 84 years (the father of Col. Walter Bartelot). Here there is no *mistake* or *sham*, for, while scores of families of past nobility have run out over and over, or, as Macaulay has it,—'Many illustrious houses have forever disappeared from history,' the Bartelot family have steadily held possession of the original grant (with large additions) for eight hundred years, from Adam Bartelot, the progenitor of the family, down to the present representative, and an accurate pedigree of the line has been kept from 1069, down to Ada Mary, the youngest daughter of Col. Walter Bartelot, who celebrated her twelfth birthday in August, 1874."

Mr. Levi Bartlett wrote to Col. Bartlett in 1873, and received a reply, dated Nov. 15, 1873, from which the following extract is taken:

"I was very glad to receive your letter, and am very proud that my kinsmen in America have so distinguished themselves and made the old name respected out there. I assure you that it gives me great pleasure to render what information I can, and it would give me greater pleasure, should you come to England, to see you here and show you what we have that is worth seeing. I was very glad to see Prof. Bartlett. He was very kind as to his descriptions of all he saw here.

"I shall send with this a short copy of the pedigree to 1428 and later under three families, or rather five, viz.: Bartelot, Stopham, D'Orley, Lewknor, Tregoz, and an extract from the Ford pedigree. The Fords lived at Stopham before the Conquest; the old Saxon proprietors. Brian, a knight, who came over with William the Conqueror, is on the Battle Abbey Roll, with his esquire Adam Bartelot, both of course being officers and gentlemen. Both received grants of land, —Stopham Sussex being the principal, of which we suppose Brian got the largest share, and Adam Bartelot[1] a smaller one; the Saxon family of Fords still retaining possession of a large part of the estate. The Fords lived on this spot before the Conquest and there is still a room, said—with more or less truth—to have been here before the Conquest. Brian, the Norman knight, assumed the name of Brian de Stopham. He was succeeded by his son Richard de Stopham. After

---

[1] The original grant from King William to Adam Bartelot, in 1066, "was a landed estate, which could neither be sold, given away, or pass out of the family."—*Levi Bartlett.*

several generations the male issue of the Ford family failed, and the estate fell into the hands of a daughter of the Fords. John de Stopham, as you will see, married the daughter of the Fords and got their share. In the fourteenth century, John Bartelot married the daughter and heiress of the Stophams, and came into possession of the whole property, the male line of the Stophams having failed. You will see by the chart of pedigree I send, that the Bartelots and Stophams have been members of Parliament for the county from the earliest times. You will also see that John Bartelot had one of our crests—the castle—given him by Edward the Black Prince, for taking the castle of Fontenoy in France, in command of the Sussex men. I also send you our coat of arms. The plates I send you are my arms quartered with those of my first wife, who was a Musgrave of Cumberland; also one of the oldest families of England. My arms quarterings—1, Bartelot; 2, Stopham; 3, Lewknor; 4, D'Orley; 5, Tregoz; 6, Camoyes; 7, Walton; 8, Syhester. I send you the pedigree down to the time when the Bartelots married the heiresses of the Waltons and Syhesters The original coat of arms of the Bratelot family was three opened left hand falconer's gloves with golden tassels about the wrist. Crest, a swan; 2nd crest, a castle. We had the old right of keeping swans on the river, a right which very few had. The Bartelots have lived here ever since the Conqueror fought at the battle of Poictiers, 1356, and at the battle of Cressy, 1346; and subscribed handsomely to the funds contributed to defend England against the attack of the Spanish Armada in 1588. The records of the church are compiled from John Bartelot, who was born early in 1300, down to the present date. There are some very curious and handsome coats of arms in the windows bearing the family names of those with whom they married; also old memorial windows of Stopham and Bartelot, the date of the oldest figures being 1273. If I can give you more information I shall be glad to do so."

On the 27th of February, 1874, Mr. Levi Bartlett received a second letter from Col. Walter Bartelot, from which the following extract is taken:

"I now send you the rest of the pedigree, not complete, but perhaps as much as you will require. You will see, as I said before, Brian, the knight, and Adam Bartelot, the esquire, came over and fought with William, at the Battle of Hastings. Both received grants of land in Stopham. And here I would say, grants were different from what would be called an estate now. Then the manorial rights, as well as the lands, gave great power, and were very valuable. There is a tradition that after the marriage first of the Stophams with the Fords, then of the Bartelots with the Stophams and also with the Lewknors and with the De Okehursts, that the family could ride on their own property from Stopham to Northam, about fourteen miles. I have always supposed that my American relations must have descended from Edmund Bartelot of Ernely in Sussex. He died, as you will see by the chart, in 1591; he was fourth son of Richard Bartelot of Stopham. The pedigree goes down to Thomas and John Bartelot living in 1634."

On the 19th of December, 1874, Mr. Levi Bartlett received a third letter from Col. Walter Bartelot, from which the following extract is made:

"I am very much obliged, indeed, for your very kind and friendly letter; and I will at once say, were I able to leave, there is nothing I should like better than to go to America, especially as I feel sure I should receive a hearty welcome from those who have descended from the same stock as well as from others in your hospitable and flourishing country.

"As to the Coat of Arms, I find in the end of the fourteenth century the castle was granted by Edward the Black Prince to John Bartelot for taking the castle of Fontenoy, after the battle of Poictiers. I find that crest used till the sixteenth century, when the swan is introduced and granted by the garter king of arms. Your seal that you sent me is substantially correct.[1] I may here mention, that upon the record of the family, a Richard, John and Thomas Bartelot, who lived here, were born between 1580 and 1590 (sons of Edmund Bartelot), and there their record ends, they having gone, and very likely to America; and John Bartelot, living at Ernely, did get rid of his property there in 1634.

"I have again just examined your seal, and it is, I may say, quite accurate. Our *name* is spelled in all sorts of ways, so I am not surprised that it is differently spelled in America."

Since writing the above, Col. Walter Bartelot has been created, by Queen Victoria, a Baronet.

Mr. Levi Bartlett says: "From the statements made in Col. Bartelot's letter, I think there can be no doubt that Richard and John Bartlett of Newbury were sons of Edmund Bartelot of Ernely and Stopham."

We learn from Mr. Levi Bartlett, that over one hundred Bartletts have graduated from the several colleges of the country; and that seven of the lineal descendants of Richard Bartlett of Newbury, Mass., have been Judges in the courts of New Hampshire.

In John Fox's Book of Martyrs, printed in 1610, Richard, Robert, Sarah and Isabel Bartlet are mentioned as Protestant martyrs, persecuted by John Longland, popish Bishop of the diocese of Lincoln, in the year 1521.

---

[1] "The seal sent was a *fac simile* of the arms of the Bartletts in this country, in red sealing wax."—*Levi Bartlett.*

POORE.

John Poore came from Wiltshire, England, to New England, in 1635. In 1638, Alice Poore, aged 20, Samuel Poore, aged 18, and Daniel Poore, aged 14, came to New England with the family of Richard Dummer, in the ship Bevis, from the port of Southampton, England. There was also a Thomas Poore, who died in Andover, Mass., in 1695. It is believed that they were all members of the same family. They are supposed to have been descendants of Philip Poor of Amesbury, Wiltshire, England; a tradition to this effect, says Major Benjamin Perley Poore, has come down in the family here, and was also transmitted to the family of Sir Edward Poore of Wiltshire, England. Mr. Joseph Fullerton, in his "History of Raymond, New Hampshire," says that he has made investigations for the purpose of connecting the American family of Poore with the old English family, and finds evidence of such a connection, although he has not as yet found positive proof of the fact. Major Poore says: "Philip Poor of Amesbury, England, who died in 1571, aged 71 years, added a final e to his name and the Wiltshire Poores have since used it. It is also certain that the first settlers of the name in New England spelled their name with the final e, although in some branches of the different families it was subsequently omitted, to be in some instances restored."

In the list of the names of those who composed the first English colony in Virginia, in 1585, is the name of Richard Poore.

John Poore settled in Newbury on the south-easterly side of the Parker River, in the part of the town called the Neck. He was one of the original proprietors of the town. The house built by him is still standing, and has always remained in the family. "Nov. 20, [1650] the town granted John Poore, twenty-two acres of upland, in consequence of his living so remote from meeting and difficulty in coming over the ferry and for his satisfaction."[1] John Poore, we are told, was attorney for his brother Daniel, in a case brought by the latter "against Jo Godfrey and Walter Wright."

John Poore married Sarah ——. Their children were: Jonathan; John; Hannah, who died young; Elizabeth, who probably died unmarried; Mary, died in infancy; Hannah, married Elisha, son of William Ilsley; Henry; a second Mary, who probably died young; Joseph; a third Mary, married John, son of Richard Clark of Rowley; Sarah, married John, son of William Sawyer of Newbury; Lydia, married Penuel, son of William and Joanna (Bartlett) Titcomb; Edward; Abigail, probably died young; and a second Abigail, who married Isaac, son of William Ilsley. John Poore died Nov. 23, 1684, aged 69 years. We are told that he lost his way while hunting for game in the woods, and perished. His wife died Dec. 3, 1702.

Jonathan, son of John Poore, married Rebecca ——. They had a daughter Rebecca; and a son John, who married Ann, daughter of Stephen and Abigail (Thompson) Longfellow; Stephen was a son of William and Ann (Sewall) Longfellow.

John, the second son of John Poore, born June 21, 1642, had his father's homestead. He was frequently appointed to offices of trust, being constable, tax collector, tything man, appraiser of estates, etc. He married Feb. 27, 1666, Mary, daughter of William and Joanna (Bartlett) Titcomb of Newbury. Their chil-

[1] "History of Newbury." Coffin.

dren were: John; Mary; Sarah; Elizabeth, married Joseph, son of William and Elizabeth Morse; Hannah; Jonathan; Judith; and John. John Poore, Jun., died Feb. 15, 1701.

Henry, son of John Poore, Sen., married Abigail, daughter of Thomas Hale, son of Thomas Hale, Sen., the first of the name in the country. Their children were: Abigail, Henry, Jeremiah, Mary, a second Mary, Hannah, Sarah, Benjamin and Daniel.

Joseph, son of John Poore, Sen., married Mary Wellington. Their children were: Joseph, Benjamin, Sarah, Mary, Abigail, Hannah, John and Lydia.

Edward, son of John Poore, Sen., married Elizabeth ——. Their children were: Stephen, Elizabeth and Joseph.

Samuel Poore, one of the brothers who came to New England in 1638, settled in Newbury, at Indian Hill. He married, but the name of his wife I have not been able to learn. His children were: Rebecca; Mary; Samuel, married Rachel Bailey; Edward; Joseph; Sarah; Benjamin, married widow Mary Hardy; and a second Mary. Samuel Poore died Dec. 31, 1683, at 60 years of age.

Daniel, the youngest of the brothers, settled in Andover, Mass. He married Oct. 20, 1650, Mary Farnum, daughter probably of Ralph Farnum. Their children were: Daniel and John. Daniel married Mehitable ——. Their children were: Daniel, Mehitable, John, Samuel, Joseph, and Thomas.

The Poores who first settled in different parts of Newbury, in Rowley and in Andover, were, almost without exception, tillers of the soil. In the early wars,—King William's, Queen Anne's, Father Rasle's, and the French,—we are told by Major Poore, "the name of Poore was honorably borne on many a muster-roll; and for three successive generations, members of the different branches of" the "family were engaged in a series of sanguinary but almost forgotten conflicts, on the frontier of Canada, the banks of the St. Lawrence, at Louisburg and in Cuba. Capt. Jonathan Poor, a hero of the French and Indian wars, was early on duty in the Revolutionary war. Capt. Joseph Poor, another veteran Indian fighter, marched at the head of his company from Byfield to Cambridge, in April, 1775. On the roll of Capt. Thomas Poor's company in Col. Frye's regiment, formed on the 2d of February, 1777, were the names of Abram Poor, Stephen Poor, Timothy Poor, Jr., Daniel Poor and Peter Poor, Jr. Capt. Thomas Poor, who had in his youth led a company against the French in Canada, was promoted during the Revolutionary war to the rank of Colonel, and his brother Enoch Poor, who had removed to Exeter, commanded one of the New Hampshire regiments at Bunker Hill. Promoted to the rank of Brigadier-General in 1775, Gen. Enoch Poor fought bravely at Saratoga and Monmouth, and was in command of a brigade of light infantry under La Fayette." He was in the camp at Valley Forge, and his brigade was among the first troops that commenced a pursuit of the British across New Jersey. He was killed in a duel with a French officer, Sept. 8, 1780. Washington, in announcing his death to Congress, said he was "an officer of distinguished merit, who as a citizen and a soldier had every claim to the esteem of his country." His funeral was attended by Washington and La Fayette. Gen. Poor was greatly esteemed by the latter, who, it is said, was much affected on visiting his grave in the church-yard at Hackensack, N. J., when in this country, in 1825.

Mary, daughter of Gen. Poore, married Rev. John Cram, who died in Exeter. Patty, another daughter, married Col. Bradbury Cilley of Nottingham; and Harriet, another daughter, married Jacob Cilley. Gen. Poore was a descendant of Daniel Poore of Andover, Mass.

Daniel Warren Poore, D. D., born Jan. 27, 1789, was

a descendant also of Daniel of Andover. He sailed from Newburyport to Ceylon as a missionary, Sept. 3, 1815. After residing a while at Tillipally, he removed to Barricotta, where he opened a Scientific Seminary. He is said to have possessed the highest qualifications for the work he was engaged in, combining good judgment with great affability of manners, and a "stock of learning that gave him rank with the best scholars." He was the author of a variety of works in the Tamil and English languages. He died of cholera, at Jaffria, Ceylon, March 23, 1816.

Major Benjamin Perley Poore, the author and journalist, was born in Newbury, Nov. 2, 1820. He published and edited the "Southern Whig," at Athens, Ga., and later was the historical agent of Massachusetts in France, where he compiled ten folio volumes of important documents. He was foreign correspondent of the "Boston Atlas;" editor of the "Boston Daily Bee," and proprietor of the "Boston American Sentinel." Since 1854, he has been the Washington correspondent of the "Boston Journal." He is Secretary of the United States Agricultural Society, and editor of its Journal. He is the author of a "Life of Gen. Taylor," "Rise and Fall of Louis Phillippe," "Agricultural History of Essex County, Massachusetts," "The Conspiracy Trial," and a "Congressional Dictionary." Indian Hill farm, in Newbury, the homestead of Samuel Poore, the ancestor of Major Poore, who came to New England in 1638, is the home of Major Poore. The ninth generation of the family is represented by Benjamin Perley Poore Moseley, the son of Mrs. Frederick Strong Moseley, the only child of Major Poore.

The following account of Bishop Roger Poor, the great-uncle of Philip of Wiltshire (see page 201), is chiefly from Major Poore's Address to the Poores, at their gathering at Newburyport, in 1881;

Prince Henry, the third and youngest son of William the Conqueror, while riding one morning at the head of his mounted men-at-arms, in the vicinity of Caen, in Normandy, approached a small chapel of the Roman Catholic faith just as its bell rang forth the call to matin-prayers. The prince, we are told, halted his men and entered the sanctuary, where he was at once recognized by the parish-priest, a tall, gaunt man known as Father Roger, who dispatched the morning service with wonderful rapidity. "Whereat they were so well pleased that the prince said to him: 'Follow my camp,' which he did." Soon after, the prince went to England, and took Father Roger with him as his chaplain. On crossing the channel, every Norman assumed a surname, and the Caen chaplain became Roger Poor. When Henry became king, he retained Roger Poor as his chaplain, and made him his private secretary, Bishop of Sarum, and eventually Chief Justician, or Lord High Chancellor, which made him in reality Prime Minister. Up to this time, we are told, the crown of England had only descended in the male line; for, although Queen Boadicea had ruled over the Britons, no female had ever sat on the Anglo-Saxon throne. Bishop Roger Poor, to please King Henry who wished to leave the crown to his daughter Matilda, "laid it down as incontrovertible doctrine 'that the crown like a private inheritance should descend to the daughter of the person last seized.' He was also greatly instrumental in obtaining from the Barons of England as well as those of Normandy, a recognition of the Princess Matilda as the successor to her father in both countries. Under the decree promulgated by Bishop Poor, Queen Victoria now occupies the British throne, and it was the origin of what is now termed 'Norman Rights.'"

Vast wealth flowing in upon Bishop Poor, he built a castle at Devizes, which is said to have been one of the largest, strongest, most sumptuous and stately edifices in England. He built a second at Sherborne, little inferior; and repaired the castle of Sarum, which had been injured by a storm soon after its dedication. In the old English chronicles, he is styled the "great builder of churches and castles." He was also called "Roger the Great." He is said to have brought several of his relations from Normandy and obtained for them honorable positions. One of his nephews, Alexander, afterwards called "Alexander the Magnificent," was made Archdeacon of Sarum, next Chancellor, and finally in 1123, Bishop of Lincoln. Another nephew Nigillus, was appointed a Prebend in the church of St. Paul's, and in 1133, Bishop of Ely..

"Late in life King Henry quarrelled with Bishop Roger Poor, and dismissed him from civil office. For this the Bishop revenged himself after the King's death in 1135, by forgetting his sworn allegiance to the Princess Matilda and aiding in giving the crown to Stephen, Earl of Blois. He defended himself by asserting that circumstances had changed, but that he remained consistent to his principles, and he was rewarded by a restoration to his position as Chief Justician." The Bishop of Ely, his nephew was appointed Treasurer of the realm, and his son Roger Poor was made Chancellor. King Stephen also gave Bishop Roger Poor extensive landed possessions yielding large revenues. "The Bishop obtained a grant of the burgh of Malmsbury, and displayed his characteristic fondness for building by commencing a stately castle there like those at Devizes and Sherborne."

We are told by Knight, that "the English Church in the reign of Stephen, had become more completely under the papal dominion than at any previous period of its history. The King attempted, rashly perhaps, but honestly, to interpose some check to the ecclesiastical desire for supremacy; but from the hour when he entered into a contest with bishops and synods, his reign became one of kingly trouble and national misery. The Norman bishops not only combined in their own persons the functions of the priest and of the lawyer, but were often military leaders. As barons, they had knight-service to perform; and this condition of their tenures naturally surrounded them with armed retainers. That this anomalous position should have corrupted the ambitious churchman into a proud and luxurious lord was almost inevitable. The authority of the crown might have been strong enough to repress the individual discontent, or to punish the individual treason of these great prelates; but every one of them was doubly formidable as a member of a confederacy over which a foreign head claimed to preside. There were three bishops whose intrigues King Stephen had especially to dread, at a time when an open war for the succession of Matilda was on the point of bursting forth.

"Roger, the Bishop of Salisbury, had been promoted from the condition of a parish priest at Caen, to be chaplain, secretary, chancellor, and chief justician of Henry I. He was instrumental in the election of Stephen to the throne; and he was rewarded with extravagant gifts, as he had been previously rewarded by Henry. Stephen appears to have fostered his rapacity, in the conviction that his pride would have a speedier fall; the king often saying, 'I would give him half of England if he asked for it, till the time be ripe he shall tire of asking, ere I tire of giving.' The time was ripe in 1139. The bishop had erected castles at Devizes, at Sherborne, and at Malmsbury. King Henry had given him the castle of Salisbury. This lord of four castles had powerful auxiliaries in his nephews, the Bishop of Lincoln and the Bishop of Ely. Alexander had built the castles of Newark and Sleaford, and was almost as powerful as his uncle. In July, 1139, a great council was held at Oxford; and hither came these three bishops with military and secular pomp, and with an escort that became 'the wonder of all beholders.' A quarrel ensued between the retainers of the bishops and those of Alain, Earl of Brittany, about a right to quarters; and the quarrel went on to a battle, in which men were slain on both sides.

"The Bishops of Salisbury and Lincoln, were arrested as breakers of the king's peace. The Bishop of Ely fled to his uncle's castle at Devizes. The king, under the advice of the sagacious Earl Mellent, resolved to dispossess these dangerous prelates of their fortresses which were all finally surrendered. 'The bishops, humbled and mortified, and stripped of all pomp and vain-glory, were reduced to a simple ecclesiastical life, and to the possessions belonging to them as churchmen.' The contemporary who writes this—the author of the 'Gesta Stephani,'—although a decided partisan of Stephen, speaks of this event as the result of mad counsels, and a grievous sin that resembled the wickedness of the sons of Korah and Saul. The great body of the ecclesiastics were indignant at what they considered an offence to their order. The Bishop of Winchester, the brother of Stephen, had become the pope's legate in England, and he summoned the king to attend a synod at Winchester. He there produced his authority as legate from Pope Innocent, and denounced the arrest of the bishops as a dreadful crime. The king had refused to attend the council, but he sent Alberic de Vere, 'a man deeply versed in legal affairs,' to represent him. This advocate urged that the Bishop of Lincoln was the author of the tumult at Oxford; that whenever Bishop Poor came to court, his people, presuming on his power, excited tumults; that the bishop secretly favoured the king's enemies, and was ready to join the party of the empress. The council was adjourned; but on a subsequent day came the Archbishop of Rouen, as the champion of the king, and contended that it was against the canons that the bishops should possess castles; and that even if they had the right, they were bound to deliver them up to the will of the king as the times were eventful, and the king was bound to make war for the common security. The Archbishop of Rouen reasoned as a statesman; the Bishop of Winchester as the pope's legate.

"Some of the bishops threatened to proceed to Rome; and the king's advocate intimated that if they did so, their return might not be so easy. Swords were at last unsheathed. The king and the earls were now in open hostility with the legate and the bishops. Excommunication of the king was hinted at; but persuasion was resorted to. Stephen, according to one authority, made humble submission, and thus abated the rigour of ecclesiastical discipline. If he did submit, his submission was too late. Within a month Earl Robert and Matilda were in England."[1]

We are told that upon the flight of Nigillus, Bishop of Ely, to his uncle's castle at Devizes where he prepared for resistance, "the king, enraged at his contumacy, marched with a body of troops to Devizes, carrying with him Bishop Poor and his son as prisoners. Bishop Nigillus refusing to surrender, King Stephen ordered a gallows to be erected, and informed Bishop Roger Poor that his son Roger, to whom he was tenderly attached, should be hung unless the castle was surrendered to him. The aged prelate supplicated for mercy, and with difficulty prevailed upon his nephew to open the gates of the castle. The bishop's sacred office protected him from violence, but the treasures which he had accumulated through long years of prosperity were seized by King Stephen, and the old man sunk under his troubles, dying in December, 1139."

"Alexander Poor, Bishop of Lincoln, succeeded his uncle as Lord Chancellor, but died while on a mission to the Pope in 1147. The great seal was then entrusted to Bishop Roger Poor's natural son Roger,

---

[1] "Knight's History of England," Vol. I., pp. 286–288.

who possessed neither the ability or pliancy of his father. Taking part with the barons who held their castles against the king, he was made prisoner, and refused to take the oath of submission even when threatened with the penalties of treason. As a singular favour he was allowed to leave the realm, and he died in exile.

"Another nephew of Bishop Roger Poor, Richard Poor, located himself in Gloucester, and brought up three sons, Herbert, Richard and Philip. The two first named were educated for the church, and were advanced by old friends of their great-uncle, Bishop Roger.

"Herbert Poor was made Arch-Deacon of Canterbury, and in 1194, was consecrated Bishop of Sarum. In 1196, he appears on the rolls as one of the king's justices, and in 1199, he attended at the coronation of King John." The consent of King John was obtained for the erection of a cathedral at Salisbury, but the work was postponed on account of civil troubles and the confiscation of the church revenues. Bishop Herbert Poor died in May, 1217."

Richard Poor, brother of Herbert, was made Dean of Sarum, and, in 1215, Bishop of Chichester. Under his direction, the cathedral at Salisbury was commenced. "The stately Gothic pile soon rose in all its fair proportions. In unity of design, and as a specimen of old English ecclesiastical architecture, it is unequalled.

"Bishop Richard Poor was translated to the see of Durham before the cathedral was completed. 'He was,' says Godwin, 'a man of rare learning in those times, and of notable integrity in his life and conversation.' Matt Paris says that, perceiving the approach of death, he caused the people to be assembled and from the pulpit addressed them in a pious discourse, desiring them to mark well his exhortations, as he was shortly to be taken from them. The next day he did the same, bidding them farewell. The third day he sent for his particular acquaintances, and calling together his family and servants, distributed among them his last benefactions. He then tenderly dismissed each individual, and having arranged his temporal affairs, betook himself to prayer, in which act of devotion he gave up the ghost, on the 13th of April, 1237.

"Salisbury cathedral contains the monument of Bishop Roger Poor, brought from Sarum, and of Bishop Richard Poor. In the library are manuscript books of the Old and New Testaments, transcribed under the auspices of Bishop Poor, and also his seal."

Philip Poor, the son of Richard Poor of Gloucester, and brother of Bishop Herbert, and Bishop Richard Poor, settled in Amesbury, Wiltshire, Eng., and from him it is believed that all of the Poores in America are descended. The Poores of Wiltshire held various local offices, and, in 1795, John Methuen Poore was created a Baronet. He was unmarried, and the provision was made for the inheritance of the title by his brother Edmund. He survived his brother and his brother's eldest son, and on his death the baronetcy descended to his grand-nephew, Sir Edward Poore.

Roger Poor, believed to have been a descendant of Bishop Roger Poor, accompanied Richard Strongbow, Earl of Pembroke, on his expedition to Ireland to reinstate Dermoid MacMurrough in his kingdom of Leinster. He was knighted as Sir Roger Le Poer, and Cambrensis says of him: "He was the youngest, bravest and handsomest of all the Anglo-Norman knights; although he was young and beardless, he showed himself a lusty, valiant and courageous gentleman. He became marshal and standard bearer to Ireland, and he had a large estate granted to him, on a portion of which the city of Waterford now stands. The family, which afterward changed the name to Power, has since been prominent in that section of Ireland, and has always been loyal to the crown of England. In 1662,

Richard Le Poer was created Earl of Tyrone, but the earldom became extinct in 1704 for want of a male heir." "Later the daughter and heiress of the last earl married Sir Marcus Beresford, who was soon after created Earl of Tyrone. In 1786, the king called him to a seat in the British House of Peers, by the title of Baron Tyrone of Haverford, and three years later he was created Marquis of Waterford. The family name of this title now is De le Poer, and there is a large family connection of Powers, Poors and Le Poers.

The arms of the Poors are: Arg. a fesse az. between three mullets, gu. Crest—A cubit arm, erect, vested sa., slashed, arg. cuff ermine charged with two mullets, in fesse or. grasping in the hand an arrow, ppr. Motto—Pauper non in Spe.

SEWALL AND LONGFELLOW.

THE name of Sewall is of great antiquity in England, particularly in the county of Warwick. In Fuller's "Worthies of England," and in Dugdale's "Antiquities of Warwickshire," it is found as far back as the eleventh century, and occurs variously spelled, as Saswalo, Sewald, Sewalle, Seawall, Seawald, and Sewall. "Saswalo, or Saswald, before the Norman Conquest in 1066, was possessed of 17 hides of land (each hide being, according to Bailey, 'as much as one plough would cultivate in a year') in the village of Nether Eatendon, Warwickshire, where he resided, besides considerable tracts of country in the counties of Northampton, Lincoln and Derby. He built and endowed a church in the place of his residence, and from the extent of his possessions there, Dugdale concludes him to be a Saxon Thane. But at the Conquest all his possessions fell into the hands of Henry de Ferriers, one of the knights, doubtless, of King William, and ancestor of the Earls of Derby by that name. His Norman lord allowed him, however, to retain his possessions at Nether Eatendon, and from him they passed down in the male line of his posterity to the year 1730, a period of about 700 years."[1] Several of his descendants were knighted.

Henry Sewall, the ancestor of the American Sewalls, was of Coventry, Warwickshire, England, and born in the year 1544, or about that time. He was Alderman of Coventry, and Mayor of the city in 1589 and 1606. He was a linen draper, and a man of large estate. He married Margaret, eldest daughter of Avery Graze-

---

[1] "American Quarterly Register," Vol. XIII., p. 249.

brook of Middleton, Warwickshire, Eng., about 1575. Their children were: Henry; Richard of Nuneaton, married Mary, sister of Sir William Dugdale; Anne, married Anthony Power of Kenilworth, Warwickshire, gent.; and Margaret, who married Abraham Randall of Coventry.

Henry Sewall died April 16, 1628, aged 84 years, and was buried in St. Michael's Church, Coventry. His will was dated Sept. 1, 1624.

Henry, the eldest son of Henry and Margaret Sewall, was baptized in St. Michael's Church, Coventry, April 8, 1576. He married Anne Hunt, and in 1623, or about that time, was residing at Manchester, Lancashire, Eng. In 1634, from dislike to the English hierarchy, he sent his only son Henry to New England "with English servants, neat cattle and provisions" to begin a plantation, and soon followed him. He settled in Newbury, at Old Town Green, where the first meeting-house stood; but, on the removal of the meeting-house, he sold his house and land, and removed to Rowley, where he purchased land. He died there in 1657.

Henry, his son, had a grant of five hundred acres of land in Newbury, and was the founder of the town. He was made a freeman, May 16, 1637, at the Court of Election held that year in Cambridge, traveling with others forty miles on foot for that purpose, that he might strengthen the hands of Gov. Winthrop against Sir Henry Vane. He was four times chosen a Representative to the General Court.

He was married, March 25, 1646, by Richard Saltonstall, Esq., to Jane, eldest daughter of Stephen and Alice (Archer) Dummer of Newbury. The following winter he and his wife returned to England with Mrs. Sewall's father and mother, the New England climate "not being agreeable" to Mr. and Mrs. Dummer. They resided first at Warwick, afterwards at Bishop-Stoke and Baddesly in Hampshire. At the last mentioned places and at Tamworth five children were born to them.

Mr. Sewall made a voyage to New England for the purpose of visiting his father, and in 1659 he came again to New England for the purpose of settling his father's estate, his father having deceased in his absence from the country. He brought with him a letter from Richard Cromwell, the Protector, to the Governor and Assistants of Massachusetts, in which he is spoken of as being "Minister of North Baddesly in our county of Southampton;" "laborious and industrious in the work of the ministry, and very exemplary for his holy life and good conversation." He purposed returning to England, but it is certain that he never did. The change in his plans may have been owing to the unsettled state of affairs in England, or to the restoration of King Charles II. and the re-establishment of Episcopacy which followed. He sent for his family, and the following account of their voyage is given by his son, Judge Samuel Sewall:

"My mother went to Winchester with 5 small Children, Hannah, Samuel, John, Stephen and Jane; and John Nash and Mary Hobs her Servants; there to be in readiness for the Pool Waggons. At this place her near Relations, especially my very worthy and pious Uncle Mr. Stephen Dummer took leave with Tears. Capt. Dummer of Swathling treated us with Raisons and Almonds. My mother lodged in Pump-yard, London, waiting for the going of the Ship, the prudent Mary, Capt. Isaac Woodgreen, Commander. Went by water to Graves-End where the Ship lay. Took in Sheep at Dover. Passengers in the Ship at the same time were Major Brown, a young brisk Merchant, and a considerable Freighter, Mr. Gilbert and his wife. He was Minister at Topsfield: Madam Bradstreet (then Gardener), Mrs. Martha, Mr. Pitkin's Sister, who died lately at Windsor, and many others. We were about eight weeks at sea, where we had nothing to see but Water and the Sky; so that I began to fear I should never get to Shoar again; only I thought the Capt. and Mariners would not have ventured themselves if they had not hopes of getting to Land again. Capt. Woodgreen arrived here on Saturday. I was overjoyed to see Land again, especially being so near it as in the Narrows. 'Twas so late by that time we got to the Castle, that our men held a discourse with them whether they should fire or no, and reckoned 'twas agreed not to doe it. But presently after the Castle fired; which much displeased the Ship's company; and then they fired. On the Lord's day my Mother kept aboard; but I went ashoar, the Boat grounded, and I was carried out in arms, July 6, 1661. My Mother lodg'd at Mr. Richard Collicotts. This week there was a publick Thanksgiving. My Father hastened to Boston and carried his Family to Newbury by Water in Mr. Lewis * * * * Brother Tappan has told me our arrival there was upon Lecture-day which was Wednesday. Mr. Ordway carried me ashore in his Canoe. We sojourned at Mr. Titcomb's."

The children of Henry and Jane (Dummer) Sewall were: Hannah, married Jacob Toppan of Newbury; Samuel; John; Stephen; Jane, married Moses, son of Capt. William Gerrish of Newbury; Anne; Mehitable, married William, son of William Moody of Newbury; and Dorothy, who married, first, Ezekiel Northend of Rowley, second, Moses Bradstreet of Rowley. Henry Sewall died March 16, 1700, aged 86 years. The Rev. Mr. Toppan, in a sermon preached after his death, gave him the character of a true Nathaniel. His widow died Jan. 13, 1701.

Samuel Sewall, the eldest son of Henry and Jane (Dummer) Sewall, was born in Bishop-Stoke, Hampshire, England, March 28, 1652. He was instructed by the Rev. Thomas Parker until he entered Harvard College, where he took his second degree in 1674. He was married by Gov. Bradstreet, Feb. 28, 1676, to Hannah, daughter of John and Judith (Quincy) Hull of Boston. Mr. Hull was master of the mint, a man of great wealth, and for several years treasurer of the province.

Samuel Sewall resided in Boston. He had a large family of children, only six of whom lived to matu.ity. They were: Samuel; Hannah, died unmarried at 44 years of age; Elizabeth; Joseph; Mary, married Samuel, son of Rev. Josiah Gerrish; and Judith, who married Rev. William Cooper, pastor of the Brattle Street Church (his son succeeded him in the same pastorate). Mrs. Sewall died Oct. 19, 1717. Samuel Sewall married, Oct. 29, 1719, Abigail, daughter of Jacob Melyen, and widow of William Tilley. She died the 26th of May following. He married, March 29, 1722, Mary, daughter of Henry Shrimpton, and widow of Robert Gibbs, who survived him.

Moses Coit Tyler says of Samuel Sewall:

"A strong, gentle and great man was Samuel Sewall, great by almost every measure of greatness—moral courage, honor, benevolence, learning, eloquence, intellectual force and breadth and brightness. . . . . He had the usual education of a New England gentleman in those days. He was graduated at Harvard College. He tried his hand for a time at preaching—a vocation for which he was well qualified, but from which he was diverted into a prosperous and benign secular career. He became a member of the board of assistants, then of the council, judge of the supreme court, and finally its chief justice, holding the latter office until 1728, two years after which date he died. He was a man built, every way, after a large pattern. By his great wealth, his great offices, his learning, his strong sense, his wit, his warm human sympathy, his fearlessness, his magnanimity, he was a visible potentate among men in those days.

'Stately and slow, with thoughtful air,
His black cap hiding his whitened hair,

Walks the Judge of the Great Assize,
Samuel Sewall, the good and wise.
His face with lines of firmness wrought,
He wears the look of a man unbought,
Who swears to his hurt and changes not;
Yet touched and softened nevertheless
With the grace of Christian gentleness;
The face that a child would climb to kiss;
True and tender and brave and just,
That man might honor and woman trust.'[1]

"He had the courage to rebuke the faults of other people; he had the still greater courage to confess his own. Having, in 1692, fallen into the witchcraft snare, and having from the bench joined in the sentence of condemnation upon the witches, five years later—when more light had broken into his mind—he made in church a public confession of his error and of his sorrow. The Indians of Massachusetts had then no wiser or more generous friend than he; and he was, perhaps, the first of Americans to see and renounce and denounce the crime of negro slavery, as then practiced in New England. In 1700, he spoke out plainly on this subject, publishing a tract named 'The Selling of Joseph;' an acute, compact, powerful statement of the case against American slavery, leaving, indeed, almost nothing new to be said a century and a half afterward, when the sad thing came up for final adjustment. In this pamphlet one sees traces both of his theological and his legal studies; it is a lawyer's brief, fortified by Scriptural texts, and illuminated by lofty ethical intuitions. Within those three pages he has left some strong and great words—immortal and immutable aphorisms of equity. 'Liberty is in real value next unto life; none ought to part with it themselves, or deprive others of it, but upon most mature consideration.' 'All men, as they are the sons of

[1] "Prophecy of Samuel Sewall." Whittier.

Adam, are co-heirs, and have equal right unto liberty, and all other outward comforts of life.' 'Originally and naturally there is no such thing as slavery.' 'There is no proportion between twenty pieces of silver and liberty.'

"It gives still another charm to the memory of this practical and hard-headed mystic of New England, this wide-souled and speculative

'Puritan,
Who the halting step of his age outran,'

to discover that in a matter of very serious concern, he had the chivalry to come forward as the champion of woman. He tells us that once, while 'waiting upon a dear child in sickness,' he took up a book to read. It was a book called 'The British Apollo.' Presently his eye fell upon a startling question, worded thus: 'Is there now, or will there be at the resurrection, any females in heaven; since there seems to be no need of them there?' Very likely he then closed the book; and there, by the death-bed of his daughter, over whose resurrection this question threw its cold shadow, his mind set to work upon the problem thus presented; and afterward he fully resolved it, in an essay bearing this delectable title: 'Talitha Cumi; or, An Invitation to Women to look after their Inheritance in the Heavenly Mansions.' He begins by quoting the question that he had met with; then he proceeds to say: 'This malapert question had not patience to stay for an answer, as appears by the conclusion of it—'since there seems to be no need of them there.' 'T is most certain there will be no needless, impertinent persons or things in heaven. Heaven is a roomy, a most magnificent palace, furnished with the most rich and splendid entertainments; and the noblest guests are invited to partake of them. But why should there seem to be no need of women in heaven? . . . . To speak the truth, God has no need of any creature. His name is exalted far above all blessing and praise. But, by the same argument, there will be no angels nor men in heaven, because there is no need of them there.' He then discusses with judge-like care and fullness, *all* the arguments on both sides, that may be drawn from reason, Scripture, and the ancient and modern theologians, reaching at last this assertion: 'There are three women that shall rise again,—Eve, the mother of all living; Sarah, the mother of the faithful; and Mary, the mother of our Lord. And if these three rise again, without doubt all will.' In the course of the discussion he meets the objection that, upon a certain branch of his subject, 'the ancients are divided in their opinions.' His answer to this objection comes edged by a flash of wit: 'If we should wait till all the ancients are agreed in their opinions, neither men nor women would ever get to heaven.' "[1]

Samuel Sewall died Jan. 1, 1730, after an illness of about a month, in a "triumphant hope of immortal life."

Samuel, the eldest son of Judge Samuel and Hannah Sewall, was the proprietor of a large landed estate in Brookline, Mass., still called "Sewall's Farm." Sewall's Point, so called, was a part of it. He married Rebecca, daughter of Gov. Joseph Dudley. They had seven children, only one of whom—Henry—lived to maturity.

Henry married Ann White of Brookline. Their children that lived beyond the period of childhood were: Hull (Harv. Col.), married Abigail Sparhawk of Little Cambridge, now Brighton; Samuel; Henry (Harv. Col.), died unmarried; and Hannah, married Edward K. Wolcott of Brookline.

Samuel, the second son, was graduated at Harvard College and became a lawyer. He adhered to the Royal cause, and left the country as a refugee in

[1] "History of American Literature," Vol. II., pp. 99-103.

1776, forfeiting a large estate inherited from his mother.

Elizabeth, the second daughter of Judge Samuel and Hannah Sewall, married Grove Hirst, a wealthy merchant of Boston. Their children were: Mary, married Capt. William Pepperrell, afterwards Sir William (see account of the Pepperrells); Samuel (Harv. Col.); Elizabeth, married Rev. Charles Chauncy, colleague-pastor at the First Church; Hannah, married Nathaniel Balston; Jane, married Addington, eldest son of Rev. Addington Davenport, an Episcopal clergyman of Boston; William, died young; and a second William, also died young.

Rev. Joseph Sewall, D. D., son of Judge Samuel Sewall, was born in Boston, Aug. 15 (O. S.), 1688. He graduated at Harvard College in 1707, and studied for the ministry. Sept. 17, 1713, he was ordained as colleague of the Rev. Ebenezer Pemberton, pastor of the Old South Church in Boston. In 1724, Mr. Sewall was chosen to succeed Mr. Leverett, as President of Harvard College, but, owing to the unwillingness of his church to part with him, he declined. He was a warm friend to the College, and for many years made a liberal appropriation for the support of pious, indigent students; and after the fire which destroyed the College library, he gave a large number of valuable books to the College. He is said to have been distinguished above almost any other man of his time for devoted fervor, and simple and earnest engagedness in his work. His degree of Doctor of Divinity was conferred by the University of Glasgow. John Eliot said of him: "He was a man who seemed to breathe the air of Heaven while he was here upon earth." He was familiarly called the "good Dr. Sewall." He married Elizabeth, daughter of Hon. John Walley. Their children were Samuel and Joseph. The former became a merchant and a deacon of the Old South Church; also a selectman and a justice of the peace.

He married Elizabeth, daughter of Edmund Quincy, Esq. Their children were: Elizabeth, married Samuel Salisbury, Esq., of Boston; Hannah, married James Hill of Boston; Sarah, died unmarried; Samuel; Dorothy; Katherine, married Henry Gallison of Marblehead; and Joseph.

Samuel Sewall, LL. D., A. A. S., the eldest son of Samuel and Elizabeth Sewall, was born Dec. 11, 1757. He was graduated at Harvard College; studied law, and began practice at Marblehead. He soon became eminent in his profession. He was a member of the State Legislature; Judge of the Superior Court, from 1800 till 1813; and in 1814 was appointed Chief Justice, in which year he died. He married Abigail, daughter of Dr. Humphrey Devereaux of Marblehead. Their children were: Samuel (minister at Marblehead), married Martha Marrett; Henry Devreaux, married Mary Norton; Joseph H., died young; Lydia, married Samuel Greele; Anne Henchman; Joseph Henchman (Harv. Col.); Edmund Quincy, married Caroline Ward of Newton; Elizabeth Quincy, married Thomas R. Sewall; Charles Chauncy (Harv. Col., who became a minister), married Amy, daughter of William Peters, Esq., of Medfield.

Dorothy, daughter of Judge Samuel and Elizabeth Sewall, married Col. May of Boston. The wife of A. Bronson Alcott of Concord, was a daughter of theirs. They are the parents of Louise May Alcott, the popular authoress.

Joseph, the youngest son of Dea. Samuel Sewall, married Mary, daughter of Thomas Robie, Esq., of Salem. Their children who lived to maturity were: Mary; Thomas Robie, married Elizabeth Q. Sewall; Samuel Edmund; Edward Bradstreet; Martha Higginson; Elizabeth Salisbury; and Frances R.

Samuel Edmund, son of Joseph and Mary (Robie) Sewall, married Louisa M., daughter of Nathan Winslow of Portland. Mr. Sewall is a counselor-at-law in Boston, and resides in Melrose. He is a firm friend and advocate of the woman suffrage movement, and has published "The Legal Condition of Women in Massachusetts."

John, the second son of Henry and Jane (Dummer) Sewall, born Oct. 10, 1654, married Hannah Fessenden of Cambridge. Their children were: Hannah, died soon; a second Hannah, married Rev. Samuel Moody of York, Me.; John; Henry; Stephen; Samuel; Nicholas; a child that died soon; and Thomas, who died at college.

Henry, the eldest son of John and Hannah Sewall, born Sept. 7, 1682, married Elizabeth, daughter of Benaiah and Sarah (Brown) Titcomb of Newbury,—Benaiah was a son of William and Joannah (Bartlett) Titcomb. Their children were: Sarah, died young; Stephen; a second Sarah; Mary; Elizabeth; and Hannah. Stephen graduated at Harvard College in 1731, and was "an eminent teacher of youth in Newbury."

Samuel, the second son of John and Hannah (Fessenden) Sewall, married Lydia Storer. Their children were: John, died in childhood; Dummer, died at 21 years of age; Lydia; Mary, died in infancy; a second Mary; and Hannah. Samuel Sewall married for his second wife, Sarah, daughter of Samuel Batchelder of Reading, and widow of Joseph Titcomb of Newbury, Mass. Their children were: Samuel (Major), died unmarried; John; Joseph; Moses; David; Dummer (Col.); Sarah and Jane, twins, who both died young.

David Sewall, LL. D., the fifth son of Samuel and Sarah Sewall, was graduated at Harvard College in 1755. He was a classmate and friend of John Adams, (afterwards President). He studied for the profession of law, and began practice in York, Me., in connection with the office of Register of Probate. In 1777, he was appointed Associate Justice of the Supreme Court of Massachusetts; and in 1789 he was appointed by President Washington, a Judge of the United States

Court for the District of Maine. This Court then had the jurisdiction of the Circuit Court of the United States. He was the second educated lawyer of that State. He was President of the Board of Overseers of Bowdoin College for fourteen years. He is said to have been a good man, as well as a good lawyer, and is spoken of as the "upright judge." He was a man of great benevolence and of great purity of character. He was unassuming in his deportment, social and amiable in his manners. He died in 1826, at the age of 90 years, having filled the office of judge for forty-one years. He left no family.

Nicholas, the fifth son of John and Hannah (Fessenden) Sewall, married Mehitable Storer. Their children were: Stephen and Henry.

Stephen was born in York, Me., April 4, 1734, and was graduated at Harvard College in 1761. He taught the grammar school in Cambridge, and later he was teacher of Hebrew at Harvard College. He was the first Hancock Professor, and continued twenty years in that chair. He was a Representative from Cambridge, in 1777. He published a Hebrew grammar, some translations and obituary discourses, a Scripture History of Sodom and Gomorrah, and left in manuscript a Chaldee and English Dictionary. He died July 23, 1804. He is spoken of as the "learned and honored professor."

Henry, son of Nicholas and Hannah (Storer) Sewall, married Abigail, daughter of Joseph and Sarah (Batchelder) Titcomb of Newbury. Henry Sewall was a religious man, and a man of strong sense. His wife is said to have been an eminently devout person, possessed of good talents, and well educated. On her devolved chiefly the task of instructing her children. Her son, Rev. Jotham, in writing of this fact, said: "The instructions thus received impressed my mind while I was very young. I recollect having had many religious enquiries respecting the existence of God, the creation of the world, and my own existence, when I was about three years old, and from that time forward I had more or less religious thoughts. In the absence of my father, my mother frequently prayed with us; and some of the expressions she used impressed me. When teaching us the catechism, she often interspersed such remarks and exhortations as made me weep." Of his brother Henry, who was a soldier, he says: "When he was at home on a furlough, our mother would converse with him so seriously, especially before he left, that he could not forbear weeping. He would sometimes express fears that his mother would spoil him for a soldier."

Gen. Henry, the eldest son of Henry and Abigail Sewall, was born in York, Me., Oct. 24, 1762. He entered the army at the age of twenty-three as a private, and served through the Revolutionary war, rising to the rank of captain, and being at one time aid to Gen. Heath. He served for twenty years as General of militia. At the conclusion of peace, he settled in Augusta, and was appointed by his cousin, Judge David Sewall, Clerk of the District Court of Maine. He was also Register of Deeds for the county. He is said to have been a thoroughly upright, conscientious and religious man. He married, first, his cousin, Tabitha, daughter of John Lowell of Georgetown; second, Rachel Crosby; and his third wife was Elizabeth Lowell of Boston. He died Sept. 4, 1845.

Daniel, the second son of Henry and Abigail Sewall, was at one time in the Revolutionary army. He was appointed by Gov. Hancock, Register of Probate for York county, and held the office thirty-seven years. He engaged in the practice of law to some extent, and was chosen Clerk of the Court of Common Pleas. In 1792, he was appointed postmaster at York, and held the office fifteen years. He married Dorcas, daughter of John H. Bartlett of Kittery, Me., by whom he had one son, William Bartlett, and seven daughters. He died Sept. 5, 1845, aged 84 years. It is said that he was a man of remarkable diligence and punctuality, of singular fidelity, probity and perseverance, and possessed great moral courage and firmness.

His son, William Bartlett Sewall, was a graduate of Harvard College, and a member of the Phi Beta Kappa Society. He studied for the profession of law, but preferred the quiet pursuits of the scholar, and devoted much time to poetry and prose composition. While in practice, he prepared and published a Register of Maine. He was Secretary of the Senate; and later, he had charge of the editorial department of the "Portland Advertiser." It is said that he was a ripe scholar, of cultivated taste, and a fine writer.

Rev. Jotham, son of Henry and Abigail Sewall, and the youngest of five children, was born Jan. 1, 1760, at York, Me. He was ordained in 1800 as an evangelist, and was employed as a missionary until near the close of his life,—first by the Massachusetts Missionary Society, and afterwards by the Maine. His field of labor embraced a territory of hundreds of miles in extent, and he is said to have been greatly venerated. His ministry was a very successful one. He married, in 1787, Jenny Sewall of Bath, Me. They had thirteen children,—seven sons and six daughters. He died Oct. 3, 1850. He preached until about three weeks before his death.

Rev. George Shepard, D. D., being at one time in Hallowell, Me., while Mr. Sewall was holding meetings in that place, thus wrote of him: "I heard at once so much of the peculiarities and excellencies of this venerable man (he was then on the border of seventy), that there was awakened within me a strong desire to see and hear him. My remembrance of that evening is one of high gratification, and even of admiration of his appearance and performance. In his person, he was tall, large, massive. Dignity, gravity, impressiveness were borne on his frame and features,—

one of those robust, compact, solidly-built men, whose very size and structure indicated the natively strong and great mind. The preaching of Father Sewall, on that evening, had as ever, its marked traits and excellencies. It was without a scrap of paper; with an uninterrupted flow, with clear, logical order; a singular, almost a conversational simplicity, an occasional quaintness of language; and was pervaded by an earnest warmth, and finished by a faithful application. . . .

"He was a man who could relish and who could give the genial, jocose remark. His wit and pleasantry will not be soon forgotten. . . . He was the instrument in the conversion of a great many souls. . . . 'What a *wide* man he is!' was once the exclamation of a little girl to her mother, as the venerable patriarch withdrew from the room—true in another sense than as applied to his singular breadth of frame—a wide man he was in the reach of his Christian heart, and in his labors for the good of souls; broad the field which under God he blessed; bright, we believe, his crown in Heaven."[1]

Major Stephen, the youngest son of Henry and Jane (Dummer) Sewall, born in England, Aug. 10, 1657, married Margaret, daughter of Rev. Jonathan Mitchell of Cambridge. Their children were: Margaret, married John Higginson of Salem (his second wife); Samuel; Susannah; Jonathan; Jane, married Rev. William Cooke; Mehitable, married Thomas Robie; Mitchell; Henry; Stephen; and Benjamin.

Samuel, the eldest son of Stephen and Margaret Sewall, born Nov. 24, 1689, was a mechanician and constructor of bridges. He possessed a vigorous and inventive mind, and was well versed in the principles of mechanics and philosophy. He was the author of a number of improvements in the arts; among which is

---

[1] "Annals of the American Pulpit," Vol. II., pp. 432–434. Sprague.

the construction of bridges on piles, which he first introduced at York, Me., in 1761. In 1786, he superintended the erection of the Charlestown bridge on this plan. He married Catherine, daughter of Samuel Lee, and widow of Henry Howell.

Jonathan, the second son of Stephen and Margaret Sewall, was a merchant. He married, first, Eliza Alford; second, Mary, a sister of Edward Payne. He had one son by his second wife—Jonathan, who was born Aug. 28, 1728, and was graduated at Harvard College in 1748. He married Esther, daughter of Edmund Quincy of Braintree. He was for some years a teacher in Salem, Mass., and afterwards practiced law in Charlestown, Mass.

In 1767, he was appointed Attorney-General of Maine. In May of the same year, he began a suit—James *versus* Richard Lechmere—to obtain the freedom of a negro from his master. The suit was decided the following year in favor of the negro,—two years before the settlement of the case of the negro Somerset, which Blackstone commends so highly.

In 1768, he was appointed Judge of the Admiralty Court for Nova Scotia, but did not remove there. At the commencement of the Revolution, he resided in Cambridge in the Vassal house, subsequently Washington's headquarters, and later the home of the poet Longfellow. Mr. Sewall was a Royalist, and, early in 1775, went to England, being one of the prescribed. He was an intimate friend of John Adams (afterwards President), and it is said that in a discussion which they had in July, 1774, upon the great questions then agitating the country, Mr. Adams terminated the conversation by saying, "I see we must part; and with a bleeding heart I say it—I fear forever; but you may depend upon it, that this adieu is the sharpest thorn on which I have set my foot." They did not meet again until 1788, when Mr. Adams, then embassador of the free American States, called upon him in London.

In 1779, Mr. Sewall removed to St. John, N. B., and continued to hold the office of Judge of the Admiralty Court until his death, which occurred Sept. 26, 1796. He was author of a number of political papers.

Jonathan Sewall, LL. D., a son of Judge Jonathan Sewall, was born in Canada, in 1760. He was a resident of Quebec. He was admitted to the bar, and was appointed Solicitor-General; in 1793, Advocate and Attorney-General; and in 1795, Judge of Vice-Admiralty. He was a member of three successive Parliaments, and in 1808, was appointed Chief Justice of Lower Canada. He was President of the Executive Council, from 1808 till his death, which occurred Nov. 12, 1839. He was author of a "Memoire of Sir James Craig," and an Essay on the Judicial History of France, so far as it relates to the law of the Province of Lower Canada.

Mitchell, the third son of Stephen and Margaret (Mitchell) Sewall, married Elizabeth Price. They had one son, Jonathan Mitchell, who was adopted by his uncle, Chief Justice Stephen Sewall, and educated for the bar. He was distinguished as a lawyer and a poet; also, as a wit.

Stephen, the fifth son of Joseph and Margaret (Mitchell) Sewall, was born Dec. 18, 1704. He was graduated at Harvard College in 1721, and was a tutor there from 1728 to 1739. He taught school in Marblehead, and preached acceptably. In 1732, he was appointed Judge of the Superior Court, and in 1752 he was appointed Chief Justice. He was also a member of the Council from 1752 till his death, which occurred Sept. 10, 1760. He died unmarried.

Ann, the third daughter of Henry and Jane (Dummer) Sewall, born in Newbury, Sept. 3, 1662, was married, Nov. 10, 1678, to William Longfellow of Newbury. Mr. Longfellow was born in Hampshire, England, 1651, and came to Newbury while young, settling in that part of the town called the Falls. He went, says Judge Samuel Sewall, in 1687, to England to obtain his patrimony in Yorkshire, and after his return was made ensign of the Newbury company. Their children were: William; Stephen, died young; Anne; a second Stephen; Elizabeth; and Nathan, who married Mary Green. In 1690, William Longfellow, as ensign of the Newbury company, was one of the expedition to Quebec under Sir William Phips. On the return of the expedition, a violent storm overtook the fleet in the Gulf of St. Lawrence, and scattered the vessels; and one of them, containing the Newbury company, went ashore at the island of Anticosti, and William Longfellow, with nine others, was drowned.

His widow married, May 11, 1692, Henry, son of Henry and Sarah (Glover) Short. Their children were: Jane; Samuel, died young; Mehitable; a second Samuel, died young; a third Samuel; Hannah, died in infancy; and Joseph. Mrs. Sewall died in 1706.

Lieut. Stephen, son of William and Anne Longfellow, born Sept. 22, 1685, married Feb. 5, 1728, Abigail, daughter of Rev. Edward Thompson of Marshfield. Their children were: William; Ann, married John, son of John and Rebecca Poore of Newbury; Edward; Sarah; Stephen; Samuel; Abigail, died in infancy; Elizabeth, died young; and Nathan, died in infancy. Stephen Longfellow was a blacksmith, and was one of the selectmen of Newbury. He died Nov. 17, 1768, at Byfield, Mass.

Stephen, son of William and Abigail Sewall, born Feb. 7, 1723, was graduated at Harvard College in 1742, and became a school teacher in York, Me. In 1745, he removed to Falmouth, now Portland, Me., to teach the grammar school of that place, and continued to be the principal instructor in the place until he was appointed, in 1760, Clerk of the Judicial Court. Mr. Willis, in a sketch of his life, says: "Mr. Longfellow filled many important offices in the town to universal acceptance." "He was parish clerk twenty-three years; town clerk twenty-two years; many years clerk of the proprietors of the common land; and from the establishment of the county in 1760 to the commencement of the Revolution in 1775, he was register of probate and clerk of the Judicial Courts." He married, Oct. 19, 1749, Tabitha, daughter of Samuel Bragdon of York, Me. After the destruction of the town by Mowatt in 1775, Mr. Longfellow removed to Gorham, Me., where he resided until his death, which occurred May 1, 1790.

Of his three sons, Stephen, Samuel and William, the latter died in early life, and Samuel left no children. Stephen, the eldest, born Aug. 3, 1750, married Dec. 13, 1773, Patience Young of York, Me. He was extensively employed as a surveyor, and received appointments to various town offices. He represented Gorham in the General Court of Massachusetts, eight years; he was for several years Senator from Cumberland County, and from 1797 to 1811, Judge of the Court of Common Pleas. He is said to have been a fine looking man, with the bearing of the old school; erect, portly, rather taller than the average, with a strongly marked face. Rev. H. S. Burrage says of him: "He was a man of sterling qualities of mind and heart, great integrity, and sound common sense." He died greatly respected, May 28, 1824.

Stephen, his second child, born in Gorham, March 23, 1776, entered Harvard College in 1794. A college friend, Daniel Appleton White, said of him: "He was evidently a well-bred gentleman when he left the paternal mansion for the university. He seemed to breathe the atmosphere of purity as his native element, while his bright intelligence, buoyant spirits, and social warmth, diffused a sunshine of joy that made his presence always gladsome." Professor Sidney Willard, his classmate, in his "Memoirs of

Youth and Manhood," says of Longfellow: "He was a young man of remarkable maturity of judgment, and of quiet, affable and gentlemanly manners and demeanor, from his first entrance within the college walls to his exit. His kindness and courtesy were so unostentatious and sincere that they seemed to be innate. So early was his ability as a counselor and advocate of his younger fellow-students perceived by them and confided in, that, in cases of doubt or difficulty in matters of conduct, his advice was often sought and followed."

He was a member of the Phi Beta Kappa Society. He graduated with a full share of the honors of his class, and studied for the profession of law. He began practice in Portland, and at once became sucessful as a lawyer, and later was a leader in the profession. In 1814, he was sent to the Legislature of Massachusetts; and while engaged in this service, he was chosen a member of the celebrated Hartford Convention. In 1816, he was made a Presidential Elector, and in 1822 he was chosen a member of the Eighteenth Congress. At the close of his congressional term, he retired from political life, and devoted his remaining years to his profession. He was President of the Maine Historical Society, and Trustee of Bowdoin College. This college conferred upon him the degree of Doctor of Laws.

He married, Jan. 1, 1804, Zilpha, eldest daughter of Gen. Peleg Wadsworth. Gen. Wadsworth was the son of Deacon Peleg Wadsworth of Duxbury, Mass., and the fifth in descent from Christopher Wadsworth, who came from England and settled in that town previous to 1632. Peleg Wadsworth, Jr., was graduated at Harvard College in 1769, and married Elizabeth Bartlett of Plymouth, Mass. Their children, through their mother, and grandmother Wadsworth, who was Susannah Simpson, inherited the blood of five of the *Mayflower* pilgrims, including Elder Brewster and John Alden.

The children of Hon. Stephen and Zilpha Longfellow were: Stephen, married Marianne, daughter of Hon. William P. Preble of Portland; Henry Wadsworth; Anne, married George W. Pierce, a young lawyer of great promise, who died a few years after his marriage; Alexander Wadsworth, a member of the United States Coast Survey, married Elizabeth, daughter of Richard King Porter of Portland; Mary, married James, son of Hon. Simeon Greenleaf, late Royal Professor of Law at Harvard; and two daughters, Elizabeth and Ellen, lovely and accomplished girls, who died young.

We are told by Rev. H. S. Burrage, that "in the domestic circle, Mr. Longfellow's noble traits of character were no less apparent. His home was one of refinement, and the purest social virtues; and she who shared its direction with him, not only adorned it with rare womanly grace, but gave to it many an added charm."[1] Mr. Longfellow died Aug. 3, 1849.

Henry Wadsworth, his second child, was born in Portland, Feb. 27, 1809. He was named for his mother's brother, a lieutenant in the United States Navy, who was killed three years before by the explosion of a fire-ship before the walls of Tripoli, in the attempt to destroy the Barbary pirate flotilla.

Henry Longfellow was fitted for college in the Portland Academy, and entered Bowdoin College in 1821, at fourteen years of age, in company with his brother Stephen. A number of his early poems appeared while he was in college, in the newspapers of the time; and among them, "The Hymn of the Moravian Nuns." He was graduated in 1825, in the class with Hawthorne, his rank being second in a class of thirty-seven. He was assigned an English oration on "Native Writers." He began the study of law in his father's office, but was soon after elected to the newly established chair

[1] In the "Portland Weekly Advertiser," March 4, 1882.

of Modern Languages and Literature at Bowdoin College, and spent three years and a half in Europe in study of the principal modern languages. In 1833, appeared "Coplas de Manrique," his first published work, and the greater part of the essays collected as "Outre-Mer."

He married, Sept. 14, 1831, Mary Storer, daughter of Judge Barrett and Anne (Storer) Potter. Mrs. Potter was a daughter of Hon. Woodbury and Anne (Titcomb) Storer (see page 178). Col. Thomas W. Higginson says: "Mrs. Longfellow was, by the testimony of all who knew her, a person of rare loveliness of person and mind. . . . Her father was a Judge of Probate, and a man of strong character, holding very decided views as to the education of his children, of whom only the daughters lived to maturity. Although himself an old-fashioned classical scholar, he believed the study of Greek and Latin to be unsuitable for girls; all else was open to them—modern languages, literature and mathematics. For all these, especially the last, his daughter Mary had a strong taste; her note-books, preserved by her family, give, for instance, ample and accurate reports, recorded as being 'from memory,' of a series of astronomical lectures; and she learned to calculate eclipses, which must have been quite beyond the average attainments of young girls of her day. She was for several years a pupil at the excellent school of Mrs. Cushing, at Hingham; and all her school papers, abstracts and compositions show a thoughtful and well-trained mind. Some exhibit a metaphysical turn, others are girlish studies in history and geography, but the love of literature is visible everywhere, in copious extracts from the favorite authors of that day—Cowper, Young, Mrs. Hemans, Bernard, Barton, and even Coleridge and Shelley. Further on in the series of note-books the handwriting becomes firmer and maturer, and notes and translations appear upon the pages in the unmistakable autograph of Longfellow, almost precisely the same at twenty-four as at seventy-four."[1]

In 1835, Mr. Longfellow was called to succeed George Ticknor as Professor of Modern Languages and Literature in Harvard College. He took another European journey, by way of preparation, and visited the north of Europe with his young wife, who died at Rotterdam, Nov. 29, 1835. Under the shadow of this great sorrow, Mr. Longfellow returned to Cambridge, and began his college duties, in 1836. In 1839, appeared the exquisite prose poem, "Hyperion."

In 1839, Mr. Longfellow was again in Europe, and there met Frances Elizabeth, daughter of Nathan Appleton of Boston, to whom he was married in 1843. Of her, Col. Higginson writes: "Those of us who can recall the second Mrs. Longfellow will never forget her distinguished and noble presence, or the rare beauty of 'those deep unutterable eyes' the poet sang."

The same year, Mr. Longfellow bought the Craigie House in Cambridge,—a house rich in associations. It was built before 1747 by Col. John Vassal, whose family stone in the Cambridge church-yard bears only the goblet and the sun—Vas-sol. At his death, the property passed to his son, a tory, who forfeited all in the Revolution; then Washington had it for his headquarters. Its next possessor was Nathaniel Tracy (see page 175), "who appears to have been," we are told, "a sort of American Vathek, emulating as far as possible in an uncongenial clime, the magnificent doings of the Eastern prince. Traditions float down to us of the lavish opulence of these the golden days of Vassal Hall; how wine flowed like water, servants lived like kings, a hundred guests sat down every day at the banquet table, and from the far-off lands of the Orient, treasures of silk and jewels and gold flowed into the coffers"[2] of Nathaniel Tracy. He finally lost

[1] From an account of Longfellow in "N.Y. Evening Post," Mar. 25, '82.
[2] From the account of Longfellow in "Poets' Homes."

his vast wealth through the inability of the government to repay the large sums advanced by him during the war. The house was next occupied by Joseph Lee, the brother of Mrs. Tracy, and then was bought by Andrew Craigie, Apothecary-General of the army, who also failed. After his death, his widow rented rooms, and here Mr. Longfellow was located on coming to Cambridge. Here were born Mr. Longfellow's five children: Charles Appleton, Earnest Wadsworth, Edith, Alice Mary, and Anne Allegra. On July 9th, 1861, occurred the terrible tragedy of Mrs. Longfellow's death from her clothes taking fire.

In 1854, Mr. Longfellow resigned his professorship that he might devote his time wholly to literary work. The books he has since written have enriched the world. In the words of a recent writer, "If it may be said of any man 'that he is known all over the world,' it may be said of Henry Wadsworth Longfellow. His words seem to travel on the swift rays of light that penetrate into the uttermost parts of the earth. . . . He has the touch of nature that makes the whole world kin, for he is not more warmly appreciated in his native land than in the hearts and homes on the other side of the world."[1] He died March 24, 1882.

"Alike are life and death,
When life in death survives,
And the uninterrupted breath
Inspires a thousand lives.

"Were a star quenched on high,
For ages would its light,
Still traveling downward from the sky,
Shine on our mortal sight.

"So when a great man dies,
For years beyond our ken,
The light he leaves beyond him lies
Upon the paths of men."[2]

---

[1] "Poets' Homes." [2] From Longfellow's poem on "Charles Sumner."

DOW.

The name of Dow occurs in the English Hundred Rolls of the thirteenth century, in the time of Edward the First, and has been a common English name ever since. "Many of that name," we are told, "trace to a Scotch ancestry; and it has been a question whether the name originated in the early English Doue,—for in this way it is spelled in the early records,—or in the Scotch Dhu—black."[1]

Thomas Dow, one of the grantees of Newbury, Mass., removed to Salisbury, and afterwards to Haverhill, Mass. He was admitted a freeman, June 22, 1642. The Christian name of his wife was Phebe, but her surname is unknown. They had five children, viz.: John, Thomas, Stephen, Mary and Martha. Thomas Dow died May 31, 1654 (O. S.) He was the first adult, we are told by George W. Chase in his "History of Haverhill," who had died since the settlement of the town. In his will, which was made two days before his death, he bequeathed to his eldest son John all of his "housing and land," after providing for his wife. John was to pay legacies to his brothers Stephen and Thomas, and his sisters Martha and Mary. His wife was sole executrix.

The name of John Dow appears on the Muster Roll of Ensign Moses Higgins; also among the names of those appointed to guard the sixth garrison. We are told by Mr. Chase that in the fifth division of town lands, Mr. Coffin's right was purchased by John Dow. John and Thomas Dow were among the thirty-seven persons

---

[1] Mr. J. J. Dow of Fairbault, Minn.

who sent a petition to the General Court asking that the sentence of Robert Pike might be revoked.[1]

Thomas Dow married, about 1668, Elizabeth Duston, a sister probably of Thomas Duston who on the memorable 15th of March, 1697, saved his seven children when attacked by the savages.

Stephen, the youngest son of Thomas and Phebe Dow, born March 29, 1642, married, first Ann Storie; second, Joannah Hutchins, a widow. Their children were: Ruannah, Samuel, Hannah, Stephen, Martha and John. Stephen Dow was made a freeman in 1668. He lived in the east part of the town, and when the common was fenced in, we are told by Mr. Chase, a gate was ordered to be by his house. After the Indians became troublesome, he and his son Stephen were stationed at the sixth garrison. Mr. Chase, in writing of those times, says: "It was truly an age of terror.... Almost every man was a soldier, and many who lived in remote parts of the town, moved with their families, into the vicinity of a garrison, or a house of refuge. This was the case with Stephen Dow and his son, who lived in the east part of the town, and moved near to the garrison of Capt. John White. The Indians had a peculiar whistle, which was made by placing both hands to the mouth, and was known to be their call. It was frequently heard in the adjacent woods, and tradition says that Stephen Dow, Jun., was the only person in the garrison who could exactly imitate it; and that he frequently concealed himself, and endeavored to decoy them within range of the soldiers' bullets. But it does not say that he ever succeeded."

"The 15th of March, 1697," we are told by Mr. Chase, "witnessed one of the bloodiest forays of the whole war, and this town was the victim. On that day a party of about twenty Indians came suddenly,

[1] See Chase's History of Haverhill, p. 80.

and without warning, upon the western part of the town, and with the swiftness of the whirlwind, made their attack, and as suddenly disappeared. The first house attacked was that of Thomas Duston. Of this attack and the heroic exploits of Duston and his wife, there have been various accounts published and traditions handed down.... After the attack on Duston's house, the Indians dispersed themselves in small parties, and attacked the houses in the vicinity. Nine houses were plundered and reduced to ashes on that eventful day, and in every case their owners were slain while defending them. Twenty-seven persons were slaughtered, (fifteen of them children), and thirteen captured." Among the slain was Martha, daughter of Stephen Dow. She was twenty-three years of age.

Stephen Dow was a selectman in 1685, and a grand juror in 1692. His signature is on the agreement made by the school-teacher, Mr. James Chadwick, and the selectmen; also on the agreement made by the Rev. Benjamin Rolfe and the selectmen. The name of Stephen Dow is in a list of the names of the company commanded by Capt. John Hazen, at the reduction of Ticonderoga and Crown Point. Stephen Dow, Sen., died July 3, 1717.

Samuel, the eldest son of Stephen and Ann Dow, born Jan. 22, 1666, married May 5, 1691, Ruth, daughter of John and Elizabeth (Maverick) Johnson of Haverhill, and widow of Timothy Ayer of that place.

John Johnson was a son of William Johnson, a brickmaker of Charlestown, who is supposed to have been a brother of Capt. Edward Johnson, author of "Wonder-Working Providence of Zions Saviour in New England." John Johnson came to Haverhill in 1657, with his wife Elizabeth, daughter of Elias Maverick of Winnisimet, now Chelsea (see account of the Mavericks), and one child—John. We are told by Mr. Chase that he was a blacksmith, and that a house lot and various town accommodations were given him to induce him to settle in Haverhill. "He was an active and useful citizen, and became the founder of one of the largest and most respectable families in town." He represented the town in the General Court; was one of the deacons in the church; an officer of the militia, and became a large land owner. He was killed by the Indians, Aug. 29, 1708. The children of Samuel and Ruth Dow were: Ruth, Abigail, Samuel, Hannah, Timothy, Hepzibah, Ann and Peter.

Samuel Dow was one of the soldiers under the command of Lieut.-Col. Saltonstall. His name appears in the list of those who had estates in the east part of Haverhill, after the new State line had been made. He died Dec. 30, 1749.

The name of Peter, his son, is on the list of those who had estates in the east part of the town. His daughters Ruth and Abigail, with nine others, petitioned for permission to build a "womans pew" in the meeting-house.

Timothy, the second son of Samuel and Ruth Dow, born May 10, 1700, married Judith Worthen. Their children were: Hannah, Samuel, Deliverance, Mary, Elizabeth, Joshua and Ezekiel. The town of Haverhill having been divided, Timothy Dow's estate was in the part called Plaistow. He was a farmer, and his farm was on Sweet Hill, one of the most delightful spots in that region. He died July 22, 1777.

Ezekiel, his youngest son, was born Sept. 23, 1747. He inherited his father's farm, and remained through life in Plaistow. He married Sarah Merrill of that place. Their children were: James, Elizabeth, married Henry Tucker of Kingston, N. H.; Hannah, married Samuel Noyes of Plaistow; Francis, married Betsey Palmer of Boston; Sarah, married James Eaton of Plaistow; and Ezekiel. Ezekiel Dow, Sen., died April 4, 1832.

Ezekiel, the youngest son of Ezekiel and Sarah Dow,

born Nov. 26, 1789, married Elizabeth, daughter of John and Elizabeth (Follensbee) Bradley (see account of the Bradleys). Mr. Dow had a part of his father's estate, and spent many years in Plaistow. He finally sold his farm, and purchased another in Hopkinton, N. H., which, under his management, was awarded the first prize at a county fair. Late in life, he exchanged his farm for real estate in Chelsea, and removed to that city, where he remained several years, but finally returned to his native town. He took a deep interest in reforms, especially the temperance reform. He was a member of the Baptist church in Plaistow. For several years before his death, he was entirely helpless from paralysis, but was never known to murmur at his fate. He died in January, 1876.

Mrs. Dow was a woman of great energy and strength of character, and possessed a cheerful and amiable disposition. She died of paralysis, Oct. 30, 1872, in her eighty-second year. They had thirteen children.

Luther, the eldest, died in infancy.

Elizabeth, the eldest daughter, resided with her parents, and was the joy and stay of their declining years.

Elvira, the second daughter, married Joshua, son of Nathan and Susan (Bacon) Merrill of Bedford, Mass. Mr. Merrill went to Lowell, Mass., in 1827, to teach school, which he continued to do for eighteen years, resigning for the purpose of entering the book and stationery business, continuing in that thirty-five years. He has been a member of the City Council and the Legislature, and for fourteen years was a member of the school committee; he is now, at the age of eighty, in full possession of his mental powers.

Martha, the third daughter, married Rev. George Washington Bailey of Springfield, Vt. Mr. Bailey was for a number of years a member of the State Legislature, and is now Superintendent of Schools. Mrs. Bailey died Sept. 15, 1844.

Jesse, the second son, removed to Cambridgeport, where he was engaged as a manufacturer. He married Emeline Patten. He died Jan. 10, 1856.

Sarah Bradley, the fourth daughter, married Louis Frederick, son of Pearson and Anne Maria (de Les Dernier) Titcomb (see page 157).

Luther, the third son, removed to Portland, Me., and was a manufacturer in that place. He married Sarah Ann, daughter of Dearborn and Elizabeth (Godfrey) Lane. He died in September, 1854.

Catherine, the fifth daughter, married Arnold Otto, son of Arnold Otto Waldeck, an attorney-at-law in the Principality of Waldeck in Germany. Mr. Waldeck purchased a tract of land in Cordova, Ill., and removed there with his family; he died some years ago.

John Calvin, the fourth son, was an early resident of Lawrence, where he was engaged in business as a merchant; he married Mary, daughter of John Woodbridge and Anne Fawcett (Grafton) Fenno of Boston. The parents of Mrs. Dow were descendants of the Rev. John Woodbridge and Gov. Joseph Dudley.

Gilbert, the fifth son, was for many years a conductor on the Rock Island and Pacific Railroad, and was afterwards a merchant in Muscatine, Iowa. He married Mary Ellen, daughter of Asa Taft and Louisa (Currier) Groendycke. Mr. Dow died in 1873.

Harriet, the sixth daughter, is unmarried.

Jane, the seventh daughter, died young.

Julia, the eighth daughter, married George Martin, son of Jesse and Hannah (Woodley) Blaker. They reside at the South.

MAVERICK.

Early in the year 1630, preparations were made in England for a large emigration of Puritans to New England, or more particularly to the Massachusetts colony, and Winthrop's fleet was getting in readiness as speedily as possible. Previous to the 20th of March, a company of the Puritans assembled in the New Hospital in Plymouth, England, and formed themselves into a Congregational Church, choosing the Rev. John Maverick and the Rev. John Wareham to be their pastors. This company set sail from Plymouth on the 20th of March, in "that great ship of four hundred tons," the *Mary and John*, the first of Winthrop's fleet of seventeen ships. They arrived the 30th of May following at Nantasket (now Hull), and settled at Mattapan, which they named Dorchester.

The Rev. John Maverick was a minister of the Established Church, who resided about forty miles from Exeter, Eng., and is spoken of as being a famous minister. William H. Sumner, A. M.,[1] says: "Judging from the scattered accounts which have come down to us, he was a godly man, a beloved pastor and a safe and trustful guide in temporal and spiritual things." He took the freeman's oath on the 18th of May 1631, "and appears to have been active in his duties as a pastor and a citizen." Mr. Sumner says: "An instance is recorded by Winthrop of the wonderful working of a kind providence, in the preservation of the life of the Rev. Mr. Maverick and the meeting-house at Dorchester of which he had charge, and which contained

[1] In his History of East Boston, from which the following account is taken.

the military stores. From his ignorance as a magazine keeper, and not having any apprehension of danger, he incautiously attempted to dry some wet gunpowder in a pan over the fire! The powder ignited from the heat of the pan, and communicating with 'a small barrel of two or three pounds,' which was kept in the meeting-house as the only place of safety, exploded. The explosion instead of blowing up the house and all its contents, as might have been expected, '*only blackened the thatch of the house a little, and singed the parsons clothes.*'"

In 1635 the greater part of the church removed to Windsor, Conn., which was very disagreeable, we are told, to their ministers. They decided, however, to go with their people, and Mr. Wareham joined them in September, 1636. Mr. Maverick intended to join them the following spring, but did not live to do so. He died on the 3d of February, 1636–7, being about sixty years of age.

Samuel, a son of Rev. John Maverick,[1] was born in England about 1620, and came to New England some years before his father came, but the date is unknown. Savage thinks that he came in 1628 or 1629, and Drake also places his name on the list of those who were here as early as 1629. Capt. Edward Johnson says the planters in Massachusetts Bay at this time [1629] were William Blackstone at Shawmut (Boston), Thomas Walford at Mishawum (Charlestown), Samuel Maverick at Noddle's Island, and David Thompson at Thompson's Island (near Dorchester). It is evident that he was in the country in 1630, for Winthrop

---

[1] "1630. The Tenth of July, John Winthrop, Esq., and the Assistants arrived in New England, with the Patent for the Massachusetts, they landed on the North side of the Charles River, with him went over Thomas Dudley, Isaac Johnson Esquires; Mr. John Wilson, Mr. George Phillips, *Mr. Maverick* (the father of Mr. Samuel Maverick, one of his Majesties Commissioners) Mr. Wareham ministers."—*Josselyn.*

32

made his house a stopping-place on the 17th of June of that year, on his excursion from Salem "to the Massachusetts." Samuel Maverick is represented by early writers as a whole-souled, generous, hospitable man, of warm impulses and courteous behavior,—a royalist and Episcopalian, living in a strongly fortified residence on Noddle's Island." Capt. Edward Johnson, one of Winthrop's company, says: "On the north side of Charles River they [Winthrop's company] landed neare a small Island called Noddle's Island, where one Mr. Samuel Maverick [was] then living, a man of a very loving and courteous behaviour, very ready to entertaine strangers, yet an enemy to the Reformation in hand, being strong for the Lordly Prelaticall power, one this island he had built a small fort with the helpe of one David Tompson, placing therein four Murtherers [small cannon] to protect him from the Indians." Josselyn, who visited New England in 1638, speaks of Mr. Maverick as "the *only* hospitable man in all the country, giving entertainment to all comers *gratis*."

It is conjectured that Mr. Maverick was one of those who came over to settle the Gorges' patent (possibly with Robert Gorges, in 1623), as he with others had a patent for lands in Maine, under the President and Council of New England in 1631, the same lands being given to him by deed, in 1638, by the Council of New England and Sir Fernando Gorges.

He was made a freeman in 1633. He was, we are told, engaged in commerce at an early date, and identified himself with the efforts made to promote the success of the colony. "Although opposed in religious sentiment, he joined with Governor Winthrop and Governor Thomas Dudley, in trading expeditions, and many instances are recorded of his being entrusted with public matters."

When, in 1632, the Governor and Council decided to send an armed vessel with twenty men to join others at Piscataqua, for the purpose of hunting for one Dixy Bull, a pirate, Samuel Maverick's pinnace was selected for the purpose, and it made a cruise of several weeks, but without success.

In 1635, Mr. Maverick went to Virginia to purchase corn, stock, etc., and remained there nearly a year. Gov. Winthrop, in a letter to his son, says: "It hath been earnestly pressed to have her [the Blessing] go to Virginia for Mr. Maverick and his corn; but I have no heart to it this season, being so perilous both to the vessel [for worms] and especially the persons." Later, in his Journal, he says: "Samuel Maverick, who had been in Virginia near twelve months, now returned with two pinnaces and brought some fourteen heifers, and about eighty goats (having lost about twenty goats by the way). One of his pinnaces was about forty tons."

In 1646, Mr. Maverick advanced a large part of the outlay required for fortifying Castle Island. In 1640, he had a grant of six hundred acres of land from the town of Boston, also an additional grant from the town of Boston of four hundred acres in Braintree. He owned or had claim upon property in Boston, as there is on record a mortgage from Robert Nash to him on a tenement near the house of the Rev. John Cotton. He was, we are told, one of the earliest (if not *the* earliest) of slaveholders in Massachusetts, he and others having purchased a number of negroes brought by Capt. William Pierce from the Tortugas in 1638. "This is the first notice," says Felt in his "Annals of Salem," "that we have of the disfranchised class."

"At the time of the exciting controversies between the Legalists and Antinomians, so-called, the differences grew so great that they tended fast to a separation, and to the breaking up of social intercourse. Gov. Winthrop, in July, 1637, invited the late Governor, Henry Vane, to accompany the Lord Ley at dinner at his house. But Vane not only refused to come (alleging by letter that his conscience withheld him), but also at the same hour he went over to Noddles Island to dine with Mr. Maverick, and took Lord Ley with him."

Although the colonial government was willing to avail itself of Mr. Maverick's services, and found him always ready to unite with the colonists and do his full share in any public undertaking, yet on account of his religious faith, he was never allowed any part in the civil rule of the colony, and this finally brought him into conflict with the government. In 1634-5, there was in England a concerted plan to uproot Puritanism and establish Episcopacy, and the colonial authorities were exceedingly apprehensive of efforts to establish Episcopacy here. This may account for the harsh treatment Mr. Maverick received at their hands. As an Episcopalian and a royalist, he doubtless received and entertained people who were obnoxious to the authorities. On the 4th of March, 1634-5, it was ordered by the General Court that he should, "before the last of December nexte, remove his habitation for himselfe and his family to Boston, and in the mean tyme shall not give entertainment to any strangers for a longer tyme than one night without leave from some Assistant, and all this to be done under the penalty of £100."[1] This injunction was not of long duration, however, and was countermanded in the September session of the Court. Felt says: "The suspicion against Samuel Maverick as a staunch Episcopalian, having lessened, the injunction for his removal to Boston is repealed."

As early as 1645, the subject of equal civil and religious rights and privileges to all citizens began to be agitated by those who like Mr. Maverick, were debarred by their religious belief from taking part in the affairs of the colony. Says Hutchinson: "A great

---

[1] Mass. Records, Vol. I., p. 140.

disturbance was caused in the colony this year [1646] by a number of persons of figure, but of different sentiments, both as to civil and ecclesiastical government, from the people in general." The principal persons engaged in the controversy were William Vassal, a man of wealth and influence in Scituate, Dr. Robert Child, a young physician of Hingham who was educated at Padua, and Samuel Maverick.

A "Remonstrance and humble petition," was addressed to the General Court which "gave great offence to the court, and the people generally." "In reply, a declaration was published by order of the court, in which the charges were freely examined and the government vindicated. The petitioners were required to attend court, and on so doing urged their right of petitioning, to which it was replied, that they were not accused of petitioning, but of using contemptuous and seditious expressions in their remonstrance, and they were ordered to appear before the court." At the November term of the court, they were heavily fined. "The petitioners then claimed the right to appeal to the commissioners for plantations in England; but this was not allowed. Yet they appealed to Parliament, and Dr. Child with others prepared in all haste to go to England to prosecute the appeal. The court judging it dangerous to allow these men to proceed to England under these circumstances, and, under the pretence of detaining Child on account of his fine, determined to seize him, and to take away and destroy whatever papers any of them might have, calculated to expose the proceedings here." In March, 1647, Samuel Maverick was arraigned by the Assistants for his active exertions in obtaining signatures to the non-freeman's petition, and bound over to appear at the General Court. At the May term of the court, he was fined one hundred and fifty pounds, and was to be imprisoned until it was paid or security given. Mr. Maverick "did not quietly submit to this heavy tax, but earnestly addressed the court on the subject." His first petition not being granted, on the 16th of May of the same year, he sent in another petition to which the deputies consented in full, but the magistrates refusing their consent, the petitioner failed in his request. He sent in still another petition, which was partially successful, for, on the 19th of June, 1650, one-half of his fine was abated.

Drake observes: "It may seem strange that Mr. Maverick should submit to so many indignities as from time to time it has been seen that he did; *a man that Boston could not do without.* He was a gentleman of wealth and great liberality. . . . He may have looked upon these and other proceedings against him as petty annoyances, to which it was best quietly to submit, not wishing to set an example of opposition to the government, or having a large property at stake, he might not wish to jeopardise it." Mr. Sumner says of him: "Considering the peculiar circumstances under which he was placed, and the evident fact that his position as a man of wealth, liberality, hospitality, public spirit, enterprise, and rank in society, demanded at least equal rights and privileges, it must be admitted that he exercised exemplary patience."

If Mr. Maverick submitted quietly to the indignities heaped upon him, it was not for long; for, upon the restoration of Charles II., he went to England to complain to the king, and to ask that commissioners might be appointed to visit New England, with authority to settle all difficulties. His efforts were finally successful. On the 23d of April, 1664, the king appointed four commissioners, to whom extraordinary powers were given to hear and determine all matters of complaint, adjust all difficulties, and to reduce "the Dutch at the Manhadoes." Samuel Maverick was one of the commissioners, and as such, appears to have been "ready and in haste" to exercise all the authority and power over the government and colonists of Massachusetts, given him.

He disposed of Noddle's Island, and is supposed to have resided in New York after the commissioners were recalled, he having been presented with a house "in the Broadway" of that town, by the Duke of York, for his fidelity to the king.

The christian name of Mr. Maverick's wife was Amias, but her surname is unknown. Their children were: Nathaniel; Mary, married, first, John Palsgrave, second, Francis Hooke, a prominent citizen of Kittery, Me.; and Samuel, who married Rebecca, daughter of Rev. John Wheelright.

It is not known where or at what time Mr. Maverick died, but it is thought that he died in New York.

Elias Maverick was born in 1604, and was an early settler in New England. He is thought to have been a son of the Rev. John Maverick; but, on account of the destruction of the records of the Maverick family[1] at the burning of Charlestown in 1776, it is impossible to know positively. It is supposed that Elias Maverick settled in Winnisimet (Chelsea), as we find by the old records of 1657 and 1662 that Elias Maverick of Winnisimet bought land on Hog Island and at Winnisimet; and the marriage of Abigail, daughter of Elias Maverick of Winnisimet is recorded. His will was dated there also. He was one of the first members of the church in Charlestown (that being the nearest to Winnisimet), being admitted on the 9th of February, 1632-3, and the records show that he was an active member, taking a prominent part in the various church proceedings. He was made a freeman in 1633, and in 1654 was a member of the Ancient and Honorable Artillery Company.

[1] So stated by N. B. Mountfort, Esq., of New York City, a descendant of Mr. Maverick.

In Winthrop's Journal is the following: "1633, Dec. 5, John Sagamore died of the small pox and almost all his people; (above thirty buried by *Mr. Maverick of Winnisimet* in one day)." "And when their own people forsook them, the English came daily and ministered to them; and yet few, only two families took any infection by it. Among others *Mr. Maverick of Winnisimet* is worthy of a perpetual remembrance. Himself, his wife and servants went daily to them, ministered to their necessities, and buried their dead, and took home many of their children."

Elias Maverick married Anna Harris of Charlestown, whose mother, Elizabeth Harris, married for her second husband, Deacon William Stitson of Charlestown.

The children of Elias and Anna were: John, married, first, Jane ——, second, Katherine Skipper; Abigail, married Mathew Clarke; Elizabeth, married John Johnson; Sarah, married —— Watson; Elias, married Margaret Sherwood, and probably a second wife Sarah ——; Paul married Jemimah, daughter of Lieut. John Smith; Peter, married Martha, daughter of Robert Bradford; Mary, married —— Way; Ruth, married —— Smith; Rebecca, married Thomas ——; and James, who is probably the one who was a member of the Ancient and Honorable Artillery Company.

Elias Maverick died Sept. 8, 1684, aged 80 years, and was buried in the ancient burial-ground at Charlestown, where, a few years since his grave-stone might have been seen. His will was dated Oct. 13, 1681.

Moses Maverick was born about 1610, and lived at Marblehead with Isaac Allerton, whose daughter Sarah he afterwards married. In 1634, he was engaged in the fishing business, and was made a freeman the same year. In May of the next year, Mr. Allerton conveyed to his son-in-law Moses, all his "houses, buildings, and stages that hee hath att Marble Head, to enjoy to him and his heires for ever." Moses Maverick became a member of the church in Salem on the 12th of June, 1637. "During the absence of Samuel Maverick to Virginia, Moses paid the Governor 40s. rent for Noddles Island, 7th June, 1636." After that, he continued to reside at Marblehead, and was licensed to sell wine there in 1638, as appears by the court records. His first wife, Sarah Allerton, died before 1656, he having been married that year to Eunice, widow of Thomas Roberts. His children by his first wife were: Rebecca, married —— Hawkes; Mary; Abigail; Elizabeth, died in childhood; Samuel; a second Elizabeth; Remember; and perhaps others. Moses Maverick died June 28, 1686. "In the settlement of his estate, in November of that year, are mentioned,—daughter Mary; wife of Archibald Ferguson, died in 1698 (probably a daughter by his second wife); Sarah, only surviving daughter, and wife of John Norman; Moses Hawks, only son of eldest daughter Rebecca; William Hughes and Thomas Jackson, married to Elizabeth and Priscilla Grafton, daughters of daughter Elizabeth Grafton, deceased; the children of daughter Abigail Ward, deceased; and the children of daughter Remember Woodman, deceased."

"Antipas Maverick is recorded as 'belonging to ye Ile of Shoals,' in October, 1647; in 1652 we find him at Kittery, Maine, appearing before the commissioners and submitting to the government of Massachusetts. This circumstance," says Mr. Sumner, "gives plausibility to the conjecture that the different individuals by the name of Maverick were of the same family, for we know that Mary Hooke, the daughter of Samuel Maverick, lived in Kittery." Antipas married ——, and had a daughter Abigail, who was married to Edward Gilman of Exeter.

"All the known circumstances," continues Mr. Sumner, "connected with the births, lives, business relations, and residences of Samuel, Elias, Moses and Antipas, lead to the conclusion that they were brothers.

"An Abigail Maverick was admitted to the church in Charlestown, 18th 12mo. 1637–8. She may have been a sister of Samuel, Elias, etc. At least, it is evident that she could not have been Abigail, daughter of Elias, as the latter was born Aug. 10, 1637."

Prior to the Revolutionary war, John Maverick, an importer of lignum-vitæ and other hard woods, resided in Boston on Middle Street (now Hanover), on the original site of the Hancock school-house. He was a man of considerable property, owned slaves, and kept a carriage. His children were: Nancy, married Nathaniel Phillips; Jemima, married a Captain White; Sally, married Judge Stoddard of Chemsford; Mary, married John Gyles; Jotham and Samuel. The sons were merchants in Boston, and highly respected.

"The name of Maverick has become extinct in New England, although descendants still remain. In New York, however, numerous persons perpetuate it."

"There was a *Peter Rushton Maverick*, an Englishman and an engraver, who resided in New York City, and owned property (No. 85) in Crown (now Liberty) Street, about one hundred feet from Broadway. It is stated by descendants that he came to this country from England (probably from the county of Kent), about the year 1774, when but eight or ten years of age. He was originally a silversmith, and is sometimes called 'Peter Maverick the first,' to distinguish him from his son and grandson, all bearing the name of Peter, and all following the same profession. Little is known of his character or circumstances. He was a free-thinker and a friend of Thomas Paine. His family through several generations, displayed an unusual talent for engraving, and made it their occupation. For many years he etched and engraved, and had pupils, some of whom attained eminence. He was the best engraver in New York, yet he had no education in the art, and owed all his proficiency to his own persevering industry. The best specimens of his work are in Brown's Family Bible, published by Hodge, Allen & Campbell in New York, and considered a great work for that time." Francis Kearney was his pupil, and in 1787–8, he taught William Dunlap (author of the History of Arts and Designs in the United States) the theory and practice of etching. "He also instructed in the art of engraving, his son Peter, who with his brother Samuel, were afterwards bank-note engravers of celebrity; the son, however, far excelled the father as an artist."

The children of Peter Rushton Maverick, as far as can be ascertained, were: Sarah, married Benjamin Montague; Rebecca and Maria, the first and second wives of James Woodhouse; Ann, married Patrick Munn; Peter; Andrew; and Samuel. "Peter Rushton Maverick died about 1807, and left a will recorded in the surrogate's office. By this, he devised his property in Liberty Street, which appears to have been all he owned, to his wife for life, with remainder to his children." His widow died Oct. 19, 1853, in the ninety-sixth year of her age. It is supposed that a connection existed between the Mavericks of Boston and Peter Rushton Maverick.

BRADLEY.

THE earliest mention of the name of Bradley, in England, was in the year 1183, at the feast of St. Cuthbert in Lent, when the Lord Hugh, Bishop of Durham, caused to be described all the revenues of his whole district. The survey of Bolton Burke, mentions in Walsingham, Roger de Bradley, who held forty acres at Bradley and rendered half a marc besides forest service. The name seems to have been given to towns and places, at a comparatively early date. There are in England a number of townships in Cheshire, Lincolnshire, Derbyshire, Southampton and Staffordshire, of that name, a township in the latter county containing between three and four thousand acres. There are also numerous parishes of that name in Suffolk and Yorkshire.

Among the early settlers of New England were a number of families of the name of Bradley, who are probably descended from a common ancestor, as the same Christian names are often repeated in the different families.

The only Bradley, the date of whose departure from England is known, was Daniel, who was born in England in 1615, and came from the parish of Alphage, Cripple Gate, in the ship *Elizabeth*, from London in 1635. He settled in Haverhill, Mass., and was made a freeman in 1642. He married, May 21, 1662, Mary, daughter of John Williams of Haverhill, formerly of Newbury. Their children were: Daniel, married Hannah, daughter of Stephen and Ann (Storie) Dow; Martha, married Ephraim Gile; Mary, died in infancy; a second Mary, married Barth Heath; Sarah, married

John Davenport; Hannah, married Joseph Heath; Isaac, and Abraham.

Mr. Bradley in 1682 leased the parsonage farm, belonging to the Rev. Mr. Ward, for twenty-one years. We are told by Mr. Chase[1] that "after the selectmen of 1685 were chosen, it was found a majority were not freemen as a law of the colony required, and without reflection or disrespect, Daniel Bradley was left out and Josiah Gage chosen in his room." From the same author, we learn that, three years after, under the arbitrary government of Andros, Daniel Bradley as selectman had to pay five pounds and one shilling for the drawing up of a bond for him to appear at Salem, because the town had not appointed a commissioner on rates to meet at the shire town to assist in making rates for the county.

On the 13th of August, 1689, a small party of Indians made their appearance in the northerly part of the town, and killed Daniel Bradley. He was killed on the Parsonage Road, not far from the present Atkinson Depot. In September following, his son Daniel sent a petition to the General Court, asking that Joseph, the brother of his father, might be appointed administrator, as his father left no will. The request was granted. Mrs. Bradley survived her husband twenty-five years.

Early in the fall of 1695,[2] a party of Indians appeared in the northerly part of the town, where they surprised and made prisoners of Isaac Bradley, aged fifteen, son of Daniel and Mary (Williams) Bradley, and Joseph Whittaker, aged eleven, who were at work in the open fields near Joseph Bradley's house. The Indians instantly retreated without doing any further violence, and pursued their journey through the wilderness until they arrived at their homes on the shores of

---

[1] Author of the "History of Haverhill."

[2] This account is condensed from Chase's "History of Haverhill."

the Winnipiseogee. "Isaac," says tradition, "was rather small in stature, but full of vigor and very active; he certainly possessed more shrewdness than most boys of his age. Joseph was a large, overgrown boy, and exceedingly clumsy in his movements."

Immediately after their arrival at the lake, the boys were placed in an Indian family, consisting of the man, his squaw, and two or three children. While they were with this family they became so well acquainted with the language, that they learned, from the occasional conversation carried on in their presence between their master and the neighboring Indians of the same tribe, that their intention was to carry them to Canada the following spring.

The spring came "with its early buds and flowers, and its pleasant south wind, and still they were prisoners." Isaac, during this time, had been very ill with a fever, but by the care of the squaw, who treated them both with considerable kindness, had recovered.

From the time the plans of the Indians had been discovered, Isaac had been planning a mode of escape, and in April, his plans being matured, he appointed a night to put it in execution, without informing his companion till the previous day. That night Joseph soon fell asleep, and began to "snore lustily;" but there was no sleep for Isaac. A little past midnight, he slowly and cautiously arose. All was silent save the deep-drawn breath of the savage sleepers. Isaac stepped softly and trembling over the tawny bodies, and secured the fire-works of his master and a portion of his moose-meat and bread, which he carried to a clump of bushes at a short distance. He then returned and bending over Joseph, carefully shook him. Joseph only half awake asked, "What do you want?" Isaac, greatly alarmed, instantly lay down in his own place and began to snore as loudly as any of them. Perceiving that they all slept, he arose and stepped softly out of the wigwam without again attempting to awaken Joseph. He had not reached the place where his provisions were concealed, when he heard footsteps approaching hastily behind him. With a beating heart, he looked back and saw Joseph. They ran at the top of their speed until daylight appeared, when they concealed themselves in a hollow log.

When their absence was discovered, their master collected a small party of Indians, with their dogs, and pursued them. The dogs struck upon their tracks, and in a short time came up to the log where the boys were, and barked loudly. The boys spoke to the dogs, who knew their voices, ceased barking and wagged their tails with delight. They gave the dogs all of the moose-meat they had taken, and while they were eating it, the Indians passed close to the log without noticing the employment of their dogs. The dogs, after their meat was devoured, trotted after their masters. They lay in the log all day, and at night took a different route from the one taken by the Indians. They made only one or two meals on their bread, and after that was gone, they lived on roots and buds. On the second day, they concealed themselves, but traveled the third night and day without resting. On the third day, they killed a pigeon and a turtle, which they ate raw, not daring to build a fire. They continued their journey night and day as fast as their wearied and mangled legs would carry them. On the sixth day, they struck into an Indian path and followed it till night, when they suddenly came within sight of an Indian encampment. They precipitately fled and all night retraced their steps. The morning found them seated side by side on the bank of a small stream, their feet torn and bleeding and they weeping bitterly over their misfortunes. The philosophy of Isaac taught him that the stream must eventually lead to a large body of water, so after refreshing themselves with a few roots they again started and followed its windings. They continued to follow it during that day and a part of the night. On the eighth day, Joseph was completely exhausted. Isaac endeavored to encourage him to proceed; he dug roots for him to eat, and brought water to quench his thirst, —but all in vain. Isaac left him with a bleeding heart. He had traveled but a short distance, when he came to a newly raised building. He immediately retraced his steps, and found Joseph in the same place and position in which he had left him. He talked encouragingly to him, and, after rubbing his limbs for a long time, he succeeded in making him stand on his feet. They then started together, Isaac part of the time leading him by the hand, and part of the time carrying him on his back. They reached Saco fort sometime in the following night, utterly exhausted, and emaciated almost to skeletons.

Isaac, as soon as he had regained his strength, started for Haverhill, and arrived safely at his father's house. His father had heard nothing from him since he was taken, and expected never to see him again. Joseph was seized with a raging fever soon after he reached the fort, and was for a long time very ill.

Isaac, son of Daniel and Mary Bradley, born Feb. 25, 1680, married Elizabeth, daughter of John and Elizabeth Clement of Haverhill. John Clement was a son of John and Sarah (Osgood) Clement, and grandson of Robert Clement who came to Haverhill in 1642. He was the first deputy of the town to the General Court, and continued to hold that office until 1654; he was also Associate Judge and County Commissioner. Mr. Chase says of him, "He was a man of rare integrity and superior talent."

The children of Isaac and Elizabeth Bradley were: Lydia, married John Heath, Jun.; John; Mehitable; Ruth; Elizabeth, married Robert Calif; Abigail; Isaac; Nathaniel; Moses; and Mirriam.

Isaac, Jun., married Lydia Kimball of Haverhill. Their children were: Elizabeth; Mary; Benjamin;

Isaac; Joseph; John; Jesse; Abigail; a second Abigail; Lydia; and Ruth, who married Josiah Chase of Haverhill.

John, the second son of Isaac and Lydia Bradley, born Feb. 4, 1756, married Elizabeth, daughter of a Mr. Follensbee, whose wife was Martha, daughter of John Huse, Esq., a merchant of Salem. Their children were: John, married Martha Peasley; Jesse, married Harriet Brown of Salem; Betsey, married Ezekiel, son of Ezekiel and Sarah (Merrill) Dow of Plaistow, N. H., (see page 241); Gilbert, unmarried; Sally, married Moses Peasley of Plaistow; and Martha, married Ladd Hazeltine of Haverhill, Mass.

Abraham, the youngest son of Daniel and Mary Bradley, born March 14, 1683–4, removed from Haverhill to Pennacook (Concord), N. H., in 1720. He was on various committees, and in 1732 was appointed together with two others, attorney for the proprietors of Pennacook. Mr. Bradley had a farm in the northern part of Concord, which has become, including what has been added by purchase, one of the finest farms in the Merrimac valley. The house built by him is not standing; but a fine old gambrel-roofed mansion, built by his son, is occupied at the present time by his descendants. Mr. Bradley is said to have been a man of sound judgment, and one of the most enterprising of the inhabitants. He married, Oct. 18, 1705, Abigail Philbreck. They had a large family of children, two of whom—Lieut. Jonathan and Samuel—were killed by the Indians at the massacre of Aug. 10, 1746. From the History of Concord, we learn that the descendants of Abraham Bradley have taken a prominent part in the affairs of the town, and been greatly respected.

Joseph Bradley, brother to Daniel Bradley (the first), was an early resident of Haverhill, and had command of the fifth fort, which was located in the northerly part of the town. He married, April 4, 1691, Hannah, daughter of John and Sarah (Partridge) Heath of Haverhill. Their children were: Mehitable; Joseph; Martha; Sarah; a child, whose name is unknown; a second Joseph; David; Nehemiah; Samuel; and William.

We are told by Mr. Chase, that three of Mr. Bradley's children—Joseph, Martha, and Sarah—were killed by the Indians in the massacre which occurred March 15, 1697. Mrs. Bradley was taken captive by the Indians the same day. Judge Samuel Sewall, in his "Diary," gives a very thrilling account of a second captivity of Mrs. Bradley, she having been taken by the Indians at the terrible massacre of Feb. 6, 1703-4. Upon the entrance of the Indians into the fort (the gate of which had been left open, as it was early for the depredations of the Indians), Mrs. Bradley seized a ladle full of soap which was boiling over the fire, and threw it over the first one who entered, killing him almost instantly. It appears that she might have been spared this second captivity, had she not generously chosen to give herself up, in order to save her sister who was ordered to come out of a hiding place in which they were both concealed, the Indians having discovered the sister only. Mrs. Bradley had one of her children in her arms, which was instantly killed by the savages. Judge Sewall tells us that she "underwent incredible hardships and famine," during her journey through the deep snow, and that she gave birth to a child before reaching Canada, the place of their destination. The Indians tortured the child by putting hot embers into its mouth when it cried, which made its mouth so sore that it could take no food for days together, and so starved to death. According to the account given by Chase, the Indians told Mrs. Bradley that if she would permit them to baptize the child with their baptism, they would suffer it to live. This baptism consisted in gashing the child's forehead with a knife. Upon Mrs. Bradley's return to the encampment one day, after a short absence, she found her child "piked upon a pole." Upon reaching Canada she was sold to the French for eighty livres, but was finally redeemed after two years of captivity by her husband, who traveled to Canada on foot, accompanied only by a dog, that drew a small sled, in which was a bag of snuff which was sent by the Governor of Massachusetts to the Governor of Canada.

We learn from Mr. Chase that, in 1706, a small party of Indians again visited the garrison of Joseph Bradley, there being no one there at the time but Mr. Bradley, his family and one hired man. Mr. Bradley armed himself, his wife and man each with a gun, and such of his children as could shoulder one. "Mrs. Bradley, supposing that they had come purposely for her, told her husband that she had rather be killed than be again taken. The Indians rushed upon the garrison, and endeavored to beat down the door. They succeeded in pushing it partly open, and when one of the Indians began to crowd himself through the opening, Mrs. Bradley fired her gun and shot him dead. The rest of the party, seeing their companion fall, desisted from their purpose, and hastily retreated."

Mirick states that, upon the retreat of the two hundred and fifty French and Indians, after the terrible massacre committed by them on the 29th of August, 1708, Joseph Bradley collected a small party in the northerly part of the town, and secured the medicine box and packs of the enemy which they had left about three miles from the village. The French and Indians continued their retreat, and so great were their sufferings, arising from the loss of their packs, and their consequent exposure to famine, that many of the Frenchmen returned and surrendered themselves prisoners of war; and some of the captives were dismissed.

In 1738, Mrs. Bradley petitioned the General Court for a grant of land, in consideration of her former sufferings among the Indians and "present low circumstances" (she was then a widow). The court gave her two hundred and fifty acres of land, located in Methuen.

Joseph Bradley died Oct. 3, 1729. His widow died Nov. 2, 1761.

PEPPERRELL.

WILLIAM PEPPERRELL,[1] a native of Tavistock Parish, Devonshire, England, emigrated at the age of twenty-two to the Isle of Shoals, where he was engaged in the exportation of fish to the Southern and European markets. He afterwards removed to Kittery Point, and became largely engaged in shipping and mercantile pursuits. He married Margery, daughter of John Bray, an extensive ship-builder of that place. Their children were: Andrew, married Jane, daughter of Robert Elliot, Esq.; Mary, married, first, Hon. John Frost, second, Rev. Benjamin Coleman, D. D., third, Rev. Benjamin Prescott of Danvers, Mass.; Margery, married, first, Peletiah Whitemore, second, Elihu Gunnison, Judge of the Court of Common Pleas; Joanna, married Dr. George Jackson; Mirriam, married Andrew Tyler, a merchant; William; Dorothy, married, first, Andrew Watkins, second, Hon. Joseph Newmarch; and Jane, married, first, Benjamin Clark, second, William Tyler.

Mr. Pepperrell for thirty-five years held the office of Justice of the Peace, and was for many years a Judge of the Court of Common Pleas. He was also a Lieut.-Colonel. He died Feb. 15, 173¾. Mrs. Pepperrell survived her husband seven years.

William Pepperrell, Jun., was born June 27, 1696. He was early taken into partnership by his father, and became one of the largest land owners in New England. We are told by Mr. Parsons that the ascendency that the Pepperrell firm enjoyed over any

---

[1] The following account is from the Life of Sir William Pepperrell, by Usher Parsons.

other mercantile house in New England gave it a large agency in the transaction of the pecuniary affairs of the province with the mother country, this branch of the business being conducted by the younger Pepperrell. As soon as he had passed his minority, he was appointed a Justice of the Peace, and was commissioned a Captain of cavalry. He was soon after commissioned a Major, and later a Lieut.-Colonel, which placed him in command of the militia of Maine. In 1730, Gov. Belcher appointed him a Chief Justice, which office he held through life. He was also a Representative from Kittery, and a Councilor, his appointment being renewed thirty-two successive years, eighteen of which he served as President of the Board. He is said to have had courtly manners, easy and affable address, and an unblemished character. He possessed a vigorous frame and a mind of firm texture, his perceptions being clear, resolution strong and judgment sound.

When an expedition against Louisburg was projected, in 1745, the command was given to Mr. Pepperrell, and upon his hesitating to accept the appointment, he was assured by Gov. Shirley that his "influence was indispensable as commander." So great was his popularity, all classes, we are told, from the hoary-headed Gov. Wolcott to the humblest axe-man of the forest, were willing and eager to enlist under his standard. The king, in reward for his services, conferred upon him the dignity of a Baronet of Great Britain, an honor never before or since conferred on a native of New England. In 1758, he was appointed Lieut.-General.

On the 16th of March, 1723, Mr. Pepperrell married Mary, daughter of Grove and Elizabeth (Sewall) Hirst. Their children were: Elizabeth, married Col. Nathaniel Sparhawk; Andrew, died in his twenty-sixth year; William, died young; and Margery, who died young. Sir William died July 6, 1759. His wife died in 1789.

William Pepperrell, a son of Col. Nathaniel and Elizabeth (Pepperrell) Sparhawk, was made Sir William's heir on condition of his dropping the name of Sparhawk. He was soon deprived of his vast possessions; for, on account of his loyalty to his king, they were confiscated at the breaking out of the Revolution. He removed to England, and was allowed an annuity by the crown.

The Pepperrell arms are: Arg. a chevron gu. between three pine-apples of a canton of the second, charged with a fleur-de-lis of the first. No crest.

MONTAGUE.

THE name of Montague, which appears in a variety of forms — De Monte Acuto, Montecuto, Montegut, Montaigue, Montague, etc., — is derived from the Latin words *Monte Acuto*, a mountain peak. The first of the name in English history was De Drogo Monte Acuto, one of William the Conqueror's warriors, whose name and arms are on the Battle Abbey Roll. He was in the immediate train of Roger, Earl of Moreton; and appears to have held of said Roger the manors of Sceptone or Shipton Montecute, and Suttone or Sutton Montecute.

Among the descendants of Drogo, many have been famous. They have filled not only every degree of the peerage from dukes to barons, but have also held most of the high offices of state and church, and have even numbered kings among them.

They may be divided into two groups: the early group, of which the Earls of Salisbury are the type; and the later group, descended from Sir Edward Montague, Chief Justice of England.

Robert Montague of Boveney, in the Parish of Burnham, Bucks County, England, is said to have been a descendant of the extinct Earls of Salisbury, whose arms he bore — three fusils on lozenges gu. in fesse on a field arg.; crest, a griffin's head—with the addition of three pellets sa., and for the crest a griffin's head erased.

Richard Montague, son of Peter, grandson of William, and great-grandson of Robert Montague of Boveney, in the Parish of Burnham, Buckinghamshire, Eng., came to New England previous to 1646, as we learn from the early records that he removed from Wells, Me., to Boston that year. In 1651, he removed to Wethersfield, Conn.; and in 1659 or 60, to Hadley, Mass., being one of the original proprietors of that place. He married Abigail, daughter of Dr. Downing of Norwich, Eng. Their children were: Mary, married Joseph Warriner; Sarah, died in infancy; Martha, married, first, Isaac Harrison, second, Henry White; Peter, married, first, Mary, daughter of William Partridge and widow of John Smith, second, Mary, daughter of John Crow and widow of Noah Coleman, third, Mary, daughter of Chileab Smith and widow of Preserved Smith; Abigail, married Mark Warner; and John, who married Hannah, daughter of Chileab Smith. Richard Montague died Dec. 14, 1681.

William, a son of Joseph and Mary (Henry) Montague, and a descendant of Richard and Abigail (Downing) Montague, was graduated at Dartmouth College, and became an Episcopal clergyman. He was rector of Christ's Church in Boston, and afterwards of St. Paul's Church in Dedham, Mass. Mr. Montague visited England, and was the first Episcopal clergyman ordained in America who preached in a British pulpit.

He married Jane Little. Their children were: Jane Little; William Henry; Sarah, married Edward Ellis, son of Pearson and Anne Maria (de Les Dernier) Titcomb; George Little; and Edward Wortly.

William Henry, the eldest son of Rev. William Montague, married Jane Brimmer Glover. Mr. Montague was an importing and dry goods jobbing merchant in Boston for many years; also, a manufacturer. He was one of the founders of the New England Historical and Genealogical Society.

George Little, the second son of Rev. William Montague, married Catherine Fraser Watson, daughter of William Pepperrell and Harriet (de Les Dernier) Prescott. Mr. Montague was in business with his brother, Mr. William Henry Montague.

SPOFFORD.

In the county of Yorkshire, England, is a town of three or four thousand inhabitants by the name of Spofforth; also, the ruins of an ancient castle, which still bear the name of Spofforth castle. Here lived, before the Conquest, a Saxon, Gamelbar de Spofforth or Spofford, lord of this manor, which was taken by William the Conqueror and given to William, Earl Percy.

Investigations made by Markham Spofforth, Esq., of London, Eng., prove beyond a doubt that John Spofford, who came to America and settled at Rowley in 1638, was a descendant of Gamelbar de Spofford. John Spofford's name appears on the record of the first division of land into homestead lots, in 1643. He had a house lot of one and a half acres on Bradford Street, near the center of the present town of Rowley. Lots were also assigned him in the "fresh meadows, the salt meadows, the village lands, the Merrimack lands, and shares in the ox pasture, the cow pasture and the calf pasture." He lived for about thirty years in Rowley, and in the spring of 1669 removed to "Spofford's Hill," where he took a farm on a lease for twenty-one years. This lease was assigned to his sons John and Samuel, March 16, 1676. The descendants of John Spofford were owners of nearly one thousand acres adjoining, at the time the lease expired, when the farm reverted to the town.

John Spofford married Elizabeth Scott of Ipswich. Their children were: Elizabeth, married Alexander Sessions; John, married Sarah Wheeler of Rowley; Thomas, married Abigail Hagget of Bradford; Samnel, married Sarah Birbee; Hannah; Mary; Sarah, died in infancy; a second Sarah, married Richard Kimball; and Francis, who married Mary Leighton.[1]

Richard S., son of Dr. Richard S. and Mrs. Frances (Lord—*nee* Mills) Spofford, of Newburyport, Mass., and a descendant of John Spofford of Rowley, was born July 30, 1833. He studied for the profession of law with Hon. Caleb Cushing. Mr. Spofford, after his studies were finished, was commissioned by the United States Supreme Court to go to Mexico, and purchase the Spanish law books for the settlement of the California land claims. He remained some years in the practice of his profession in Newburyport, and represented that city two years in the State Legislature. He has since resided in Washington.

Mr. Spofford married, Dec. 19, 1865, Harriet E., daughter of Joseph Newmarch and Sarah Jane (Bridges) Prescott of Newburyport. Mrs. Spofford was born in Calais, Me., April 3, 1835. Richard S. and Harriet E. Spofford had one son, Richard S., who was born Jan. 30, 1867, and died Sept. 10, 1867.

While yet a school-girl, Mrs. Spofford captivated the public by a story, "In a Cellar," which appeared in the *Atlantic Monthly*. Her published books are: "Sir Rohan's Ghost," "Amber Gods, and Other Stories," "Azarian," "New England Legends," "Thief in the Night," and "Poems." Mrs. Spofford, in the words of Mr. Woodman,[2] "stands at the head of the word-painters; so far indeed as to be solitary and alone. . . . Her work has the glow of a New England Autumn; at times, it is wild as 'New England's September gale,' and then suddenly there will fall upon it the hush of a New England Sabbath. . . . Her descriptions are always faithful to nature. She paints scenes as they are,—then calls up their souls for us

---

[1] Taken from the Spofford Family Record, by Jeremiah Spofford, M.D.

[2] In "Poets' Homes."

to commune with." In her sea-scenes, she "surpasses all women who have ever written." She "is a genuine product of our New England coast. The east winds have blown her through and through,—not to chill her powers but to sweep the cords of her heart into a rare, rich melody."

The following specimen of her word-painting is the account of the night on the lake, in "Mid-Summer and May:"

"Ever and anon they passed under the lee of some island, and the heavy air grew full of idle night sweetness; the waning moon with all its sad and alien power hung low,—dim, malign and distant, a coppery blotch on the rich darkness of heaven. They floated slowly, still; now and then she dipped a hand into the cool current,—now and then he drew in his oars, and, bending forward, dipped his hand with hers. The stars retreated in a pallid veil that dimmed their beams, faint lights streamed up the sky,—the dark yet clear and delicious. They paused motionless in the shelter of a steep rock; over them a wild vine hung and swayed its long wreaths in the water, a sweet-brier starred with fragrant sleeping buds climbed and twisted, and tufts of ribbon grass fell forward and streamed in the indolent ripple; beneath them the lake, lucid as some dark crystal, sheeted with olive transparence a bottom of yellow sand; here a bream poised on slowly waving fins, as if dreaming of motion, or a perch flashed its red fin from one hollow to another. The shadow lifted a degree, the eye penetrated to farther regions; a bird piped warily, then freely, a second and third answered, a fourth took up the tale, blue-jay and thrush, cat-bird and bobolink; wings began to dart about them, the world to rustle overhead, near and far the dark pines grew instinct with sound, the shores and heavens blew out gales of melody, the air broke up in music. He lifted his oars silently; she caught the sweet-brier, and, lightly shaking it, a rain of dew-drops dashed with deepest perfume sprinkled them; they moved on. A thin mist breathed from the lake, steamed round the boat, and lay like a white coverlet upon the water; a light wind sprang up and blew it in long rags and ribbons, lifted and torn, and streaming out of sight. All the air was pearly, the sky opaline, the water now crisply emblazoned with a dark and splendid jewelry;—the paved work of a sapphire; a rosy fleece sailed across their heads, some furnace glowed in the east behind the trees, long beams fell resplendently through and lay beside vast shadows, and giant firs stood black and intense against a red and risen sun; they trailed with one oar through a pad of buds, all unaware of change, stole from the overhanging thickets through a high walled pass, where on the open lake, the broad silent yellow light crept from bloom to bloom and awoke them with a touch. How perfectly they put off sleep! with what a queenly calm displayed their spotless snow, their priceless gold, and shed abroad their matchless scent! He twined his finger round a slippery serpent-stem, turned the crimson under side of the floating pavilion, and brought up a waxen wonder from its throne to hang like a star in the black braids on her temple. An hour's harvesting among the nymphs, in this rich atmosphere of another world, and with a loaded boat they returned to shore again."

FULLER.

"In 1638, Thomas Fuller[1] came over from England to America, upon a tour of observation, intending, after he should have gratified his curiosity by a survey of the wilderness world, to return. While in Massachusetts, he listened to the preaching of Rev. Thomas Shepard of Cambridge who was then in the midst of a splendid career of religious eloquence and effort, the echo of which, after the lapse of two centuries, has scarcely died away. Through his influence, Mr. Fuller was led to take such an interest in the religion of the Puritan school, that the land of liturgies and religious formulas, which he had left behind, became less attractive to him than the 'forest aisles' of America where God might be freely worshiped. He has himself left on record a metrical statement of the change in his views which induced him to resolve to make his home in Massachusetts."

Lieut. Thomas Fuller (so styled in the probate proceedings on his will) purchased and settled upon a large tract of land in New Salem (afterward Middleton), which is still owned by his descendants. "He did not reside continuously at Middleton, but for some years dwelt in Woburn, and was one of the first settlers and most active citizens of that town."

He married, June 13, 1643, Elizabeth Tidd, probably a daughter of John Tidd of Woburn. His second wife was Sarah Wyman, whose maiden name was Nutt, and his third wife was Hannah ——. His children were all by his first wife. They were: Thomas, married,

---

[1] Taken from the "N. E. Hist. and Gen. Register," Oct., 1859.

first, —— Richardson, second, —— Durgy; Elizabeth, married Joseph Dean of Concord; Ruth, married, first, —— Wheeler, second, —— Wilkins; Deborah, married, first, Isaac Richardson, second, —— Shaw; John, married —— Putnam; Jacob, married Mary Bacon; Joseph, died young; Benjamin, married Sarah Bacon; and Samuel, who died young. Lieut. Thomas Fuller died in 1698.

Timothy, son of Jacob and Abigail (Holton) Fuller, —Jacob was a son of Jacob and Mary (Bacon) Fuller, and grandson of Thomas Fuller,—was born at Middleton on the 18th of May, 1739. He entered Harvard University at the age of nineteen, and graduated in 1760. He was ordained the first minister at Princeton, and was successful as a minister, his people being united in him till the war of the Revolution broke out. "He declared at the time and ever afterwards, that he was friendly to the principles of the Revolution, and anxiously desired that his country might be liberated from its dependence on the British Crown. But he was naturally a very cautious man, and believed this result would be certain to come if the country reserved itself for action till its strength was somewhat matured and its resources in a better state of preparation.... Such views, however, were by no means congenial to the heated zeal of his townsmen," and, "as he was not a man to swerve from his own cool and deliberate views, through the pressure of public opinion," he was dismissed, in 1776, from his pastorate, by an ex-parte council, his parish refusing to agree with him upon a mutual council. He removed soon after to Martha's Vineyard, and preached to the society in Chilmark, till the war was ended. He then removed to Middleton, and later to Princeton, "where he applied himself to the careful education of his children, in connection with the cultivation of a large farm, which embraced within its bounds the Wachusett Mountain."

"None of his children attended any other than this family school; all were carefully taught, and several fitted for college at home. Those in the town who had been opposed to him soon became reconciled and even warmly attached. He was very active in town affairs, and represented Princeton in the convention which approved and adopted the present federal constitution. He himself, with his characteristic firmness, voted against the constitution, mainly on the ground of its recognition of slavery, and he has left his reasons against it on record." In 1766, he removed to Merrimac, N. H., where he continued to reside till his decease. He married Sarah, daughter of Rev. Abraham and Ann (Buckminster) Williams of Sandwich, Mass. Their children were: Sarah, died unmarried; Nancy Buckminster, married Henry Titcomb, Esq., of Farmington, Me.; Elizabeth, died unmarried; Timothy; Anna, died in childhood; Deborah Allen, married Clifford Belcher of Farmington, Me.; Abraham Williams, died unmarried; Martha Williams, married Simeon C. Whittier of Hallowell, Me.; Henry Holton, married Mary Buckminster Stone; William Williams; and Elisha, who married Susan Adams. Mrs. Fuller is said to have possessed "a vigorous understanding, and an honorable ambition which she strove to infuse into her children." She died in 1822. Mr. Fuller died in 1805.

Hon. Timothy, the eldest son of Rev. Timothy Fuller, born in Chilmark, Martha's Vineyard, July 11, 1778, was graduated at Harvard University, 1801, with the second honors in his class. He studied for the profession of law, and practiced in Boston, where he attained great distinction. He was a member of the Massachusetts Senate, Speaker of the Massachusetts House of Representatives, a Representative in Congress, and a member of the Executive Council. "He was always an ardent advocate for freedom and the rights of man," and was a man of "strict integrity, warmth of heart, and a liberal benevolence." He married Margaret, daughter of Major Peter Crane of Canton, Mass. Mrs. Fuller is said to have been "amiable, gifted, yet unpretending, with a rare intellect, lively fancy, and ardent imagination; with warmth of sentiment and affectionate benignity of heart." She had a rare conversational gift, and in youth was possessed of great personal beauty. She died July 31, 1859. Mr. Fuller died suddenly, of Asiatic cholera, Oct. 1, 1835.

They had a large family of children, of whom the eldest, Margaret Fuller Ossoli, "is well-known to fame." "The brightness of her genius, the nobleness and heroism of her life, are set forth in two volumes of Memoirs from the pens of R.W. Emerson, Horace Greeley, W. H. Channing, J. F. Clarke, and other friends, which have been widely circulated, and have presented the story of an extraordinary life."

Hon. Thomas James Duncan Fuller, son of Martin and Letitia (Duncan) Fuller, and grandson of Deacon Thomas Fuller, one of the earliest settlers of Hardwick, Vt., and a descendant of Lieut. Thomas and Elizabeth (Tidd) Fuller, was born in Hardwick, Vt., March 17, 1808. He was left an orphan when seven years of age, and spent his boyhood and youth with an uncle upon a farm. On attaining manhood, he studied for the profession of law, and was admitted to the bar in 1833. He settled in Calais, Me.

"He was State Attorney for his county for three years; was elected Representative from Maine to the Thirty-first, Thirty-second, Thirty-third, and Thirty-fourth Congresses, serving as an active member of the Committee on Commerce. In 1857, he was appointed Second Auditor of the Treasury by President Buchanan, which office he filled until 1861. As Second Auditor, he discovered the Floyd defalcation. From

1861 to the time of his death, he practiced his profession with success in the courts of the District Supreme Court of the United States, and the Court of Claims.

The following is from the *Washington Tribune*, Feb. 15, 1876: "Hon. Thomas J. D. Fuller, a prominent member of the Washington bar, died at the residence of his son in Upperville, Va., on Sunday last, whither he had gone in perfect health some ten days ago on a visit, and while there, contracted a severe cold, which turned to a fatal case of typhoid pneumonia. Mr. Fuller was a man of great ability and genial disposition, and his death will be mourned by a large circle of friends and acquaintances."

"Yesterday in the Circuit Court his death was announced by Mr. James G. Payne, and the court adjourned in respect to his memory."

Mr. Fuller was twice married. His first wife was Elizabeth Dordin, daughter of Pearson and Anne Maria (de Les Dernier) Titcomb. Mrs. Fuller was a woman of great strength of character, and of a genial and social disposition. She died after a lingering and painful illness, in September, 1864; Mr. Fuller married for his second wife Jennie Elizabeth, daughter of Rev. Nelson and Catherine D. (Stephenson) Doolittle.

AYER.

John Ayer settled in Salisbury, in 1640. He removed to Ipswich, and later to Haverhill, Mass., his name being on the list of those who held land in that place in 1645. In 1652, he received a share in the second division of "plough-land." His name appears in the list of freemen in Haverhill, in 1646. This list has the valuation of each man's property; and John Ayer's is put down at £160, being the largest amount but one on the list. He married Hannah ——. Their children were: John, Nathaniel, Hannah, Rebecca, Mary, Robert, Thomas, Obadiah and Peter. John Ayer died March 31, 1657. His will was made March 12, 1657, and probated the following October. John Ayer had a large number of descendants. We are told by George W. Chase, in his "History of Haverhill," that, in 1700, one-third of the inhabitants of Haverhill were of the name of Ayer.

Capt. John, the eldest son of John and Hannah Ayer, was born in England. He removed to Brookfield, Mass., being one of the first settlers, and received large grants of land, some two thousand acres in all. He kept the inn of that place. He married, first, Sarah, daughter of John Williams; second, Susannah, daughter of Mark Simonds of Ipswich. He was killed by the Indians when they destroyed the town, Aug. 3, 1675.

Nathaniel, the second son, received land on his father's right in the fifth division of land, which was made in 1721.

Robert, the third son, born probably in England, was made a freeman in 1666. He received land in the second and fifth divisions of "plough-land." He was a Selectman in 1685, also under the new charter in 1692, where he is called Sergeant. He was one of a committee of three who were appointed to see about settling Rev. Benjamin Rolfe, the second minister in Haverhill. He married, in 1650, Elizabeth, daughter of Henry Palmer, of Haverhill. Their children were: Elizabeth, Samuel, Mehitable, Timothy, Hannah and Mary.

Thomas, the fourth son, was a land owner in Haverhill in 1650, and received nine acres in the second division of "plough-land." He was a freeman in 1666. He was one of seven who were appointed to defend the garrison commanded by Sergeant John Hazeltine. He married Ruth Wilford. They had five children. Mrs. Ayer and her daughter Ruth, three years of age, were killed by the Indians, Aug. 20, 1708. Mr. Ayer married for his second wife, Mrs. Blaisdell, a widow. They had one child, Ruth, who died young.

Obadiah, the fifth son, received land on his father's right in the fifth division of the common land.

Peter, the sixth son, was made a freeman in 1666. He was a land owner in 1650, and received land in the fifth division of town lands. He lived in the northerly part of the town, in the West Parish. He was one of a committee of three to see about building the first school-house, and was also one of a committee for building a new meeting-house and settling the Rev. Benjamin Rolfe. He was one of three chosen to designate what houses should be garrisoned, and was on a committee for "examination of the rights that any have in common land." He was chosen a Selectman under the new charter, and was one of the first Assessors. In 1689, he was chosen to represent Haverhill at the convention called in Boston by the "Council of Safety," which was organized upon the imprisonment of Gov. Andros. In 1690, "Cornet Peter Ayer" was "particularly made choice of to present, prefer and prosecute" the petition made by Haverhill as a frontier town, to the Council or General Court for "40 men at least to be a constant daily scout," etc. He was chosen a Representative to the General Court, in 1683-5-9 and 90. He married Hannah, daughter of William Allen. He died in Boston, Jan. 3, 1699, aged about sixty-six years.

Capt. Samuel, the eldest son of Robert and Elizabeth (Palmer) Ayer, was born in Haverhill, Nov. 11, 1654. He resided near the house of Capt. Ayer (2d). His name appears in the list of those who built cottages in 1677. He was a Selectman, a Constable, a Deacon, and was also Captain of Haverhill. During the arbitrary government of Andros, the condition of Haverhill, we are told by Mr. Chase, "was critical in the extreme. None knew when or where another attack would be made by the Indians, and it is not to be wondered at that their hearts were oppressed with the gloomiest forebodings. The following extract from a letter of Samuel Ayer, constable of Haverhill, to the General Court, under date of February 11, 1689,—in answer to a citation for the town to appear and answer to the charge of 'withholding the one-half of their proportion of rates,'—touchingly represents the condition of the town: 'I pray you consider our poor condition. There are many that have not corn to pay their rates, more which have not money: to strain I know not what to take: we are a great way from any market, to make money of anigh thing we have: and now there is not anigh way to transport to other places: I pray consider our poor condition.'"

In 1695, Haverhill for the first time chose a Town Treasurer, and Capt. Samuel Ayer was the person selected. In 1700, he was chosen to fill the vacancy in the committee for the "examination of the rights of any in common land," made by the death of Cornet Peter Ayer. His name is in the list of snow-shoe men.

Capt. Samuel Ayer married, Dec. 14, 1680, Mary

Johnson. Their children were: Peter, Mehitable, James, Obadiah, Timothy, Lydia, Hannah, Ruth, Abigail, and John.

On the 29th of August, 1708, occurred the terrible massacre of the people of Haverhill by the French and Indians. After the retreat commenced, as we are told by Mr. Chase, "Capt. Samuel Ayer, a fearless man and of great strength, collected a body of about twenty men, and pursued the retreating foe. He came up with them just as they were entering the woods, when they faced about, and though they numbered thirteen or more to one, still Capt. Ayer did not hesitate to give them battle. These gallant men were soon reinforced by another party, under the command of his son: and after a severe skirmish which lasted about an hour, they retook some of the prisoners, and the enemy precipitately retreated, leaving nine of their number dead. Capt. Ayer was slain before the reinforcement arrived. He was shot in the groin, and being a large, robust man, bled profusely. When his son arrived, he was told that his father was killed, and the informant pointed him out. He looked at the corpse awhile, as it lay on the grass, all covered with blood, and told his informant that that person could not be his father, for he (meaning the person slain) had on a pair of red breeches. Capt. Ayer was buried near Rev. Benjamin Rolfe, Capt. Wainright and Lieut. Johnson, who were killed the same day. The inscriptions on their stones have become nearly illegible." Mr. Chase says of Capt. Ayer: "He was one of the most worthy, active and intelligent citizens of the town."

James, the second son of Capt. Samuel Ayer, born Oct. 27, 1686, married, May 10, 1711, Mary, daughter of John and Lydia (Gilman) White of Haverhill. John White was a son of William White, whose name was signed to the deed of the town of Haverhill, he being one of the pioneer band of settlers in that town. Lydia Gilman, the wife of John White, was a daughter of Hon. John Gilman of Exeter, N. H.

The children of Deacon James were: Samuel, John, William, Jane, Mary, Hannah, Joanna, Abigail, Ruth, Elizabeth and James.

James Ayer, Sen., was a deacon, and was frequently appointed on important committees. In 1721, owing to trouble between Massachusetts and New Hampshire about the boundary line, a royal order was issued in response to a petition to the king, referring the matter to a board of commissioners. The town of Haverhill chose a committee, consisting of Col. Richard Saltonstall, Mr. Richard Hazen and Deacon James Ayer, "to wait upon the Commissioners, and represent the affairs and boundaries of the town to them, provided the proprietors of the undivided lands pay the expenses of the said Committee."

Deacon James Ayer lived south of the new State line, and east of the West Parish line. Ayer's Hill, in Haverhill, was named for him. He was a large land owner. He was, like his father, a very large, strong man, and tradition says that he once climbed a tree to kill a wild cat, and with the aid of dogs killed it.

William, the third son of Deacon James Ayer, was born June 18, 1716. He is said to have been a tall, grave, religious man. He removed to Plaistow, N. H. He married Sarah Little. Their children were: William and Mary, twins, Daniel, Abigail, James, Joseph, Mary and Lydia, twins, and Sarah.

Daniel, the second son of William Ayer, was born Jan. 28, 1743. He married Sarah Adams of Rowley. Their children were: Sarah, married David Gyle; Samuel; and Daniel.

Samuel, the eldest son of Daniel Ayer, was born Dec. 13, 1777. He was a man of superior natural ability and of fine personal bearing. In early life, he was a farmer, his farm bordering upon the beautiful lake named by Whittier, Lake Kenoza. He removed from Haverhill to Andover, Mass., and became a manufacturer. Later, he removed to Albany, N. Y., where he remained for many years engaged in mercantile pursuits. He married Polly, daughter of Deacon William and Abigail (Gove) Chase of East Haverhill.

William Chase was a son of Dea. Ezra and Judith (Davis) Chase of East Haverhill; Dea. Ezra was a son of Jacob and Joanna (Davis) Chase of East Haverhill, formerly of West Newbury; Jacob was a son of John and Elizabeth (Bingley) Chase of Oldtown, Newbury; John was the third son of Aquila and Anne (Wheeler) Chase of Newbury (see account of the Chases).

The children of Samuel and Polly (Chase) Ayer were: Sarah Ann, married Dustin Dunham; Charles Coffin, married Ellen Melcher; Frances Somerby, died young; John Varnum; Elbridge Gerry; Mary Ann, died unmarried; and Ruth Somerby, who died young. Samuel Ayer died in Kenosha, Wisconsin, in 1847. His wife died in Kenosha, also.

John Varnum, the second son of Samuel Ayer, married, first, a lady from Philadelphia whose name I have not learned; second, Miss Lynch, a daughter of Judge Lynch of New Orleans; third, Elida Manney. He was a resident of Chicago, where he carried on an extensive business as an iron merchant and manufacturer. He died a few years since.

Elbridge Gerry, the third son of Samuel Ayer, married Mary Dean, daughter of Pearson and Anne Maria (de Les Dernier) Titcomb. Mr. Ayer, when twenty-one years of age, entered into partnership with his father, but, after remaining two years with him, emigrated to the West. He settled in South Port, afterwards called Kenosha, where he remained many years engaged in mercantile pursuits, becoming a large land owner. His eldest child was the first white child born in the town. Mr. Ayer finally removed to the Prairie of Big Foot in Wisconsin, thinking a less changeable climate would improve his failing health. When the North-western Railway was built, he removed to the flourishing little village of Harvard, Ill., where he became the owner and proprietor of the Harvard Hotel. Mr. Ayer, like his ancestors, is a man of large frame, and of large heart, as well, as very many can testify, especially the soldiers of the North-west who were engaged in putting down the late rebellion.[1] The following letter was taken from the *Wisconsin State Journal:*

"EXECUTIVE OFFICE,
MADISON, July 12th, 1865.

"E. G. Ayer, Esq., Harvard, Ill.:

"Dear Sir:—I am informed that on several occasions sick and wounded soldiers from Wisconsin have been detained at your place, and that you have at all times treated them with great kindness, furnishing them with food when they needed it, and otherwise administering to their necessities, and that you have done this without pay or expectation of reward, and that you still decline to receive any pay for the many meals furnished this class of persons, or for your services in their behalf.

"Few as marked cases of disinterested benevolence and goodness of heart have occurred within my observation, and I could not allow it to pass without assuring you of my appreciation of your services to these sick and wounded heroes. Permit me, sir, in behalf of these noble men whom you have comforted and served, and in behalf of the people of Wisconsin, to tender to you their sincere thanks, and to assure you that your kindness to Wisconsin soldiers will not soon be forgotten.

"Yours Truly,
"JAMES T. LEWIS,
"Governor of Wisconsin."

---

[1] Many of the above facts relating to the Ayer family, are from Chase's History of Haverhill.

CHASE.

The late Mr. Theodore Chase of Boston, "being the possessor by inheritance of a voluminous collection of the family papers of Aquila Chase, one of the first settlers and grantees of Hampton, submitted them to Mr. Somerby [the genealogist] for classification, and for the purpose of taking full notes for investigations to be pursued by him in England." The result of Mr. Somerby's investigations is as follows: Thomas Chase of Hundrich, in the Parish of Chesham, Buckinghamshire, England, had five children, viz.: John, Richard, Agnes, William, and Christian.

Richard, son of Thomas of Chesham, baptized Aug. 3, 1542, married Joan Bishop. Their children were: Robert, Henry, Lydia, Ezekiel, Dorcas, Aquila, Jason, Thomas, Abigail, and Mordecai.

Aquila, son of Richard, married, and it is supposed that his wife's name was Sarah. They had two sons: Thomas, and Aquila.

Thomas, the eldest son, emigrated to New England as early as 1636, and settled in Hampton, Mass., being one of the original grantees of that town. He married Elizabeth, daughter of Thomas Philbric. Their children were: Thomas, who had an original grant of one hundred acres in Hampton, was Selectman, and died unmarried; Joseph, married Rachel, daughter of William Partridge of Salisbury; Isaac, married Mary, daughter of Isaac Perkins, and resided in Edgartown; James, married Elizabeth Green; and Abraham, who "was slain in ye wars." Thomas Chase died in Hampton, in 1653.

Aquila, the youngest son of Aquila, also came to New England, and was one of the grantees of Hampton, where he remained for about six years, when he removed to Newbury, Mass., and received several grants of land in that place on condition that he "do goe to sea and do service *in the town* with a boat for four years."

Aquila Chase married Anne, daughter of John Wheeler. Their children were: Sarah; Anne; Priscilla, married Abel Merrill; Mary; Aquila, married Esther, daughter of John Bond of Newbury; Thomas, married Rebecca, daughter of Thomas Follensby; John; Elizabeth; Ruth; Daniel; and Moses, married Anne, daughter of Thomas Follensby.

Mr. Chase says: "Soon after the disappearance of the Chase family from the Parish of Hundrich, their estate passed into the hands of the lord of the manor of Chesham, whose estate adjoined, and by whose family it has since been leased." In a visit to Chesham, Mr. George B. Chase learned that "it was the intention of Mr. William Lowndes, the present lord of the manor, and a gentleman of much antiquarian feeling, to repair and refit for the use of his tenants in that neighborhood" the "chapel, the only building left upon the estate as it existed when in the possession of the Chase families in the sixteenth and seventeenth centuries." [1]

John Kirby, son of Robert and Martha Jane (Noyes) Chase, and said to have been a descendant of Aquila and Anne (Wheeler) Chase, was born in West Newbury, Mass., Sept. 7, 1813. When twenty years of age, Mr. Chase went to Lowell, Mass., and entered the employ of Samuel Burbank (who then and for many years afterwards kept a clothing and hardware store on Central Street) as a clerk. In 1842, he was admit-

---

[1] The above is from an account published by George B. Chase.

ted as a partner, and remained connected with the business until his death. He married, in 1840, Adeline Ann, daughter of Pearson and Anne Maria (de Les Dernier) Titcomb. Mr. Chase died of pneumonia, after a short illness, March 5, 1879.

From the *Lowell Daily Citizen*, March 5, 1879, the following is taken:

"Mr. Chase's death deprives some of our local business institutions of one whose counsels have long been appreciated. He was in the directorship of the Prescott Bank, and a Trustee in the City Institution for Savings. High Street Church and Society and other religious organizations will miss his co-operation and liberality.

"The sudden ending of such a life is the occasion of wide-spread sorrow to which we can give no adequate expression. In a population of fifty thousand, we know not one who can be pointed out as a fitting substitute for him, who has left so bright a record of good citizenship, of Christian activity, of unselfish devotion to the material and spiritual welfare of his race. Endowed with talents which fitted him for almost any position, he chose the quiet offices of charity rather than posts of honor, and declined rather than sought places of civil trust. The Belvidere Mission for twenty-five years has witnessed his self-sacrificing zeal for thousands of ignorant and poor children, who but for his painstaking care might have been left to drift with the tide of waywardness and sin. Deacon Chase was on the alert in every good cause:—a Christian without ostentation; a man over whose loss our community has cause to mourn. If the good that men do lives after them, we may be well assured that his memory will be tenderly cherished among a people who for half a century have looked upon his beautiful life as radiant with good deeds—a perpetual benediction."

A PARTIAL INDEX.

INDEX.

INDEX.

INDEX.

ERRATA.

PAGE 16.—In eleventh line from top, for "sable between three fleurs-de-lis, argent," read "sable *a chevron* between three fleurs-de-lis, argent."

PAGE 32.—For "State Senator," read *Representative*.

PAGE 37.—Read "anddaughters" as two words.

PAGES 157, 158, 159, 160, 161.—For "Pierson," read *Pearson*.

PAGE 158.—For "Adelaide," read *Adeline*.

PAGES 175 AND 179.—For "Wordsworth," read *Wadsworth*.

PAGE 197.—For "Col. Bartlett," read *Col. Bartelott*.

PAGE 198.—For "Bratelot," read *Bartelott*.

PAGE 258.—In tenth line from bottom, for "trembling," read *tremblingly*.

www.ingramcontent.com/pod-product-compliance
Lightning Source LLC
Chambersburg PA
CBHW020505270326
41926CB00008B/747

* 9 7 8 3 3 3 7 0 1 3 4 9 3 *